ANGELS

Also by Peter Stanford

Martin Luther: Catholic Dissident

Judas: The Troubling History of the Renegade Apostle

How to Read a Graveyard:
Journeys in the Company of the Dead

The Death of a Child (editor)

The Extra Mile: A 21st Century Pilgrimage

C Day-Lewis: A Life

Why I Am Still a Catholic:
Essays in Faith and Perseverance (editor)

Heaven: A Traveller's Guide to the Undiscovered Country

Bronwen Astor: Her Life and Times

The She-Pope: A Quest for the Truth
Behind the Mystery of Pope Joan

The Devil: A Biography

The Outcasts' Outcast: A Life of Lord Longford

Cardinal Hume and the Changing Face of English Catholicism

Catholics and Sex (with Kate Saunders)

Believing Bishops (with Simon Lee)

ANGELS

*A Visible and
Invisible History*

Peter Stanford

HODDER &
STOUGHTON

First published in Great Britain in 2019 by Hodder & Stoughton
An Hachette UK company

1

Copyright © Peter Stanford, 2019

Biblical references are taken from *The New Jerusalem Bible*
published and copyright © 1974 by Darton, Longman and Todd Ltd
and Doubleday, a division of Random House Inc.

References from the Qur'an are taken from English translation by
M.A.S. Abdel Haleem, published and copyright © 2004 by Oxford University Press.

A CIP catalogue record for this title is available from the British Library

ISBN 978 1 473 62208 1
eBook 978 1 473 62210 4

Typeset in Sabon MT by Hewer Text UK Ltd, Edinburgh
Printed and bound in Great Britain by Clays Ltd, Elcograf S.p.A.

Hodder & Stoughton policy is to use papers that are natural, renewable
and recyclable products and made from wood grown in sustainable
forests. The logging and manufacturing processes are expected to
conform to the environmental regulations of the country of origin.

Hodder & Stoughton Ltd
Carmelite House
50 Victoria Embankment
London EC4Y 0DZ

www.hodder.co.uk

To Orla
– a 'divine spark'

Contents

PRELUDE

Loving Angels Instead

'Rather than words comes the thought of high windows:
The sun-comprehending glass,
And beyond it, the deep blue air, that shows
Nothing, and is nowhere, and is endless.'
                    Philip Larkin, 'High Windows' (1967)[1]

I grew up with angels. Mostly guardian angels, who inhabited my
night-time prayers, repeated from under a candlewick bedspread
in my Catholic home near Liverpool, all the while gazing up at
the 'holy picture' of Jesus on the wall with his copiously bleeding
heart. 'Angel of God, My guardian dear, / To whom his love
commits me here, / Ever this night be at my side, / To light and
guard, To rule and guide. / Amen.'

The place I remember angels best, though, was not in my
bedroom but on the drive at the front of our house. Not that I ever
saw them, but I knew they were there. My mother had been diag-
nosed with multiple sclerosis just before she found she was pregnant with me. By the time I could walk, she couldn't. Or only with
help: first the support of one wooden stick and her other hand resting on my shoulder; later, two sticks; and then a frame. Her declining mobility is how I measure out my childhood. When I was ten,
she began to use a wheelchair, but refused ever to be confined by it.

To which end, in the early 1970s, she took delivery of a sky-blue
three-wheeler Invalid Carriage (however much we now moan about
the clumsiness of politically correct language, it is surely an

improvement on calling anyone, or anything, in-valid), a Reliant-Robin-without-the-styling provided by the British taxpayer in the first flickerings of the disability revolution. The design allowed the driver to transfer across from their wheelchair onto a car seat, which then slid across on rails to lock into position behind the handlebars that controlled the whole contraption. In the space left once the seat had moved over, there was room to haul aboard a folded-up wheel-chair, but hers was heavy and the manoeuvre awkward, so most of the time she didn't bother with the faff. Her empty wheelchair stayed behind on the drive, while she parked outside shops where the assistants would come out and serve her through the Invacar window.

My father was forever telling her that, one day, some 'young buck' would 'walk off' with the wheelchair while she was out 'gallivanting', leaving her stranded. 'Oh Reg,' I can still hear her rebuking him, refusing to rise to the bait, 'cheer up. My guardian angel is looking after it.'

And for the fifteen years she used that Invacar, her empty wheel-chair was always there, awaiting her return. So, though never seen, her guardian angel must have been taking care of it, and her. At least, that is what we concluded at the time, using the same logic as the Scottish actor and comedian, Billy Connolly, when he told the tale in one of his stand-up shows about the 'wee parking angel' on the dashboard of his car. If he wound it up and its wings flapped, he said, it was supposed to find him a parking space. At which point the audience would laugh, before he added that, in his experience, it always worked.[2]

*

My first adult brush with visible angels came in 2000, when I published a biography of Bronwen Pugh, the 1950s supermodel whose marriage to one of the super-rich Astors was described as a 'fairy-tale romance' by the newspapers, but who was then drawn unwittingly into the notorious sex-and-spying drama of the Profumo Scandal that began around the Astors' swimming pool at Cliveden, their stately home outside London.[3] By her own description, before and during her marriage Bronwen had lived a very different inner life from outward appearances. Away from the catwalk and high society, it was one shaped by intense spiritual experiences, when she felt herself to be in the overwhelming presence of God's unconditional love. One episode she recounted challenged me as I was researching the book. It was her description of what happened two days after the birth, in December 1961, of her first daughter, Janet.

> Bill [her husband] had gone on a shoot. I was lying in my bed and I suddenly saw these angels. They were tiny and going up and down, as if on a ladder. They were in brilliant colours and they were looking at me and smiling a wonderfully merciful smile. They had brought me a message. 'You forget that the dynamic of the universe is self-sacrifice.' I was appalled. They were right. It had been a difficult labour and I had been afraid for my own life. If I'd put myself to one side, I'm sure I would have relaxed more and the labour would have been easier.[4]

I pressed her for more explanation. Had she actually seen angels, or was it that, exhausted after a prolonged birth, and under the influence of heavy medication, she had been half-dreaming? 'No,' she insisted, 'I was awake and that is what I saw. They were there in the fireplace in my bedroom.' Angels were, for her, real and tangible and unremarkable. The point of the story, as far as she was concerned, was the message they carried from God – of self-sacrifice, linked to the theme of unconditional love that shaped all of her religious experiences. For me, though, it was the angels' physical presence that beguiled. For all my faith in them at the time, the guardians who had watched over my mother's wheelchair had remained invisible.

*

My own faith is, essentially, a dull, practical one, so Lorna Byrne proved still more challenging to my default scepticism about any sort of supernatural manifestations. If Bronwen Astor saw angels once, Lorna reported having them in plain view all the time. There is also something of the mystic about her, I found out in 2008 when I was sent by the *Daily Telegraph* to interview her about *Angels in My Hair*, her book that had become a word-of-mouth, international bestseller.

In it, this fifty-something mother-of-four from County Kildare in Ireland told how, since childhood, she had seen guardian angels as 'spirals of light, usually three paces behind people', usually with wings closed together, and therefore not fully revealing themselves. More than that, she could on occasions go beyond the accepted bounds of this visible domain and communicate with them. She lived, she explained, in a 'parallel' world, 'between spirit world and human world';[5] in other words the 'endless nowhere' that Philip Larkin saw through high windows in the poem that opens this prelude.

There was undeniably something 'other' about Lorna, though not in any contrived or flamboyant way. Indeed, quite the opposite. Her sheer ordinariness of appearance and manner made it hard for me (and presumably her millions of readers) to doubt her sincerity. When recounting any sort of religious experience in our ever more secular and sceptical world, there is always a risk of being labelled (and dismissed) as deluded. To a Western society that increasingly places its faith only in those things that can be empirically measured, religion is mumbo jumbo because it doesn't fit the scientific 'proof' model. So talk of angels is at heart no more off-the-scale than any other aspect of believing in God. 'If I had told people what I was seeing when I was a child,' Lorna recounted to me, 'I would have been locked away.'

So was Lorna telling the truth? She talked of angels as if discussing old friends and I felt myself drawn in, almost in spite of myself, carried back to the unchallenged convictions of my childhood and its unseen but ever-present guardian angels. How does she deal with it when people demand that she prove her claims, I asked? 'I point to the response from my website. My book has given people back hope and belief in life itself, and that for me is wonderful. There are people who tell me they haven't prayed for years, since they left school, but now . . . It's the hope the world is crying out for.'[6]

Though she surely did not know it, since she has had very little formal education and reads with difficulty because of severe dyslexia, Lorna's remark to me that day echoed that of Saint Teresa of Avila, a sixteenth-century Spanish theologian and mystic who reformed her own Carmelite order and the first woman to be accorded the honour of being declared a 'doctor of the church'. Yet in her lifetime, she faced many more doubters. Doctor Teresa wrote in her autobiography about how angels visited her, on one occasion piercing her heart with a flaming spear that was God's pure love, and sending her into a state of ecstasy.[7] Challenged by the church authorities to prove her claims of angelic visitations, she reputedly replied that the evidence of the moral effect on her should be sufficient.

A few months after my meeting with Lorna, I got a call from her agent. Would I interview her again, this time on stage in front of an audience at Friends' House, the vast Quaker headquarters in central London? I had said yes almost before I knew the word had come out of my mouth.

It was full to its 800-seat capacity, all ages, all backgrounds. On the podium, Lorna and I ran through the same questions as before, and then the audience joined in. The most remarkable moment of the evening came only after it was officially over. For a good ninety minutes, I watched as a large proportion of those 800 people waited patiently in a queue that trailed out of the door of the main auditorium and round into the entrance hall.

They wanted to be able to spend a moment one-to-one with Lorna.

I assumed they were seeking a description of their own guardian angel. It is what I'd asked her when first we met (she wouldn't say). But those waiting to see her wanted something different. They asked no questions. They simply wanted this woman to put her arms round them in a hug. She offered them no cure, no special blessing, no therapeutic insight, no two-way channel to the angels, or beyond them to God. It was just, many told me subsequently when I stopped them on their way out of the building, that they recognised in Lorna's unshakeable acceptance of angels something that they too felt, a connection with something bigger, something that violated every law of science, but that they too experienced as a reality.

*

There is a terrible arrogance in the widespread confidence today that we are cleverer in all things than past ages. Angels are, for a sizeable minority, part of the present. In a 2016 poll of two thousand people, one in ten Britons stood shoulder to shoulder with Lorna Byrne and Bronwen Astor in saying they have experienced the presence of an angel, while one in three, like my mother, remain convinced that they have a guardian angel (39 per cent among women and 26 per cent among men).[8] These are significant numbers that shouldn't lightly be written off. They mean that, on some counts, angels are actually faring better than God. In a 2015 YouGov survey on British religious attitudes, only 23 per cent described themselves as 'very' (3 per cent) or 'fairly' (20 per cent) religious.[9]

While belief in God is on the wane, belief in angels is flying high. One survey reports that 21 per cent of Britons who never participate as worshippers in religious services, as well as 7 per cent who describe themselves as atheists, say they believe in angels,[10] a clear case at first glance of drawing on capital that is just not there. Nevertheless, we seem to be, in the lyric from Robbie Williams' hugely popular 1997 song, 'loving angels instead'.[11]

The Lion-man – or *Löwenmensch* – figure, with the head of a lion and the legs of a man, is the oldest-known evidence of religious belief in the world, predating every holy book, part of the unwritten religions, traditions without texts and without hierarchies that have existed across the world and across the whole of human time. Carbon-dated to forty thousand years ago, this ivory carving was unearthed in the Stadel cave in south-west Germany in 1939.[12] Its combination of human and animal features, painstakingly shaped used a flint knife, testifies that our earliest ancestors craved a relationship both with the natural world and with things unseen. Angels are central to that same history of yearning and the search to connect visible with invisible. In cultures stretching back tens of thousands of years, there have been winged creatures who serve the gods and who make a bridge, or ladder, between the divine realm and the earthly one.

Now, when in the West, at least, the statistics for formal religious attachment are dropping like a stone, angels remain. How has that come about? The decline in organised religion, which in some avowedly secular circles is on occasion accompanied by a virulent dislike of its remaining manifestations, is part of a wider anti-authoritarian trend in Western society, and beyond, that has seen the election of populist politicians on tickets that promise sweeping away long-established rules, alliances and experts who tell us what to do. And organised religion, too, suffers as part of that anti-authoritarian groundswell, because it is, in part at least, about laying down rules and regulating human freedom.

But only in part. Angels represent the other side of the coin to the claims to authority made by religious institutions. Unlike any formal attachment to a faith, with its doctrine, dogma and theological complexities, angels demand from those who place their trust and hopes in them no signing up to membership of a church, synagogue, mosque or temple, no attendance at rituals, no deference to the earthly representative of the gods. They are religious, or – if you like, though it is an overused word at the moment – spiritual, yet their make-up and history is such that they fit just as comfortably into the individualistic, anti-institutional mood of modern times as they have into more conventionally and collectively religious eras in the past. Indeed, one of the features of the contemporary upswing in interest in angels is that the formally non-religious are often happier talking about them than those who are part of a religious institution.

Angels have moreover shown a remarkable ability to chime with very different ages. Their history is full of examples of them being recruited, even dragooned, to suit the immediate needs of particular times. They seem endlessly adaptable, their very shape and form so often debated, and so often changing. When the Jewish people despaired at apparently losing their place as God's chosen people in the wake of a series of defeats that began with forced exile – or captivity – in Babylon in the sixth century BCE, they turned to angels and gave names – Michael, Gabriel, Raphael – to these hitherto shadowy figures. It was a way of investing in them their hopes of a renewed relationship with Yahweh and of the dawn on earth of the kingdom of God in which they would defeat all-comers. Likewise, when the 'angelologists' of the twelfth century CE ambitiously sought to develop a comprehensive explanation of the relationship between the earth, the heavens and the cosmos – in essence between God and emerging science – they hit upon angels as providing the key. When the artists of the Renaissance wanted to give expression to new notions of how every individual could have a one-to-one relationship with the divine, rather than be treated as part of a collective endeavour, they painted and sculpted and wrote about disarmingly human angels.

8

By the same measure, today's angels introduce a spiritual dimension into a material reality that for the many, personally and as societies, has become tattered, especially in the developed world where it is now commonplace to reject religion, deeming it a force for division, and as inimical to individual liberty and choice.

Down the ages, this same process of turning to angels has kept on happening. 'It is fruitless', wrote the great American critic and thinker, Professor Harold Bloom, on the eve of the second millennium CE, 'either to literalise or dismiss spiritual experience, whether ancient, medieval or contemporary.'[13]

If I were asked if I believed in angels, what would I say? Probably something mealy-mouthed such as, 'What do you mean by believe?' It is not just a neat side step. It also goes to the heart of the discussion that lies ahead in this history of angels. We are in inexact territory and invisible worlds.

So that word belief, found in the question 'Do you believe in angels?', can mean many things. In the secular societies of the West, it is a challenge to present incontrovertible evidence of their physical existence. I cannot. Yet angels have been, for millennia, in scriptures and myths, hearts and minds, an expression of human aspiration, hope and expectation, an in-built instinct to engage not only with invisible worlds, but with invisible beings too, as a way of relieving anxiety about living, and about the inevitability of death. Angels speak of and to something all too real and all too urgent in the human experience.

The ancient Greeks made better use than we do of language to enable them to hold two concepts at once: *mythos* and *logos*. Both were crucial in life, they believed, but each had its particular sphere of competence. *Logos*, which translates as reason, was the equivalent of today's scientific orthodoxy, a pragmatic mode of thought that was shaped by external realities, but had little to offer those who were stressed or suffering, and nothing at all that resonated with people's intimations that their lives had a larger meaning. Instead, all of that side of life was covered by *mythos*, in some ways an early form of psychology, and just as respected, all about the less easily measured or quantifiable aspects of human experience.

The classical stories of ancient heroes descending to the under-world, with which many are still familiar today, were not regarded by the ancient Greeks as fact, as *logos*. They were about teaching those who heard them how to navigate their psyche – *mythos*. In the same way, the Bible's creation narrative of Adam and Eve and the Garden of Eden was understood for centuries, until the Scientific Revolution, not as a factual explanation of our origins, but rather as a kind of poetic cosmology, to be recited at times of crisis or sickness, to give energy, courage and reassurance. Nobody was required to 'believe' it. Certainly not in the sense that we use the word today. Belief was about commitment, not credulity.

Nowadays, however, scientific *logos* is all-conquering and the world of *mythos* is discredited and discarded. The rise of the novel in the eighteenth century arguably marked a further but associated shift. When we were perfectly able to understand and applaud the 'fiction' that was told in the pages of a novel as meta-phor for the reality of life and human experience, simultaneously (and curiously) we became progressively unable to continue to accept the same thing about the narrative we read in the scrip-tures. For believers, an embattled tendency began to develop, by way of reaction, that insisted on presenting scripture as literal truth, and gave rise to a new and distorting fundamentalism within religions. It contributed to scripture being sidelined as 'just' myth, as if myth had no value in the modern way of looking at the world and its challenges.

Since angels seem unlikely ever to be proven to 'exist' in any rational or scientific way, they too should, logically, be on their way out; but they are not. One explanation is that their survival against the odds says something about what some scientists like to refer to as the 'God circuit' in our brains – a part of the hippocampus that has been shown to be activated when we feel love. In that same maze of patterns of nerve cells and neural pathways, angels just cannot be extinguished.

Yet science is not clear-cut on the structure of the brain. The British psychiatrist Iain McGilchrist, in his landmark 2009 book *The Master and His Emissary*, argued that the modern age has seen a shift in the balance between the brain's right and left hemispheres, with the left – which processes into expression thought that originates in the right, and then returns it to the right to be integrated – having become more dominant in Western culture. Though the left hemisphere may be the domain of language, McGilchrist argues, the right is that of poetry and metaphor, so what he is saying is that in recent times our collective ability to grasp the meaning of ideas such as angels has been reduced.[14]

Reduced but absolutely not eliminated. The urge, many would suggest, remains. The Anglican theologian Jane Williams has written: 'In what we think about angels, it is as though we allow ourselves access to needs that normally we would deny or suppress. Angels give us a way of expressing our longing for beings who are more powerful than ourselves, and who care for us.'[15]

It is once again that time-honoured hankering to narrow the distance between us and the beyond, to find a way of connecting with that untenanted void beyond our planet, somewhere that also beguiles the half of Britons, Americans and Germans who believe in aliens.[16]

In 1923, the German poet-mystic Rainer Maria Rilke envisaged an unknowable species of angel in his *Duino Elegies*. They had a remoteness, a terrible beauty that lies beyond human limitations, a perfection towards which we can only aspire. 'Who,' he wrote, 'if I cried out, would hear me among the angels' hierarchies? And even if one of them pressed me against his heart: I would be consumed in that overwhelming existence.'[17]

Human beings, nevertheless, continue to pit their finite minds against the infinite.

Part One

The Authorised Version of Angels

'And as imagination bodies forth
The form of things unknown, the poet's pen
Turns them to shapes, and gives to airy nothing
A local habitation and a name.'
Duke Theseus, in *A Midsummer Night's
Dream*, by William Shakespeare (V.i.8–23)

A

A is for **Asa Vahista**, one of the six Amesha Spenta (or 'Beneficent Immortals') of Zoroastrianism, the predominant religion of Persia from 1500 BCE until it was displaced by Islam in the seventh century CE. Each of the six were 'divine sparks' created by the good god, Ahura Mazda, to watch over his people, and protect them from the bad god, Angra Mainyu. They were a type of guardian angel, with the elevated status of archangels. Though technically all are gender neutral, Asa is usually regarded as masculine. To his name is added Vahista – a word used of him in the sacred Zoroastrian text the *Gathas* by the prophet Zoroaster himself and meaning simply 'the best'. Asa represents truth, justice and righteousness, the combination of which embodies what it is to be a good Zoroastrian. Each Amesha Spenta is also allocated a specific domain. In the case of Asa, it is fire – still an integral and distinctive part of Zoroastrian rituals.

B

B is for the **Bulgarian** angels, who local legend has it inhabit the Devil's Throat Gorge in the Rhodope Mountains in the south-eastern European country. Amid marble cliffs is a deep cave through which an underground waterfall plunges deafeningly over forty metres. It was here that, Christian legend has it, based on a passage in the Book of Genesis, the fallen angels retreated once they had come down to earth and impregnated the daughters of men. It was as good as a prison, not least because of the constant thundering sound of the waterfall inside the cave, caused by their tears of regret. An alternative, possibly earlier, legend has it that this was the spot where the Greek god Orpheus came to enter the underworld and find Eurydice.

Holy Books – the First Angels

'And yet, as angels in some brighter dreams
Call to the soul when man doth sleep,
So some strange thoughts transcend our wonted themes,
And into glory peep.'

Henry Vaughan, 'They Are All Gone
Into the World of Light' (1655)[1]

For almost three thousand years, the words 'Holy, Holy, Holy,
Lord God of Hosts / Heaven and Earth are full of your glory /
Hosanna in the highest' have been set to music by believers as
part of their liturgies and rituals in synagogues and churches.
The origins of what is called 'The Song of the Angels' rest in the
Jewish tradition, an approximation of it having first been
recorded in the Hebrew Scriptures in the Book of Isaiah, one of
a series of prophets sent by God to the Jewish people in their
hour of need.[2]

The early sections of the book date back to the eighth century
BCE, and it is here that the 'Holy, Holy, Holy' rings out to herald
Isaiah's extraordinary vision of the Almighty seated on a throne
in the Temple in Jerusalem. Accompanying him is an honour
guard of mighty angels known as seraphim, 'each one with six
wings: two to cover its face, two to cover its feet, and two for
flying'.[3]

As these seraphim sing their hymn of praise, the very foundations of the Temple – the holiest of holies in Judaism – shake and

it fills with smoke. Then, with great ceremony, one of their number takes a red hot lump of coal from the altar and touches Isaiah's lips with it, burning away his sins and anointing him as God's messenger.[4]

Many of the details given in Isaiah – including the words of 'The Song of the Angels' – are repeated in chapter four of the Book of Revelation, the final, apocalyptic instalment of the Christian New Testament, written towards the end of the first century CE.[5] Now, though, there are four creatures, still with six wings, not angels but three animals – a lion, a bull and a flying eagle – and a fourth with a human face. All of them have 'eyes all the way round as well as inside; and day and night they never stopped singing: "Holy, Holy, Holy is the Lord God Almighty; he was, he is and he is to come." '[6]

In Jewish ritual today the words of 'The Song of the Angels' continue to be heard in the *Kedushah* (or sanctification), part of the daily prayer service. Traditionally those reciting them rise onto their toes with every '*kadosh*' or 'holy', a little higher each time, as if straining to reach up towards the angels above.

Among the early Christians, too, the Book of Isaiah was regarded with a special reverence because of the prophet's promise that God would come among his people. Christians took this as an early promise of Jesus. So much so that Isaiah is still sometimes referred to as the 'fifth gospel'.[7] 'The Song of the Angels' was incorporated by the Western Church in the fifth century CE into the officially approved text of the mass, with the 'Holy, Holy, Holy' repeated in the *Sanctus* (the Latin for 'Holy'). Meanwhile, in the East, Orthodox Christians continue to recite the angels' words, as part of their liturgy, in the *Trisagion* (or 'Thrice Holy'). In all these traditions, which together cover over 1.5 billion of the world's population, it is understood that human voices join in song with those of angels in a single choir that transcends the boundaries of heaven and earth.[8]

Of all the words included in 'The Song of the Angels', it is arguably their collective 'Hosanna' – in Hebrew *yasha na*, or 'O, Save!' – that has been most often placed on the lips of angels, or hung around their person. It is there, for instance, in the popular early sixteenth-century Christmas carol, 'Ding Dong Merrily On High', where 'the sky / is riv'n with angels singing: / Gloria, Hosanna in excelsis!' And 'Hosanna' is spelt out, too, on the banners that the angels unfurl from their trumpets on Christmas cards (though any sense of it being a plea to be saved is lost). Meanwhile, in Dante's *Paradiso*, the final leg of the poet's journey through the next world that makes up his three-part *Divine Comedy*, the narrator only manages to work out that the millions of 'scintillating sparks' that encircle him in the upper realms of heaven are in fact angels when he hears the sound of their hosannas.

> I heard them sing hosanna choir by choir
> To the fixed point which holds them at the 'Ubi',
> And ever will, where they have ever been.[9]

The Song even gives us the word 'host' – our collective noun for angels. The origins of host predate even Isaiah and belong to the period around the eleventh century BCE when the Jewish king, Saul, established a united kingdom of Israel, with his successor David making its capital at Jerusalem. In the Hebrew Scriptures concerned with that time (for example, at the very start of the First Book of Samuel), Yahweh is credited with playing an active part in these victories, and is regularly referred to as 'Lord of Hosts'.[10] The Hebrew word *sabaoth*, translated as 'hosts', also means armies, and carries with it therefore the sense of massed ranks of supporters. In earthly terms, that becomes the Yahweh-inspired troops who brought Saul and his successors victories on the battlefield against their opponents, the Philistines. Mixed in with them, it was believed, were angels, sent from heaven to assist.

Beyond music, liturgy and scripture, the lines of 'The Song of the Angels' open out to reveal how entwined the history of angels is with the Israelites' relationship with their God. Indeed, the story goes back to the very beginning, and the creation story of the Garden of Eden. When God expels Adam and Eve from paradise for eating the apple from the tree against his instructions, 'He posted the cherubs, and the flame of a flashing sword, to guard the way to the tree of life.'[11] And later in the same Book of Genesis – the first text in both the Pentateuch, taken by Jews as the work of Moses and containing the Jewish law, *and* of the Christian Bible – three angels appear at Mamre to Abraham,[12] regarded as a founding father by Judaism, Christianity and Islam alike.

In understanding the origins of humankind's enduring relationship with angels, the overlapping holy books of Judaism, Christianity and Islam are one obvious starting point. Yet, though they present themselves – or are often presented by religious literalists – as the start of everything that ever was, these are neither the first holy texts, nor the first ones to feature angel-like creatures.

Those six-winged seraphim that Isaiah described so memorably in the eighth century BCE in his vision of Yahweh entering Jerusalem have no obvious forerunners in earlier sections of the Hebrew Scriptures. Only much later in Revelation do they appear again in the Christian Bible. And yet the seraphim have gone on to figure large in theological debates about angels and their hierarchies, as well as in art and in literature. In *Paradise Lost*, Milton even gives his seraphim individual personalities, with Abdiel – a name he borrowed from a minor, Old Testament character[13] – described as the seraph 'than whom none with more zeal adored / The Deity and divine commands obeyed'.[14, 15]

So where did Isaiah's description of the seraphim come from? Their curious gesture in covering their eyes and feet with their 'extra' pairs of wings may be understandable as an act of protection in the first case – unable to look directly at the glory of God – and modesty in the second. Some interpretations in Jewish rabbinical literature suggest that the reference to feet was a euphemism for their genitals.[16] But when God chose to reveal the seraphim for the very first time in Isaiah's vision, how did the prophet know what to call them? If he was not instructed by God as to the proper name to use for these extraordinary creatures (and that may be implicit, but is not stated in the text), are there other origins, both for the word *seraph*, and for the strange creatures it describes in the world that Isaiah would have known? Or even in that which was beyond his ken?

There are, according to scholars, two possible sources for the word *seraph* in ancient Hebrew: the first from the verb to burn, hence these six-winged angels were burning with love for God; and the second from the verb to exalt. They exalted God and were in their turn the exalted ones, on a higher level than other angels.[17]

The first option – from the verb to burn – is the most intriguing in exploring the history of angels, because it connects the seraphim with other creatures who inhabit the Book of Isaiah. The *saraf* were bewinged serpents, deadly on account of their burning venom,[18] and were in their turn linked with the serpent cults that existed at the same time, and earlier, both among the Israelites and in other belief systems.

The Book of Numbers, for example, which in origin predates Isaiah by several centuries and comes fourth in the five texts of the Pentateuch, tells of the desert journeys and first settlements of the Israelites. In it, the travellers are regularly assailed by *saraf*, or fiery, flying serpents, whose bite could cause death. That doesn't seem, at first glance, to have any sort of connection to the angels of modern imagination, all balm and smiles. Yet the *saraf* are, like other angels in the Old Testament, sent by Yahweh as emissaries to advise the Israelites of their first loyalty to him. The reminder these *saraf* deliver may be anything but gentle, much more the sting of the stick than the incentive of the carrot, but it comes nonetheless from God as a message that should not be ignored.

And Moses does not ignore the *saraf*. His response is to fashion a bronze serpent, 'which he put on a standard, and if anyone was bitten by a serpent, he looked at the bronze serpent and lived'.[19] Later in the Second Books of Kings, though, we read that this bronze serpent has to be destroyed because people have begun to make sacrifices to it and treat it as a deity in its own right.[20]

There is certainly something fierce and terrifying, menacing as well as magnificent, about the mysterious seraphim that Isaiah describes as accompanying Yahweh's throne. So this etymological and physical connection between seraphim and the flying *saraf* may well have contributed to the particular awe that the six-winged seraphim inspired when Isaiah recounted his vision.

And that resonance extends into the deities of Canaan and Baal, which ran alongside, and in places predated, the history of the Jews as told in the Hebrew Scriptures. They had winged serpent gods, as did the Egyptians, from whose overlordship and exploitation Moses freed the Israelites. In the crowded pantheon of the highly advanced Egyptian civilisation that thrived along the River Nile and its delta from the fourth millennium BCE, the *saraf* or serpent would have been well known as a benign symbol of power and protection. The goddess Wadjet, guardian of Lower Egypt, for instance, was depicted as a flying serpent.

She was not alone in the ranks of the minor – and sometimes major – Egyptian gods in having wings like Isaiah's seraphim. Isis (in Greek) or Asset/Eset (the latter curiously the ancient Egyptian word for the sort of throne occupied by Yahweh in Isaiah's vision) was one of the most important deities in Egypt, subsequently to be taken up by the Greeks and Romans, with her cult spreading across their empire from Britain to Afghanistan, and still found today in pagan belief systems. Beside her more familiar depiction with her infant son, Horus (said to be one of the influences behind Christian depictions of Mary and Jesus as Madonna and Child), Isis was often shown with wings as one of the four protector goddesses.

The first references to Isis date back to the Fifth Dynasty of Pharaohs, around 2500 BCE, and over the millennia Isis was given many roles, among them using her wings to spread a heavenly scent across the land, or to bring fresh air into the underworld, where she acted as guide to the dead on their journey into the afterlife.

In addition to annexing Isis, the ancient Greeks had many other winged emissaries of the gods, among them Hermes, who features in the writings of both Homer and Hesiod around the eighth century BCE, the same date given to the early section of Isaiah where 'The Song of Angels' appears. One of Hermes' tasks, like Isis, was to accompany the souls of the dead on their journey.

Both Homer and Hesiod also refer to daimons, lesser deities, somewhere between humans and the gods, who act as benign guiding spirits, and sometimes have wings or winged sandals, though often they cannot be seen at all. They were, Hesiod states in his epic poem *Works and Days*, 'good beings who dispense riches [but who also] remain invisible, known only by their acts'.[21]

It is a description that could easily be applied to a guardian angel and, just as angels later became a subject of endless speculation in Jewish, Christian and Muslim thought, so too the daimons of ancient Greece evolved over time through debate and discussion. Hesiod, for example, connected them with veneration of ancestors, suggesting the great and powerful should continue to be honoured after death in the form of daimons. In their local communities, some Greeks would build shrines to the daimons of their dead heroes.

Where Homer argued that daimons were closer to the gods than to humans, several centuries later Plato (427–347 BCE), the philosopher credited with founding the Academy in Athens as the world's first seat of higher learning, maintained that the daimon was inextricably tied to humans, the rough equivalent of each individual's immortal soul, and there with him or her from birth, but separate from the body.[22] In particular, Plato recalled in *Phaedo* how his teacher, Socrates, widely considered as the founding father of Western philosophy, had been able to hear the voice of his personal daimon. It was the source of his genius,[23] guiding him away from errors, though never directly instructing him what to do or say. Its role was to inspire human thoughts and actions, Plato suggested, rather than prescribe or enforce them.

The nature of daimons was subsequently further refined in the later Hellenistic period (300 BCE to 30 BCE) to encompass the idea that daimons could be both benign and malign guiding spirits. Such a division, in turn, went on to influence Jewish and early Christian writers. The Jewish philosopher Philo of Alexandria (*c.* 20 BCE–50 CE), for example, laboured to reconcile Greek ideas with the Hebrew Scriptures. 'The beings whom other philosophers called daimons,' he noted, 'Moses usually called angels.' Emphasising the overlap, he added that 'souls, demons and angels differ in name but they are identical in reality'.[24]

'The angels' names came from Babylon'

The blueprint for the various parts played by angels in Judaism, and hence Christianity and later Islam, can already be glimpsed in these accounts, but we are skipping ahead in our story at the risk of losing sight of other potential influences on Isaiah and that striking description he offers of the seraphim in 'The Song of the Angels'. Casting the net more widely, among the Sumerians, Akkadians and later Assyrians and Babylonians – connected, highly developed agriculturally based civilisations that grew and then spread outwards from 4000 BCE from a core in the rich fields between the Tigris and Euphrates rivers in what is today southern Iraq[25] – there were mighty, intimidating winged figures who were both used as symbols of quasi-divine earthly power, and regarded as deities.

They were featured in the fabric of the stone-built palaces of worship that became common for the first time in these parts, forerunners of temples, synagogues, churches and mosques. These buildings expressed a physical link with the often-invisible power of the gods, rooting it physically in the material world. Among the figures used to decorate them was Pazuzu, a flying composite of human and animal parts, who was simultaneously the demon bringing famine in the dry season[26] *and* the guardian protecting those who worshipped him from other more malign spirits.

Often, too, the shape and size of these buildings could express a yearning to get closer to the gods. Ziggurats (or temple towers), like that of Marduk, in the Babylonian epic poem of creation, the *Enuma Elish*, provided a summit, halfway between heaven and earth, where humans could encounter the divine face to face.[27]

Arguably the greatest influence on the angels that feature on our Christmas cards today, though, came from the winged spirits of Zoroastrianism, the religion of the followers of the prophet Zoroaster, who is thought to have lived in modern-day Iran sometime between 15,000 and 10,000 BCE.[28] The belief system he inspired thrived across the whole region in various forms until the seventh century CE, when the rise of Islam displaced it. The most obvious parallels with 'our' angels are provided by Zoroastrianism's *fravashi*, sometimes described as patrolling the ramparts of heaven before descending to earth to act as guardian spirits to believers.

Like many aspects of Zoroastrianism, their exact role and status is now the subject of much debate among scholars, since they are not mentioned in those sections of the *Avesta*, the most sacred book of Zoroastrianism, that have survived (estimated at around a quarter of the original). There are references to them, according to some readings, in extant sections of the *Gathas*, a collection of 'hymns' and other texts reputedly written by Zoroaster. These describe an army of *fravashi* helpers created by Ahura Mazda, the Lord of Light and Wisdom, to assist him in his struggle against Angra Mainyu, Lord of Evil and Destruction. In positing a good god against a bad god, Zoroastrianism was one of the world's first dualist belief systems, portraying believers as caught up in a cosmic battle between equal and opposite divine powers.

Like the daimons of ancient Greece, it is hard to be truly precise about the angel-like *fravashi* because they rise and fall in significance, and in how they are described, over the sweep of Zoroastrian history. Our ability properly to understand those developments is dented by the relative scarcity of surviving materials. What does seem to have happened, however, is that a strand of Zoroastrianism, known as Zurvanism and allied to geo-political power in Babylon, dominated from at least the fourth century BCE onwards. In it, the *fravashi* came to the fore as models – or mirrors – of spiritual perfection, rather than heaven-sent guardians to individual believers.

Among today's direct descendants of the Zoroastrians, the 200,000-strong community of Parsees, found mainly in India (where they fled when persecuted by Islam), there is a slightly different view again, with the *fravashi* more likely to be characterised as protective spirits of ancestors watching over their surviving relatives. To add to an already far from clear picture, the *Faravahar*, the depiction of a winged angel-like creature as the infinite human spirit that is usually taken as the symbol of Zoroastrianism, is believed, in its current form, to be a nineteenth-century-CE invention, created as a reaction to European colonialism, and designed as a national rallying point for Iran, its history and culture, rather than a specifically religious image.

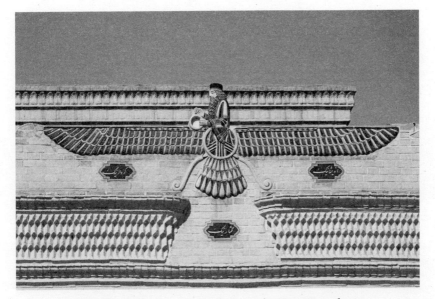

The Faravahar *– as seen here at the Fire Temple at Yazd in Iran – is a representation in Zoroastrianism of the human spirit as a winged angel-like figure.*

The *fravashi*, then, offer no easily read clues as to their potential influences on the seraphim of Isaiah's imagination. The sections of the book that contain 'The Song of Angels' were written earlier than the passages that reflect a much stronger Zoroastrian influence over Judaism. These parts of Isaiah were completed during the Jews' long exposure to Zoroastrian beliefs and practices during their exile in Babylon from 587 to 539 BCE. This 'captivity' was the result of their defeat by Nebuchadnezzar, King of Babylon, who added to the Jews' trauma and sense of being abandoned in their hour of need by Yahweh when he destroyed their Temple in Jerusalem. That Zoroastrian influence on Judaism found in later parts of the Book of Isaiah is part of a wider impact exile had on Jewish ideas. For this history of angels, that is best summed up by a striking adage from the Talmud (the written compilation of Jewish law and rabbinic discussions around it, which first started to be compiled in the second century CE). It states that 'the angels' names came from Babylon'.[29]

The named angels in question are the archangels Gabriel and Michael, found in the Book of Daniel, one of the final books in the Hebrew Scriptures and dated to 165 BCE, as well as Raphael and others in the Book of Enoch, who we will explore in detail later. The claimed Babylonian/Zoroastrian inspiration for these named archangels is its six (three male and three female) Amesha Spenta, or 'Beneficent Immortals'. In the *Yasna* – the main Zoroastrian act of worship – it is told how Ahura Mazda creates each of the six to line up alongside him as 'divine sparks' (an echo of that description, 'scintillating sparks', later used of angels by Dante in his *Paradiso*). They are the visible form taken by a creator God who is invisible, and are akin to putting a series of faces on the divine. Each of the six Amesha Spenta has individual virtues and associations – good purpose, truth and righteousness, power, devotion, wholeness, and immortality – and all guard creation in the cosmic battle with the malign Angra Mainyu. They are, in this capacity, more powerful than the mere *fravashi*, and so equate to a better class of angel.

How ideas are shared

It was through human interaction between different religions and belief systems – in exile, at war, or simply different peoples encountering each other as neighbours and trading partners – that the angels emerge who fill the pages of Hebrew Scriptures, the New Testament, and later the Qur'an. The physical links created by the East–West trading routes linking Asia to Europe may not have developed until the second century BCE into an established network, known as the 'Silk Road' between the Mediterranean and the Himalayas,[30] but some sort of exchange of ideas had been going on long before that date. Geographical or commercial proximity, though, is not the only factor to consider.

Historians have in the past half-century increasingly high-lighted the importance of the period between 800 and 300 BCE, a time that they call the Axial Age because it was when many of the world's great religions burst into life around a common axis of beliefs.[31] It witnessed the dawn of the great traditions that continue to nourish humanity: Confucianism and Daoism in China; Hinduism and Buddhism in India; the one God ('mono-theism') of Judaism, which was later to nurture both Christianity and Islam; and the philosophical rationalism of Greece. This was the period of the Buddha, Confucius, the Hindu mystics of the Upanishads, and Socrates, among others, as well as some of the prophets of the Hebrew Scriptures. The overlap of ideas between these different and disparate teachers, and the systems they repre-sent, cannot simply be explained by physical contact. Some of them worked anonymously, others in isolation. It must also have been part of a shared human reaction to the particular circum-stances of those centuries, the dilemmas they threw up, and the appetites they created.

In the case of the Axial Age sages, one of the things that united them was impatience with the doctrinal codes, rules, prescrip-tions and carefully plotted hierarchies that we nowadays tend to associate with organised religion. They were much more inter-ested separately but – with hindsight – severally in pushing forward the frontiers of human consciousness in search of a transcendent dimension to life, something that went beyond the here and now, and connected them with a higher principle, whether it be a god or gods, a state of perfection, or higher being, an afterlife or the cycle of reincarnation.[32] Part of that endeavour included, in all sorts of different and not so different shapes, a cast of messengers, lesser deities, spirits, intermediaries or guard-ians, who closed the gap between the gods and the rest of us. Why? Because such go-betweens answered a shared human need for some way of approaching or feeling the presence of deities.

And so, while it would be stretching a point to say that Isaiah's vision of six-winged seraphim in the eighth century BCE owed any sort of obvious debt to emerging ideas in evolving Hinduism, nevertheless its angel-like figures should form part of the wider backdrop to this story. Hinduism is often described as the world's oldest religion, stretching back to the civilisation that thrived in and around the Indus Valley – the 'Land of Seven Rivers' (or Sapta-Sindhu, the origin of the word Hindu) – between 2500 BCE and 2000 BCE. From it sacred texts emerged, written in Sanskrit, and known collectively as the *Vedas* ('knowledge'), of which the *Rig Veda*, dated between 1500 and 1200 BCE, is the best known. It describes Gandharva as a god who guards the moon and holds the secrets of heaven. By the time of the Upanishads, from the eighth to the fifth century BCE, however, the *gandharva* had become male nature spirits, half human, half animal, usually bird, and hence with wings. They also acted as messengers between the gods and humans, but were most celebrated for their musical gifts, their voices, and the songs they sang that were able, it was said, to carry their listeners into ecstatic trances, just as the choirs of angels in Judaism and Christianity could reach down in 'The Song of Angels' to those on earth.

Significant, too, in the Hindu pantheon are the male *deva* and female *devi*, 'dwelling with glory in mid-air' according to the *Rig Veda*.[33] They are often represented as the bringers of light (as opposed to the *asuras*, spirits who bring darkness) and have their place in the cycle of rebirth that is part of Hinduism as the guardian of souls between each death and rebirth.

The parallels with the history of angels are striking. To their number should also be added the *bodhisattvas* of Buddhism, guides to meaningful spiritual life, mythical, awesome in power, radiance and wisdom, but simultaneously as ordinary as your next-door neighbour.

How far, though, did that shared but separate Axial Age search for a transcendent dimension in life connect peoples in distinct and distant parts of the world? Why the overlaps and echoes – in our case around angel-like figures – in what historians argue was often a spontaneous human inclination to make 'transparent the transcendent'? That phrase is one associated with the American writer and academic Joseph Campbell (1904–87), who was less interested in the technicalities of how ideas were passed from hand to hand, head to head, or heart to heart, and preferred instead to see any connections between peoples in different parts of the world at the same time as part of a more instinctive joint human endeavour to make sense of life. All religions, he argued in his 1949 book *The Hero with a Thousand Faces*, created gods who were aspects of a shared 'mono-myth'.[34] Drawing heavily on the insights of the analytical psychologist Carl Jung, Campbell proposed that many of the shared details of religions – angelic beings among them – are better seen as remnants that 'line the walls of our interior system of belief, like shards of broken pottery in an archaeological site', a road map of existence generated largely from inside rather than from outside connections and influences.

In other words, in the case of Isaiah's winged creatures, the first choir to sing 'The Song of Angels' three thousand years ago, they were part of a response that arose spontaneously and separately in all religions to human psychology and its need for this life not to be everything, and for there to be something in that space between earth and sky, and beyond. As Campbell put it, we just didn't want to be alone.[35]

C

C is for Angel **Clare**, the son of a clergyman in Thomas Hardy's 1892 novel *Tess of the d'Urbervilles*, who starts out as a 'freethinker'. His first name suggests a free spirit as well. Unlike his more conventionally christened brothers Felix and Cuthbert, Angel disdains following in his father's footsteps into church ministry, and instead opts to be a lowly farmer, preferring, as Hardy puts it, 'sermons in stones to sermons in church'. Of Tess, he writes, 'there was hardly a touch of earth in her love for Clare'. Yet this Angel is not there when the woman he loves, and who loves him in return, is raped by the libertine Alec Stoke-d'Urberville. 'Where was Tess's guardian angel?' the narrator pointedly asks, as if damning the very notion that such a thing exists. And Angel Clare turns out to be no 'freethinker'. Instead his residual conventional, church-based morality means he abandons Tess on their wedding night when she tells him what Alec did to her. By the time he finally returns to guard her in the book's poignant ending at Stonehenge, fate has intervened and it is too late.

D

D is for **Damiel**, mentioned in the Book of Enoch as one of the 'Watcher Angels' who betray God, fall to earth and introduce evil into the world. He is perhaps better known, though, as one of the two trench-coat-wearing guardian angels assigned to assist the people of Berlin in Wim Wenders' award-winning 1987 film, *Wings of Desire*. Of the two, Damiel (played by Bruno Ganz) is the one who grows tired of a role that never allows him to cross the boundary between the material and spiritual, a frustration exacerbated when he falls for a lonely trapeze artist called Marion. He discards his immortality, and his wings, and so gets to meet Marion, his world no longer the sepia-infused black and white landscape seen by angels, but a full-colour bar in Berlin where Australian rocker Nick Cave is playing.

Wrestling with Angels – Genesis and the Hebrew Scriptures

'The angels keep their ancient places;—
Turn but a stone and start a wing!
'Tis ye, 'tis your estrangèd faces,
That miss the many-splendoured thing.

But (when so sad thou canst not sadder)
Cry;—and upon thy so sore loss
Shall shine the traffic of Jacob's ladder
Pitched betwixt Heaven and Charing Cross.'
Francis Thompson,
'In No Strange Land'[1]

The Book of Genesis records an extraordinary night spent by Jacob, grandson of the biblical patriarch Abraham, at a ford on the River Jabbok. He is assailed and then locked in physical combat with a figure who, in the text, is described first as a man, then is revealed as God, but later in the Jewish and Christian tradition was recast as an angel.

Jacob wrestling with the angel is one of the best-known episodes in the epic saga recounted in Genesis of the foundation of Israel and of Abraham, Isaac, Jacob and his twelve fractious sons who form the tribes of Israel (and fall out over a technicolour dreamcoat). The man/God/angel is so rough that he ends up dislocating Jacob's hip, leaving him limping. It has ever after beguiled theologians,[2] poets,[3] hymn-writers[4] and artists, including Rembrandt, Delacroix, Gaugin and Chagall, as well as Jacob's twentieth-century namesake, the British sculptor Jacob Epstein. His arresting 1940 alabaster carving in primitive style in Tate Britain in London has the two wrestling figures in a tight grasp that is half embrace, and half attempted murder.

Jacob Epstein's 1940 Jacob and the Angel *is an alabaster carving of the sculptor's biblical namesake wrestling with what is variously described in Judaism and Christianity as a man, an angel or God.*

Genesis chronicles how Jacob is journeying home. On arriving at the River Jabbok, he sends on ahead his wives, servants and eleven children, but spends the night there himself.

And there was one that wrestled with him until daybreak who, seeing that he could not master him [Jacob], struck him in the socket of his hip, and Jacob's hip was dislocated as he wrestled with him. He said, 'Let me go, for day is breaking.' But Jacob answered, 'I will not let you go unless you bless me.'

He then asked, 'What is your name?'

'Jacob,' he replied.

He said, 'Your name shall no longer be Jacob, but Israel. Because you have been strong against God, you shall prevail against men.'

Jacob then made this request. 'I beg you, tell me your name.'

But he replied, 'Why do you ask my name?' And he blessed him [Jacob] there.

Jacob named the place Peniel, 'because I have seen God face to face,' he said, 'and I have survived'.[5]

Some of the details jar, certainly for a contemporary audience, brought up on New Testament notions of a loving God. Why would he, under cover of night, turn aggressor?[6] And would he have gone further still and killed Jacob if the latter hadn't put up such fierce resistance? God appears to be the first one to blink in the stand-off. He was 'worsted' by Jacob, as the poet Emily Dickinson wrote in her reflection on the episode.[7]

Yet Genesis – and indeed the Hebrew Scriptures – is full of similar violence, destruction and death, meted out by God, or by his representatives, often angels, with his explicit approval. The question then becomes, why does he hold back here mid-struggle?

Theologians and historians of the Bible have debated at length over the centuries whether this passage (and indeed most accounts of angels) is best treated as a dream. Sigmund Freud was not the first to recognise that what we dream of as we sleep reveals what we are thinking when we are awake. The idea was part of earliest rabbinic teaching and 'significant' dreams feature in the Hebrew Scriptures.

Jacob, in particular, has form in this regard. Earlier in Genesis, Yahweh has appeared to him in a dream and shown him a ladder, 'standing on the ground with its top reaching to heaven: and there were angels of God going up it and coming down'.[8] This was the ladder that Bronwen Astor saw after she gave birth to her daughter, and is a familiar and recurring image in the Judeo-Christian imagination, for instance on the extraordinary pair of carved stone ladders that ascend to heaven on either side of the West Front of sixteenth-century Bath Abbey in Somerset, with six angels on each.

On another occasion, Jacob is again visited in his sleep by 'the angel of God', who warns him to 'leave the country' as part of his bloodthirsty row with his brother, Esau, from which neither emerges with much credit.[9]

At the Jabbok, though it is explicitly nightfall, when sleep should come naturally, there is no mention of a dream, but Jacob is all alone with no one to prevent him dozing off. Does God, or someone on God's behalf, appear in Jacob's dreams, and then go away when he wakes? It is, after all, the text makes clear, daylight when the fight ends.

But what of the dislocated hip? Dreams may leave you traumatised. On rare occasions, they might even cause you to fall out of bed and bruise yourself, but rarely does a physical injury sustained in a dream remain once you are fully awake.

That may be taking it all too literally. And literal readings of the Book of Genesis can produce strange results. In her *Angels and Ministers of Grace*, for example, the well-known twentieth-century anthropologist M.J. Field – who described her work as 'ethno-psychiatric' – set out to 'prove' that all the angels of the Bible were either human beings or hallucinations. Taking the former approach with the angel who tussled with Jacob, she concluded that he was a land agent, 'some obscure little man' patrolling a border between different land holdings at the ford, 'whose co-operation and ritual blessings immigrants were passionately anxious to secure'.[10]

Perhaps the dreams of Jacob – and others – are instead best seen as moving the scriptural narrative from the actual to the metaphorical, or even the metaphysical. Those who study the Hebrew terms used by the writers of Genesis suggest that there could also be some sort of word-play going on here: that using the River Jabbok is of symbolic significance, because Jabbok means 'crooked', and Jacob has been 'crooked' in his past dealings with his brother, deceiving their father to receive a blessing intended for Esau.

And what, in this context, of the parallels in other belief systems for such an encounter? In Greek mythology, there is Achilles, who has a duel (one of three) next to flowing water with the river god Scamander, whose name in some (but not all) translations echoes the fate of Jacob because it can be broken down into *skado*, from the Greek to limp, and *andros*, or man.

Such speculation, though, pales next to another 'meaning' of this resonant wrestling match. God wants to test Jacob's mettle, in order to decide which of the brothers in the Esau–Jacob battle should get his blessing. So he creeps up on him in disguise, slogs it out with him, punishing him (with a dislocated hip) for any past misdeeds, and only then reveals himself, absolves Jacob, and finally anoints him as his chosen vessel on earth, the one who will build Israel.[11]

Significantly, Jacob names the place where their tussle takes place as Peniel, which means the face of God. The spiritual yearning to see the face of God – in modern terms to receive tangible proof that God exists – has always been a powerful but usually unsatisfied urge among believers.[12] Here, then, is what truly seems extraordinary about the whole story to all who come after it – that Jacob, a mere mortal, and a flawed one at that given his dealings with his brother, gets up close and personal with God, not just in conversation (via an angel, as is often the way in Genesis), but also body-to-body in combat. This is the same God, remember, who tells Moses in the Book of Exodus (which follows Genesis in the running order of the Old Testament), 'man cannot see me and live'.[13]

Jacob, though, does both, and it is – at least, in part – the uneasiness this causes that was, many centuries later, to cause Jewish teachers anxiety, so much so that this incident would be recast in the tradition and the text tweaked (then passed on to Christianity) so that Jacob wrestles not with God himself, but with an angel as the representative of God. This 'editorial vision', writes the thinker and connoisseur of angels, Harold Bloom, was inserted because it was felt in subsequent ages that the earliest recorder of Genesis 'was being too daring in his depiction of God'.[14]

Where Abraham, Isaac and, in this case, Jacob appeared in these Genesis accounts to be living on familiar terms with their God – who guides them in their wanderings, tells them whom to marry, and speaks to them in their dreams – later generations of Jews saw an unthinkable intimacy with a God who, to them, for reasons we will go on to explore, had come to be regarded as a faraway figure. So insignificant was humanity, their teachers now instructed them, that such direct contact was no longer possible, or even desirable, lest it somehow diminish God to lower himself to the human level. He would have delegated such things to his angel messengers. Theirs was the task – as in Jacob's vision of a ladder – of bridging the gulf between heaven and earth.

This new orthodoxy is reflected most clearly towards the end of the Hebrew Scriptures in the Book of Hosea, whose writers had revisited many centuries later the Genesis account of that encounter at the ford on the Jabbok and labelled it explicitly and unambiguously as Jacob 'wrestling with an angel'.[15]

Genesis – the book of angels

As Jacob illustrates, angels are commonplace in the Book of Genesis, making it the logical stepping-off point to discover how and why angels have come to play such a significant part in the religion, culture and history of the Judeo-Christian West. The angels of Genesis are plain in their attire, unremarkable in their bodies (they have no wings), and blend in as essentially part of the furniture. They have nothing on the many-winged seraphim of Isaiah who came later.

The main purpose of Genesis is to convey the events between three and four thousand years ago in the land of Canaan, designated by Yahweh as the home to his chosen people, the Israelites. It is therefore about the relationship between the two. Angels feature in the narrative only as part of the backdrop to that central drama: doing tasks; following orders from on high; and delivering messages – often private, one-to-one messages, conveyed to individuals rather than crowds, though just as often their words have a public resonance. They are, essentially, facilitators. The Hebrew word that is rendered so often in Genesis as angel is *malach*, which in everyday usage refers to messengers. (The same is true in Greek and Arabic.) And, in Genesis, the message is more important than the messenger.

If one of the roles of angels in the Bible (and beyond, in the human psyche) is to be there when the going gets tough, then it doesn't get much tougher than the trials and tribulations of the Israelites as chronicled in Genesis. So, as they struggle to survive, and to establish their homeland in territory surrounded by – and often in the possession of – hostile forces, there are necessarily angels everywhere. They are never given individual names, and it was only much later that specific identities would be projected back in the Jewish tradition onto these anonymous angels in Genesis. Indeed, the text's essential vagueness about who exactly the angels are, and what they do, is only accentuated by the fact that they are interchangeably referred to as men, as angels, or as God himself – often all three in a single episode.

As we have already seen, the very first angels to appear in Genesis are not called messengers, but cherubim. They are the sentries placed on the gates of Eden to stop Adam and Eve from ever re-entering. Their role is to punish humans, not help them, by being actively hostile to what the Bible tells us are our earliest ancestors. This puzzled subsequent generations. In his *Paradise Lost*, Milton portrays Adam and Eve as angel-like themselves, able to talk with the Archangel Michael, whom Milton places in Eden and whom they refer to as a 'heavenly instructor'.[16] Many others, too, would later labour to discern quite what part the angels played in God's creation – were they his co-workers or were they fashioned by his hand just as he made Adam and Eve? Their speculations – and their arguments – will be examined later in the chronology of this book.

For now, our focus is on the text of Genesis, which gives little direct sustenance to such detailed speculation. In it, of the many angelic appearances, the most celebrated comes when three unremarkable desert travellers pitch up unannounced as an elderly man sits in the shade of an oak tree, sheltering from the noonday sun at the entrance to his tent. The old gent at the oak of Mamre is Abraham, Jacob's grandfather, and the three men are, albeit intermittently as is the way with Genesis, described as angels.

'He looked up and there he saw three men standing near him. As soon as he saw them he ran from the entrance of the tent to meet them, and bowed to the ground.'[17] The depth of his bow, and his haste in getting to his feet, suggest that Abraham can see behind the veneer of normality and knows that they are messengers sent by God. Or are they God himself?

'My Lord,' Abraham continues, apparently convinced he is in the divine presence, 'I beg you, if I find a little favour with you, kindly do not pass your servant by. A little water shall be brought; you shall wash your feet and lie down under the tree.'[18]

The men – still here being referred to in the text as 'they', as if the narrator has a different, more earthbound perspective from Abraham on their identity – accept what was typical Middle Eastern hospitality. As they eat the feast that is hastily prepared for them, they tell Abraham that the following year his wife Sarah will have a child. She is eavesdropping on the conversation from inside the tent and, at this revelation, 'laughed to herself, thinking, "now that I am past the age of child-bearing, and my husband is an old man, is pleasure to come my way again!" '[19]

The visitors – now called Yahweh by the narrator – overhear her chuckle and rebuke Abraham. 'Is anything too wonderful for Yahweh?' they ask him. And so Sarah speaks up. 'I didn't laugh,' she says. She is, the narrator adds, 'lying because she was afraid'. Yahweh, though, is having none of it. 'Oh yes, you did laugh,' he replies.[20]

It is an episode that has been picked over many times. When it is retold in the Qur'an, the visitors – 'our messengers' as they are called there – refuse the feast that Abraham lays before them, their abstinence from food being a sure sign that they are angels.[21] And in the rabbinic tradition, the three were allocated the names of Gabriel, Michael and Raphael.[22]

Something as specific as individual names, however, sits uneasily with these three ill-defined, ambiguous visitors, who are otherwise devoid of personality. They appear like a mirage in the midday sun of the desert. Yet that lack of sharp lines has not deterred theologians, teachers or artists. In the Eastern Orthodox tradition, for example, one of the most celebrated of all icons is an early fifteenth-century work by Andrei Rublev, known variously as *The Trinity* and *The Hospitality of Abraham*. It depicts the three visitors as winged angels, each with a halo – neither detail is in Genesis – sitting in a circle in silent contemplation round a table. There is no sign of Abraham or Sarah. Where Jewish teachers came to regard the three as archangels, Rublev's icon offers a still more radical projection. It casts them as the Holy Trinity, the three-persons-in-one-God that is central to Christian belief. In the very precise symbolism of icon painting, Rublev indicates through the colour of the clothing each angel is wearing that one is God the Father (shimmering white), one God the Son (blue cloak with red robe) and one God the Holy Spirit (green). Another of the conventions of icon painting is that God cannot be depicted. Through his interpretation of the visitors at the oak of Mamre, Rublev managed to circumvent this ban.

Andrei Rublev's early fifteenth-century Orthodox icon, The Trinity, *transforms the mysterious angels who meet Abraham at Mamre into the three-persons-in-one-God – Father, Son and Holy Spirit.*

It is a mighty step from three shadowy men to the Holy Trinity. One reason that these figures at Mamre were subsequently so often taken as angels, when the actual word is not used in standard English translations of this passage from Genesis, lies in the context in which their visit comes. Three chapters earlier, Yahweh has already spoken to the then Abram (later Abraham) in a vision, promising to make him 'heir to this land' of Canaan[23] and telling him – then already in his eighties, as is his childless wife Sarai (later Sarah) – that their 'flesh and blood' descendants will be as numerous as the stars in the night sky.[24]

What follows is that Abram gets his wife's servant, Hagar, pregnant, initially with Sarai's blessing (as an early example of surrogacy), but then Sarai turns against Hagar and treats her so badly that Hagar runs away. It is neither messengers, nor God, who appear to Hagar in the wilderness, but specifically 'the angel of Yahweh',[25] who makes Hagar promise to return and submit to Sarai. Her child will be a boy, the angel tells Hagar, and should be called Ishmael, and Hagar's descendants also will be 'too numerous to be counted'.[26]

At which stage, typically of Genesis, the writer ceases to refer to 'the angel of Yahweh' addressing Hagar, and speaks instead simply of Yahweh talking to her. In the next chapter, Yahweh appears again to Abram, now aged ninety-nine, and proposes a covenant in perpetuity between them that will make him, now to be renamed Abraham (and his wife Sarai, Sarah), 'the father of a multitude of nations'.[27] When Abraham mentions his own great age, and that of Sarah who is well beyond childbearing years, Yahweh explicitly promises him a son who should be called Isaac. Abraham, though, doesn't pass this news on to Sarah, presumably incredulous, which is why the three men come a-calling at the oak of Mamre.

If there are angels in the run-up to this key encounter at Mamre, there are also angels in its aftermath. 'The men' next set out for the city of Sodom, which Yahweh intends to punish for non-specific acts of ungodliness.[28] Traditionally, Christianity has held that Sodom and its neighbouring city, Gomorrah, were punished because their inhabitants were gay – homosexuality being labelled as 'the sin of Sodom' – but this has little explicit basis in the actual biblical text, the most obvious sin of the people being lack of hospitality.

Abraham pleads on behalf of Sodom, but still 'two angels' arrive there that evening to carry out God's orders.[29] As they stay overnight with Abraham's nephew Lot, who feeds them, they are besieged by a menacing crowd outside the house. The two avenging angels show no restraint in their response and 'strike' those gathering at the door 'with blindness, from the youngest to the oldest'.[30]

Next, the pair – now once again referred to as 'the men' – evacuate Lot and his family from Sodom before destroying it with 'brimstone and fire from Yahweh'.[31] The angels instruct their charges not to look back but, unable to resist natural human curiosity, Lot's wife sneaks a glimpse and is turned to a pillar of salt. It is, even by Old Testament standards, a disproportionate punishment, and the whole episode shows angels as being ruthless in reacting to provocation.

Being messengers who carry out orders, the Genesis angels inevitably bring good news as well as bad, and their next appearance is a happier one. Yahweh has been as good as his word. Abraham, aged one hundred,[32] and Sarah, not far short of her century, do have a child, a miracle baby, the son who, as instructed, they call Isaac. But Yahweh gives and Yahweh takes, and he puts Abraham's faith to the test by insisting that he delivers this beloved boy to a mountain and offers him as a human sacrifice.

Abraham does as he is told, his heart no doubt almost unbearably heavy as he builds a fire and tells Isaac that they are to sacrifice a lamb. He picks up a knife to kill his flesh and blood, so strong is his faith in God. 'But the angel of Yahweh called to him from heaven. "Abraham, Abraham . . . do not raise your hand against the boy . . . Do not harm him, for now I know you fear God. You have not refused me your son." '[33]

The angel who has announced Isaac's arrival is now, mercifully, the one who steps in at the last minute to save his young life. Once again, in the detail there is that ambiguity – not about the lesson that the episode teaches about absolute faith in God, but rather about who is talking from heaven. The text says it is an angel, but the words seem to come from God himself – 'you have not refused *me* [my italics] your son'. And it gets more confusing still because, a few sentences later, it states: 'The angel of Yahweh called Abraham a second time from heaven. "I swear by my own self – it is Yahweh who speaks – because you have done this, because you have not refused me your son, I will shower you with blessings" . . .'[34]

The angel is becoming less a messenger than a town crier, reading out proclamations from Yahweh in a loud voice in heaven so that they can be heard on earth. Yet that is maybe to take it too literally. What this whole angel-strewn narrative is seeking to convey is not a blow-by-blow list of historical details but rather – with first Abraham, now Isaac, and next Jacob, Isaac's son – the deepening of the special relationship between God and his chosen people. It does that by telling stories that require an imaginative leap. And when an imaginative leap is required, angels are on hand.

Taking wing

Exodus, the book that follows Genesis, is the first in the Hebrew Scriptures to give angels their trademark feature, their wings. It tells the story of Moses: the great, great grandson of Jacob according to the family tree it helpfully includes near the start.[35] It

is Moses who leads the Israelites out of slavery in Egypt on a journey towards the Promised Land.

Exodus also contains the first of two biblical versions of the
Ten Commandments,[36] the most basic statement of how to live
out faith in Yahweh. Among the ten is a clear injunction against
any 'carved image or likeness of anything in heaven'. That should
rule out detailed depictions not only of God, but also of his
ministering angels. Yet a few chapters further on in Exodus God
instructs Moses to 'build me a sanctuary so that I may dwell
among them'. At the heart of this temple – the first incarnation of
the Temple that became so central to Jewish identity and belief –
he asks for an 'ark', or ornamental box, to hold the stone tablets
on which he has handed down to Moses the law and commandments by which the Jews must live.[37]

'Further,' Yahweh continues, 'you are to make a throne of
mercy, of pure gold . . . For the two ends of this throne of mercy,
you are to make two golden cherubs . . . The cherubs are to have
their wings spread upwards towards the throne of mercy. They
must face one another, their faces towards the throne of mercy.'[38]

These two winged angels, then, are to be decorations on the
'throne of mercy' – or lid – of what is usually called the Ark of the
Covenant, which to the Jews represented physical evidence of
God's binding agreement with them and was placed at the heart
of King Solomon's Temple, built in Jerusalem in around 950 BCE.
The 'throne of mercy', more usually now known as the 'mercy
seat',[39] also had symbolic significance.[40] It was the place where,
between two cherubs standing guard, God's 'presence' rested.
And it is from this 'presence' that later 'a flame leaped out and
consumed' two sons of Aaron in the next book of the Bible,
Leviticus. The brothers, it is recorded, 'perished in the presence of
Yahweh'.[41] Did their demise come at the hands of these fierce
cherubim, so far removed from the cuddly cupids that we now
associate with the name? The text is not clear on this point.

What is striking, though, is the clanging irony to this whole passage. Inside the Ark are the tablets, brought down the mountainside by Moses after his audience with God, on which are inscribed words saying that images of all things in heaven are forbidden. Yet on the lid of the Ark are images of angels. To square the circle, some Jewish rabbis were later to teach, without gaining any great traction, that cherubs should not be categorised as angels, but as something different altogether. Still, their home would seem to be heaven, so they were forbidden images. For their part, the builders that King Solomon employed to create the First Temple were in no doubt that the cherubs were angels, and – according to the First Book of Kings, the best surviving record of their existence – fashioned for them giant wing spans out of olive wood, so wide that they touched the Temple walls on either side, and met each other in the middle, like a canopy.[42]

What, though, of the exact form of the two book-ending cherubs? What were their origins and symbolism? In carrying out God's orders, Moses may have been drawing inspiration in commissioning them from the gold-covered boxes that he would have known in his time in Egypt (and which can still be seen in the Museum of Cairo). These feature fierce winged figures at either end, placed there to protect valuable contents. Biblical scholars, though, have also speculated that the cherubim may have been inspired by the *lamassu* of the Assyrians, Akkadians and Babylonians – a quasi-divine mystical creature that dates back to 3000 BCE with a human head on the body of a bull or lion and bird's wings. Or by the winged sphinx, or griffins that, in the other contemporaneous faiths of the Near and Middle East, would guard the sanctuaries being built to the gods. We are back to that overlap between different, often competing, religious systems. In some scholarly accounts, there is even a theory that links the curious word cherub (plural cherubim) with griffin.[43]

And what of the purpose of the cherubim, beyond issuing flames to scorch those who came too close to Yahweh? The Second Book of Samuel later suggested one possible use, beyond standing guard. David, the one-time shepherd who became the king and united the divided kingdoms of Israel somewhere around 1000 BCE, is, in the text, describing Yahweh's role in his triumph, and pictures him coming down from the heavens, 'a dark cloud under his feet', mounting a cherub and 'soaring on the wings of the wind'.[44]

Some have also argued it was significant that Yahweh insisted there be two angels, not one. If there had been only one, said (among others) the Spanish rabbi, Maimonides, one of the most prolific and influential Jewish scholars of the Middle Ages, the single cherub could have been mistaken as an object of worship in its own right and caused idolatry.[45] According to Jesus' near contemporary, the Jewish philosopher Philo of Alexandria, the two cherubim on the mercy seat were placed there to represent the two sides of God – The Father and The Mother.[46] And three centuries later, in Talmudic commentaries, the respected Jewish teacher Rabbi Qetina spoke of festival days when the veil that normally covered the cherubim in the Temple was rolled back to show them as intertwined male and female figures, their shared love a metaphor for God's love for humankind.[47]

This, in its turn, was a theory with great appeal for the Kabbalists, Jewish mystics who are first recorded in Spain in the twelfth century CE. They saw in the cherubs' embrace a mysterious, intense, sexual expression of the union between earth and heaven. If angels today have become for many a flexible, unregulated receptacle for a range of ideas that we want to project onto them, the same process has apparently been going on continuously since the earliest biblical times.

The Lord's Army

The cherubim on the mercy seat mark a key development in this history. Angels put in other appearances in Exodus, but most fit with that less defined, more ambiguous impression created already by Genesis. When 'the angel of Yahweh' appears to Moses in a burning bush on Mount Horeb, for instance, it is very quickly replaced in the narrative by the voice of God himself, sending Moses to rescue the Jews living in slavery in Egypt.[48]

The Decalogue, that first version of the Ten Commandments that is found in Exodus, is followed by a much longer set of instructions from God to Moses that culminates in the divine commission for the Ark and the mercy seat. Before that, however, comes the Bible's first explicit promise of a guardian angel. 'I myself will send an angel before you to guard you as you go, and to bring you to the place that I have prepared,' Yahweh tells Moses as he leads the Israelites out of Egypt and into the land of Canaan.[49] This, though, is not one of the cosy guardians with which we are now so familiar. 'Give him [the angel] reverence and listen to all that he says. Offer him no defiance; he would not pardon such a fault, for my name is in him. If you listen carefully to his voice and do all that I say, I shall be enemy to your enemies, foe to your foes.'[50]

In a few short sentences, God is succinctly summing up the role that angels play throughout these early sections of the Hebrew Scriptures/Old Testament, and beyond. They guard, albeit more like a strict parent than a friend in the hour of need. They speak for God, as his messengers, conveying his words. And they deploy military force against those who challenge God's chosen people.

After the first five 'Books of Moses' come a series of narrative accounts – Joshua, Judges, the two Books of Samuel and the two Books of Kings – that cover the period during which the Jewish people begin the conquest of Canaan. The Book of Judges attempts to clear up the confusion that occurs in these Old

Testament accounts each time an angel appears and then Yahweh speaks. It tells of the 'angel of Yahweh' appearing to Gideon,[51] a hardworking farmer among the Israelites at a time when they are suffering at the hands of their opponents, the Midianites – camel-riding Bedouins who preyed on the crops they had been planting as they sought to make permanent settlements. But it is Yahweh, according to the text, who speaks to Gideon. So, at the end of their encounter, Gideon addresses Yahweh, and tells him, 'I have seen the angel of Yahweh face to face.' The voice of God, in Gideon's description, comes out of the physical body of his messenger. No longer is it possible, as Jacob had done in Genesis, to see God face to face; only his representative the angel.

And that angel, increasingly, unleashes violence and death on a monumental scale. In the Book of Joshua, which follows directly after the first five 'Books of Moses' in the Hebrew Scriptures, the Israelites cross the River Jordan near Jericho. Their leader, Joshua, meets a man on the road, 'grasping a naked sword. Joshua walked towards him and said, "Are you with us or with our enemies?" He [the man] answered, "No, I am captain of the army of Yahweh."'[52] In some translations this is rendered by the resonant phrase 'commander of the Lord's Army'.

Again there is that elision of man and angel. 'Take your sandals off your feet,' he commands, 'for the place you are standing is holy.'[53] Then the angel gets down to planning military tactics with Joshua so that the sound of the trumpets of the priests who accompany him in his siege of Jericho will finally bring its walls tumbling down.

Yahweh is turning increasingly war-like in support of the Jews and against those who stand in their way. 'That same night,' it is reported in the Second Book of Kings, as the Israelites fought the Assyrian king Sennacherib at the start of the eighth century BCE, 'the angel of Yahweh went out and struck down 185,000 men in the Assyrian camp. In the early morning, when it was time to get up, there they lay so many corpses.'[54]

On occasion, too, Yahweh is full of wrath with his chosen people. In the Second Book of Samuel, his anger 'blazed out'[55] against the Israelites themselves, to such an extent that he sent his angel who 'stretched out his hand to Jerusalem to destroy it'. It goes on, 'but Yahweh thought better of this evil, and he said to the angel who was destroying the people, "Enough! Now withdraw your hand." '[56]

The angel, this episode makes clear, has no independent powers. It does as it is told, whether that means carnage on a colossal scale, or staying the sword in its hand. And its target can be hundreds of thousands of lives, or just one, even if it is one who is, ostensibly, on a mission for God, as happens in the peculiar story of Balaam's ass that appears in the Book of Numbers.[57] The tale has aspects of the popular animated *Shrek* film franchise with its talking donkey, but also a distinct feeling of a horror story in the making.

Balak, King of Moab, summons a dodgy-sounding sorcerer, Balaam, to utter one of his reputedly potent curses on the Israelites, with whom he is in dispute. Yahweh then appears to Balaam and first instructs him not to go to Balak, then changes his mind and sends him on his way. For reasons unclear, Yahweh next gets angry with Balaam while he is en route to Balak and so dispatches a warning angel to stop him in his tracks by any means, up to and including killing him.

Balaam seems doomed when he cannot even see the angel standing in his path with a drawn sword, but fortunately his ass can, and so saves the day, and his master's life, by swerving to avoid it. Angels, this drama appears to make plain, are not only for the well-connected in their communities. Indeed, every trapping, real and psychological, that goes with earthly esteem can only make it harder for the powerful to admit the presence of God's messenger. This vivid story – Balaam furiously whipping the creature, the ass finally and miraculously being given the power of speech, and the angel hovering with a sword – has held great appeal for artists down the ages, notably a young Rembrandt van Rijn in 1626.

Rembrandt's Balaam and the Ass *(1626), from the Book of Numbers, where a sorcerer is told by his donkey, miraculously given the power of speech, to sidestep an angel hovering with a sword.*

And then there are the angels whose messages sound like those of a health visitor. In the Book of Judges, the angel of Yahweh is once more coming to a childless woman to reassure her she will conceive a son, but this time round it provides the wife of Manoah with specific instructions as to what to do to make it happen. 'Take no wine or strong drink, and eat nothing unclean.'[58] She follows this prescription to the letter and produces Sampson, a biblical colossus whose physical strength – and hair – was legendary.[59]

Meanwhile, in the First Book of Kings, the prophet Elijah, lost in a desert wilderness and so despondent that he is willing his own death, is visited by an angel who offers him hot scones and a jar of water. Judging that to be insufficient sustenance to get Elijah up and running, the angel returns and makes another meal for him. 'So he ate and drank, and strengthened by that food he walked for forty days and forty nights until he reached Horeb, the mountain of God.'[60] Quite what the angel gave him to eat is not specified – could this passage have been the inspiration for my childhood treat of butterscotch Angel Delight? – but Christians came to see the angel in this passage as the precursor of Jesus at the Last Supper providing believers with the bread of life in the form of the Eucharist.

Chariots of fire

Details are steadily attaching themselves to those previously blank angel figures of Genesis. This, then, is the proper context in which to see Isaiah's six-winged seraphim that opened Chapter 1. The scale and detail of his visions are matched by those of another prophet, Ezekiel.

The exact dating of the book that carries Ezekiel's name is disputed. It contains a number of reproaches to people living in Jerusalem, which suggests parts of it were written before military defeat in 586 BCE caused the Jews to be sent to a life of exile in

Babylon. Yet it explains itself from its opening words as an account of the priest-prophet Ezekiel's ministry among the Jews who had been carried off into captivity by the Babylonian king, Nebuchadnezzar. The whole text is created (like the Book of Isaiah) from the assembly of different parts written at different times before and during the exile.

It starts with Ezekiel, 'the priest son of Buzi',[61] standing with the exiles on a river bank, five years after they have been wrenched from their homeland. Suddenly, amid storm winds, illuminated clouds and flashes of lightning, Ezekiel is given a glimpse of heaven.

> In the centre I saw what seemed [to be] four animals. They looked like this. They were of human form. Each had four faces, each had four wings. Their legs were straight; they had hooves like oxen, glittering like polished brass. Human hands showed under their wings; the faces of all four were turned to the four quarters. Their wings touched each other; they did not turn as they moved; each one went straight forward. As to what they looked like, they had human faces, and all four had a lion's face to the right, and all four had a bull's face to the left, and all four had an eagle's face. Their wings spread upwards; each had two wings that touched, and two wings that covered his body; and they all went straight forward; they went where the spirit urged them; they did not turn as they moved. Between these animals something could be seen like flaming brands or torches, darting between the animals; the fire flashed light, and lightning streaked from the fire. And the creatures ran to and fro like thunderbolts.[62]

Once his gaze moves on from these bizarre creatures, Ezekiel glimpses the sapphire throne of God. Sitting in it is 'a being that looked like a man. I saw him shine like bronze, and close to and from all around him from what seemed his loins upwards was what looked like fire; and from what seemed his loins downwards I saw what looked like fire, and a light all around.'[63] The man – God – starts speaking, ordaining Ezekiel a prophet and entrusting the care of the Jews in exile to him.

It is a striking description – bold, mind-spinning and at the same time tentative, with its repeated use of 'seemed' and 'looked like'. Ezekiel is attempting to put the ineffable – as God was believed to be – into words, but some of what he saw can potentially be grounded in a more tangible reality. There is, for example, an echo in his description of living beings with outstretched wings of similar creatures found in Zoroastrianism and carved onto the buildings of Babylon. And his debt to the seraphim from the earliest sections of Isaiah, too, seems plain, not least in the awesome majesty of what he attempts to convey.

Yet in the details Ezekiel shares there is also an agenda. He is reminding his exiled audience of the mercy seat, and its cherubim, on the Ark of the Covenant, which was seized and then lost in 586 BCE by the invaders. Yahweh, he comforts them, wants the Temple rebuilt and its treasures returned. (And indeed, Ezekiel subsequently reports a second vision where he is guided by an angel around a ruined temple being restored.[64]) He never specifically calls the four-faced 'creatures' angels at the time he recounts his vision, but later in the text he does finally identify them as cherubim.[65]

If these cherubim are hard to envisage, stranger still are the wheels within wheels (ofanim) that accompany them. Though in one sense, Ezekiel's influence is felt every time artists have depicted angels, such is the sheer unearthly complexity of his descriptions that successful efforts to capture the totality of his vision are hard to find in either the Orthodox East or the Latin West. Indeed, the best-known application in modern culture of what he writes of the heavenly angels has come from the pens of writers, such as the Swiss author Erich von Däniken, who in his 1968 international bestseller *Chariot of the Gods?* claimed to have identified in Ezekiel confirmation of his own beliefs that alien beings are trying to make contact with earth.[66]

The chariot of von Däniken's title refers to the name, 'Merkabah' or 'The Chariot', often given to Ezekiel's vision on account of those wheels within wheels. In Judaism from around 100 BCE to 100 CE there was even a school of 'Merkabah' or 'Chariot Mysticism', wholly inspired by Ezekiel, and focusing on a spiritual ascent through heavenly palaces towards a vision of God's throne. Details from Ezekiel's account of his brush with cherubim continued to attract later mystics eager to know more intimate details about angels. 'I heard the noise of their wings as they moved,' he writes. 'It sounded like rushing water . . . when they halted, they folded their wings, and there was a noise.'[67]

The concentration on thrones and palaces also reflects the different stages of the history of the Jewish people. After those early days recounted in Genesis of the Israelites wandering, and later of their fighting battles to establish their own homeland, by the time of Saul and then David in the eleventh century BCE there was a settled Jewish state ruled over by a king who made Jerusalem his capital. The parallels between his court and his courtiers, and that of God in heaven, with his ranks of angels, inevitably became of much more interest – and use in reinforcing the king's leadership.

The prophet Micah, in the First Book of Kings, which begins with David's last days, is among those who share a vision of the right order of things. 'I have seen Yahweh seated on his throne; all the array of heaven stood in his presence, on his right and left.'[68] Like God, the Jewish king sits on a throne, and just as there is a heavenly army of angels to sustain God, the king has his own army to secure the Jews' destiny as God's chosen people.

In such an ordered world, calibration and measurement starts to become more important. No longer can angels exist as shadows. There has to be a hierarchy. Psalm 8 describes humankind, in a phrase still regularly repeated, as made by God as 'a little lower than the angels'.[69]

That hierarchy, though, was swept away with the defeat by the Babylonians and the experience of exile. The Jews were left feeling lowly and abandoned by God, and so sought to find new ways to win back his favour. Principal among them was a greater focus than ever before on angels, collectively and as named individuals, and it is to that we now turn.

E

E is for **Emmanuel** and **Eligius**, two angels who appeared to Alberic of Settefrati (1101–54), a monk in the Benedictine monastery at Monte Cassino in Italy. He shared with his brothers his memories of a vision he had experienced as a ten-year-old while in a coma for nine days. Saint Peter appeared to him, accompanied by Emmanuel and Eligius (sometimes He'los). The pair then took him on a tour of hell, purgatory and the seven heavens. His account was subsequently widely circulated, and is sometimes cited as having inspired Dante's *Divine Comedy*, which features a similar voyage.

F

F is for **Faax**, an angel name that re-emerged and was recorded when John Dee (1527–1609), the eminent English polymath, Elizabethan courtier and insatiable enquirer, spent much of the last three decades of his life trying to communicate, via a medium, with angels so as to learn their language. The name was not one plucked at random by Dee in these hard-to-imagine conversations, for it is also mentioned in the Book of Enoch, written between the third and second centuries BCE by Jewish teachers and given the name of a biblical patriarch, believed at the time to be one of only a handful of humans to have gone to heaven after his death. In the book that carries his name, Enoch meets multitudes of angels in the seven heavens, including Faax, who is reputedly a minor angel, serving under more senior ones, and using his skills in medicine.

3

Call Us by Our Names –
Michael, Gabriel and Raphael

'When I go to the gate [of heaven], I'll play a duet with Gabriel. Yeah,
we'll play "Sleepy Time Down South" and "Hello, Dolly!" Then he
can blow a couple that he's been playing up there all the time.'
Louis Armstrong on the welcome awaiting him in heaven[1]

The Babylonian exile is a pivotal moment in both the chronology
and the context of the Hebrew Scriptures, and in the story of angels.
Defeat by King Nebuchadnezzar, the tearing down of the walls of
Jerusalem, and the destruction of Solomon's Temple in 586 BCE saw
a brutal end to the Promised Land of a Jewish kingdom of Israel,
and its replacement by the Babylonian province of Yehud. The Jews
didn't return home again until 539 BCE, when the Persian king, Cyrus
the Great, freed them following his victory over the Babylonians.

That almost half-century of exile was a catastrophe for a nation
that had regarded itself, up to that point, as God's chosen people,
with its eventual victory over all-comers divinely assured. How had
such a calamity happened? they were forced to ask themselves. Why
had Yahweh abandoned them? And how, now they were free once
more, were they to rekindle and re-establish their bond with him?

A Second Temple was built in Jerusalem in 516 BCE after the
exiles had returned. Visitors[2] report that mighty cherubim were
once more in place behind a veil in the inner sanctum, but the Ark
of the Covenant itself was lost.[3] During the decades of exile,
though, and afterwards, even when the new Temple was there, the

focus of Jewish belief shifted from a place that signified their connection with God, to a new emphasis on the word of God. One of the tasks undertaken by the scribes among the Jews in exile was to set down in writing a definitive version of the Hebrew Scriptures all the way back to Genesis. Some texts had been lost, or were feared lost; others existed only in the oral tradition. Only by creating a permanent written record could the nation's history, and special status, be preserved in perpetuity.

It was a major undertaking. Part of the process inevitably led to some re-ordering, even revision, of what had existed before, done in the light of present circumstances. Today's biblical scholars pick over the early sections of the Hebrew Scriptures as we have them today, trying to discern passages or details that may have been re-shaped in the crisis of the Babylonian captivity. More broadly, too, this concentration on the word of God prompted a great outpouring of new texts, to augment those in existence already, reflecting both on the experience of defeat and exile, and on the way forward for the Jewish nation.

Once restored to their lands, and then to their Temple, this literary debate and discussion continued. Featuring prominently in its pages was a new kind of angel. The pre-exile angels had largely been varieties of servants of God, but in Babylon, in the practice of Zoroastrianism, which they were able to observe at close quarters, the Jews had seen something different. The Zoroastrian 'angels' were a step up from servants, more aides and assistants to the good god, Ahura Mazda, with at least six of them being divine beings, or 'sparks', created not to run errands but to shoulder the burden of the fight with the evil god. These were angels with a new sort of power. How might that be harnessed, it was asked post-exile, so that Yahweh's angels could emerge from the shadows to centre stage and so help bring his people back under his protection?

This is the backdrop to texts such as the Book of Daniel, which for the first time made angels specifically male by giving them the names of Michael and Gabriel that we use to this day (though here should be noted a fleeting and inconclusive reference in the Book of Zechariah, which predates Daniel, to 'two women with the wind in the wings' who are likened in the text to storks, but have been claimed by some scholars as the first female angels in Judaism[4]). Daniel went further with Michael and Gabriel. They were not just allocated names but also identities, admittedly lightly sketched, yet nevertheless sufficient for them from that point forward to be allotted distinctive roles.

The text of Daniel ostensibly tells of its eponymous hero as one of a number of well-born, Jewish boys, 'without any physical defect, of good appearance and trained in every sort of wisdom',[5] who were picked during the exile decades to serve at Nebuchadnezzar's court in Babylon. It reads as a simultaneous account of goings on there, but in reality its first six chapters are a legend, written around 165 BCE, of a distant hero 400 years after the events they claim to chronicle. In these post-exile centuries, the exile experience, and those who suffered it, was being constantly recycled to offer succour in what remained for the Jews troubled times, when they continued to feel themselves under siege and searching in vain for signs of God's protection.

After the victory of Alexander the Great of Macedonia over the Persian king Darius III in 332 BCE, the Jews had come increasingly under the influence of the Greeks, who had colonised Asia, Africa and the Middle East. Among the Hellenistic successors of Alexander, Antiochus Epiphanes (*c.*215–164 BCE), in particular, the ruthless, self-regarding Greek king (Epiphanes means 'God-made-manifest') and ruler of the Seleucid Empire, exerted an ever-tighter grip over Jerusalem. He regarded the Jewish god, Yahweh, as just one more among the pantheon he was prepared to tolerate, and actively encouraged an elite of 'Hellenised' Jews, keen to win his favour, to abandon traditional religious rituals such as circumcision in favour of Greek ways.

He even went so far as to introduce the cult of Zeus, the Greek god of the sky, into the Jewish Temple, challenging long-established patterns of Jewish worship – or 'overthrowing the foundation of the sanctuary' as it is referred to obliquely in the Book of Daniel.[6] His actions prompted two reactions. The first was military. The Maccabean Revolt, from 167–164 BCE, was led by two brothers, Judah and Jonathan Maccabee, who raised and directed a Jewish resistance army in a guerrilla war against the mighty military machine of Antiochus. Their tactics ultimately triumphed and led to a cleansing of the Temple, the reinstatement of Jewish laws of purity, and Jonathan becoming High Priest.

The second was a redoubling of the literary tradition that had grown up in Judaism since the exile. A fresh wave of texts sought to rally the people by countering Antiochus' Greek 'cleverness' and reason, along with its multitude of gods, redirecting the attention of those Jews seduced by the incomers back onto their own people's distinctive experience of suffering and the need to mend their fractured relationship with Yahweh.

The Book of Daniel was mostly written, it is thought, at the height of the Maccabean Revolt. Once more, it warns its readers, the Jewish people were incurring God's displeasure because of their lack of faith. The only way to see off the invader, who threatened the very essence of their way of life, was a return to God's ways. To encourage them to do so, Daniel offers a new sort of happy ending to the current crisis that is not just about victory on the battlefield. The apocalyptic second half of the book – in a style typical of this period, full of fear of God and accounts of frenzied, fantasy battles fought out by angels, but mitigated by a promise of distant end-times when God will finally exalt his chosen people and destroy their enemies – provides a revelatory vision. Though they are currently on the back foot, and will be tested to their very limits, it pledges that the Jews will one day be able to live in peace and security with God's blessing and protection in a cleansed Jewish kingdom, a heaven on earth.[7]

Crucial to the realisation of Daniel's pledge to the Jews are angels. They are plentiful in the text, but Michael and Gabriel stand head and shoulders above the massed ranks. Michael – which in Hebrew means 'who-is-like-God' – is 'the great prince who mounts guard over your [God's] people' in what is going to be 'a time of great distress, unparalleled since nations first came into existence'.[8] And Gabriel – 'God-is-my-strength' in Hebrew – is the winged creature who flies down suddenly to Daniel at the hour of the evening sacrifice with the reassuring message for him, and by association the Jewish people, 'I have come to teach you how to understand.'[9]

And guidance is certainly required with the confusing series of visions and dreams found in the Book of Daniel. Both Michael and Gabriel appear for the first time almost indirectly, as if details in a larger canvas revealed by the 'Ancient of Days', the term used for God-made-manifest.[10] In the case of Michael, Daniel is standing on the banks of the River Tigris in Babylon, while undertaking a three-week fast, when he sees a vision of the Ancient of Days, 'a man dressed in linen, with a girdle of pure gold round his waist'. Next he hears a voice that introduces Michael. It is the opposite of what has happened in the earlier books of the Old Testament, where it has been the angels appearing to announce God's presence.

Two chapters further on, that same voice of God sets out Michael's precise role as Israel's guardian in the 'time of great distress' that is coming, and makes a promise unheard until now. Michael will oversee a resurrection of the dead 'who lie sleeping in the dust of the earth'. Some of these 'will awake to everlasting life, some to shame and everlasting disgrace'.[11]

This is the first significant mention in Judaism of the dead facing any sort of judgement, and of the possibility of individual resurrection. Hitherto, Jewish views on afterlife had pointed to Sheol, a place of the dead, its name borrowed from other religions in the region, and a blank, subterranean domain for the whole Jewish people once they had died, with no distinctions made between individuals, regardless of their merits or vices in earthly life. Heaven, the place of God, was the domain of angels, and unobtainable for all but the exceptional – only the prophet Elijah in the Hebrew Scriptures unquestioningly got to go there, carried on a 'chariot of fire' by 'horses of fire' in a 'whirlwind'.[12]

Now, though, the Book of Daniel casts Michael as the guardian of a new process by which individuals will be held to account for their lives in death and the gates of heaven will be thrown open to righteous individuals. It marks another significant shift in the history of angels. No longer are they simply travellers on a ladder between heaven and earth. Now they are taking an active role in closing that chasm between this world and the next, not just for the nation as a whole, but also for individuals.

Another book, 3 Baruch, is a Jewish text in the same style as Daniel, sometimes called The Greek Apocalypse of Baruch, and, like Daniel, is set at the time of the Babylonian captivity but written between the first and third centuries CE. Excluded from the canon by both Christianity and Judaism, it is nonetheless significant in our story because the angel Michael's paramount role in this transition from earth to heaven is even more embellished than in Daniel. 'We cannot enter until Michael comes, who holds the keys,' Baruch is told in his revelation of 'ineffable things' by another angel.[13] Such a gatekeeper role fits with the cherubim standing guard on the Garden of Eden in Genesis, though their orders were to exclude, not admit. And, later, Christianity was to reallocate that particular task of granting or refusing admission at the gates of paradise to Saint Peter, the first pope. The keys of heaven remain part of the papal crest.[14]

Gabriel's introduction in the Book of Daniel is likewise made by divine fiat. Daniel is struggling to make sense of a vision in which he has heard 'a holy one' speaking of a ram and a goat. This time 'someone who looks like a man' appears to him. God is once more taking tangible form. 'Gabriel,' he urges, 'tell him [Daniel] the meaning of the vision.' At which point the Angel Gabriel, also in the person of a man, approaches Daniel, and explains to him that the vision of the ram and goat is a glimpse of 'the time of the End'.[15]

With this new channel of contact now established, God can retreat and leave it to his designated representative. In the next chapter, unheralded by any voice, Gabriel reveals his own method of operation when he 'flies down' to share with Daniel a vision of the challenges that lie ahead for Israel. These named angels henceforth will explain, elaborate, interpret and even act without God having to be present.

The notion of a guardian angel was, of course, nothing new. It was there, as we've seen, in God's promise to Moses in Exodus. Nor was there anything novel in introducing an angel into the battles being waged by the Jews. Joshua was given instructions by an angel on how to bring down the walls of Jericho. But Michael and Gabriel, in the Book of Daniel's descriptions, represent something more: intermediaries as well as guardians, a conduit between a beleaguered Jewish people and their national God who will ultimately set them free forever.

The commander and the herald

Though the formal promotion of Michael and Gabriel to the rank of archangel, higher than all other angels, was yet to come, their new-found influence was quickly retrofitted to earlier Old Testament events. So Jewish teachers began to argue that it was Michael, the great protector, who is the nameless angel in the Book of Joshua who announces himself as 'commander of the Lord's army'; Gabriel and Michael who approach Abraham and Sarah at the oak of Mamre; and Gabriel who wrestles with Jacob at the ford on the River Jabbok.

Gabriel's role as 'herald' between God and humanity, conveying messages that give birth to new religions, is part of the story that lies ahead, but Michael's rank as a quasi-military commander, 'one of the leading princes' as the Book of Daniel puts it, was quickly and enthusiastically embraced. Because the cherubim at the gates of Eden in Genesis were accompanied by 'the flame of a flashing sword', it was, for instance, deduced that one of them must have been Michael.

The connection between the princely status he enjoys in God's eyes, and the military prowess assumed to go with such a role, has echoed down the centuries. Catholicism has traditionally cast Michael as a hybrid between a warrior saint and an angel, with his vast, intimidating, corporeal wings paired with military garb and a mighty sword, as in the celebrated 1636 *The Archangel Michael Defeating Satan* by the Italian master of the high Baroque, Guido Reni, commissioned by the family of Pope Urban VIII for the Church of Santa Maria della Concezione in Rome.[16] And Michael has been regularly drafted in to rally the faithful in the Church's own wars. The Jesuit hymn that became a battle cry for the foot soldiers of the sixteenth-century Counter-Reformation begins, '*O heros invincibilis, Dux Michael, adestro nostri proelis*' ('O hero invincible, Commander Michael, aid our battles').[17]

And Michael, Daniel's 'great prince who mounts guard' over the Jews, has also been purloined by Christian knights in search of similar protection as they fought what they presented as God's battles on earth. Among those to have claimed his personal intervention in their military victories was the teenaged 'Maid of Orléans', Joan of Arc. From the age of twelve or thirteen, this unlettered young peasant girl from a pious family reported seeing visions of angels and saints, notably the Archangel Michael, who spoke to her out of a cloud of mist, illuminated by bright lights. Initially, his instructions concerned the staples of attending mass and leading a godly life, but later he was to entrust her with a grander, bespoke mission – to deliver France from the invading English and establish Charles VII, the uncrowned heir to the French throne, as the country's rightful king.

In Guido Reni's high Baroque The Archangel Michael
Defeating Satan, *based on a passage in the Book of Revelation,
Michael is simultaneously angel, warrior and saint.*

'When I was thirteen,' Joan recounted,

I had a voice from God to help me to govern myself. The first
time, I was terrified. The voice came to me about noon: it was
summer, and I was in my father's garden. I heard this voice to my
right, towards the church; rarely do I hear it without its being
accompanied also by a light . . . I saw it many times before I
knew it was Saint Michael . . . He was not alone, but duly
attended by heavenly angels.[18]

Inspired, Joan left her home at sixteen and managed in 1429 to
convince Charles (who initially tried to seduce her) that she was
sent by the angels. He dispatched her to rally the French and lift
the long-running English siege of the strategic city of Orléans.
Within nine days of her arrival, the English were driven back. She
was hailed as the heroine of the hour and acclaimed as, in her
own terms, God's messenger. An angel had inspired her, but to the
victorious French she was the angel.

The following year, though, she was captured at the Battle of
Compiègne, imprisoned by the English, and tried and convicted
by a church court. During her interrogation, she was asked repeatedly about Archangel Michael – had he been dressed or naked
when he appeared to her? 'Do you think God cannot afford to
clothe him?' she replied. And his hair, was it cut long or short?
'Why should they have cut it?' she answered.[19] It did her no good.
In 1431, she was burnt at the stake for heresy. As the flames
engulfed her, she was heard calling out to the Archangel Michael
for his protection on her journey into the next life.

Another famous military victory attributed to Michael was
that of Constantine in the fourth century CE in his campaign to
establish a new capital for his Roman empire at what became
Constantinople. Legend has it that the man who had already
established Christianity as the religion of empire paid a visit to an

ancient pagan temple at Sosthenion (modern-day Istinye) on the banks of the Bosphorus, dedicated to a winged pagan deity and reputedly a place of healing. In the images that decorated the temple, Constantine is said to have recognised the figure of the archangel. That very night, as he was camped out in the temple among the sick pilgrims, he had a dream in which Michael came to him and offered his support in the campaign that lay ahead. When, in the days that followed, Constantine triumphed over all-comers, he publicly credited the archangel and built a new and magnificent church on the site, to be known as the Michaelion.

It became a place where pilgrims would take the waters, in search of a cure, Michael by that time also being associated with healing.[20] One explanation for this addition to his portfolio is another legend, wherein a Christian church was established in the first century CE at Cheretopos in Phrygia (modern-day south-west Turkey) on the site of a spring of healing water that the Archangel Michael had sent to cure a young girl, in answer to her father's prayers. 'An angel cult' grew up there, with pilgrims coming to bathe in the waters, but it so annoyed local pagans that they plotted to divert rivers in an effort to wash the church away. Once again Michael, it was told, stepped in and, with his sword held high, blasted a gorge (known as Chonae) in the rocks to drain away the rising tide of water.[21]

States of otherness

The same Jewish scholars who identified the warrior Michael and the virtuous Gabriel as two of the angelic visitors who appeared to Abraham and Sarah at the oak of Mamre also named the third as Raphael. He is the final one of the trinity of angels identified in the later books of the Old Testament, this time in Tobit, where he announces himself as 'one of the seven angels who stand ever ready to enter the presence of the glory of the Lord'.[22] He doesn't say who the other six are, his reticence causing endless

Andrea del Verrocchio's 1475 Tobias and the Angel *is based on the*
Book of Tobit, *where Raphael first appears. In the text, Raphael hides
his identity, but the Italian Renaissance knew no such restraint.*
The Book of Tobit *is a disputed text in the Christian canon.*

speculation thereafter, as we shall see. In the pages of Tobit, Raphael takes on the mantle of the smiling, benign angel.

Since the sixteenth-century Reformation, Protestants have tended to relegate it to a section at the end of their bibles labelled 'Apocrypha' – the Greek word for hidden, and used to denote works deemed to be of doubtful origin compared with those in the preceding pages. Article Six of the Thirty-Nine Articles, the 1571 key doctrinal statement of the Church of England, specifically outlaws Tobit. And, more widely, there remains a slightly condescending attitude among biblical scholars to Tobit, as articulated by Professor David Albert Jones in his history of angels. 'It has more in common with the colourful folklore of the Arabic *Book of One Thousand and One Nights*,' he writes, 'than the much more restrained biblical encounter between Abraham and the angels.'[23]

Perhaps that lack of restraint is why Tobit, with its tale of a pious Jewish couple, Tobit and Anna, and their extended family, besieged by the forces of evil in the world but rescued by God through the active intercession of his angel Raphael, has remained so popular and so vivid. It is so very human, and recognisable, and has long appealed to artists – Andrea del Verrocchio's 1475 version, said to include details painted by his pupil, Leonardo da Vinci, hangs in London's National Gallery, while Rembrandt's 1632 *Interior With Tobit and Anna* is in the Louvre in Paris.[24]

In the Catholic and Orthodox branches of Christianity, Tobit *is* included among the books in the main body of the Bible. Saint Jerome, the fourth-century CE compiler of the Vulgate, or Latin Bible, was an enthusiast and saw in it echoes of Homer's *Odyssey*. In Judaism, it is again treated with caution. One point of dispute is the dating of the text. Though it describes events taking place in the seventh century BCE, and therefore before the exile, traditionally Tobit has been said to belong in written form to the fourth century BCE (i.e. after it). It is ascribed to Jews living in Egypt. That is why, when included in the Bible, Tobit comes roughly halfway through the standard running order of the Old Testament, grouped among the 'historical' books with those of Judith and Esther, with which it shares a literary form akin to a religious novel.

When, however, fragments of Tobit were discovered among the Dead Sea Scrolls, the stash of ancient holy texts unearthed in the late 1940s and early 1950s from caves at Qumran in the Judean desert on the West Bank of the River Jordan, they contributed to the overturning of conventional wisdom on dating and pointed instead to somewhere nearer 200 BCE; in other words, roughly contiguous with the Book of Daniel. Indeed, one of the 'crimes' cited against its principal character, Tobit, is his insistence on following Jewish traditions in the burial of the dead, something that the Hellenised Jews under Antiochus would have rejected as no longer relevant or necessary.

The link with Qumran is particularly illuminating because the Essenes, the Jewish sect widely held to have lived there and collected what we now call the Dead Sea Scrolls, were by all accounts ascetics. At a time when external threats to their independence, beliefs and way of life had caused the Jews to fragment into different, competing groups, each with a different solution to Israel's problems, the Essenes took the view that Yahweh's protection could be won back only by embracing a devout life that eschewed worldly goods, included celibacy, emphasised piety and valued, above all, mystical insights. In short, they tried to imitate as far as they could the angels so as to draw close to God. They made a point, the Jewish-Roman historian Flavius Josephus tells in 75 CE in his *The Jewish War*, of 'preserving' in their books 'the names of the angels'.[25] Prominent among them would have been Raphael.

The story in the Book of Tobit is of a righteous Jewish refugee living in Nineveh (in present-day Iraq). Tobit had kept to his faith even in times of persecution, and 'walked in paths of truth and in good works all the days of my life'.[26] After the authorities seize his goods as punishment for sticking to Jewish rituals, his troubles increase when he is accidently blinded by sparrows' droppings getting in his eyes. And to complete the bleak (and resonant of the times in which it was written) picture of the triumph of evil over good, he then hears from his niece, Sarah, that though she has been 'given in marriage' seven times, on each occasion a demon called Asmodeus had killed her grooms, 'before ever they had slept with her as man with wife'.[27]

Tobit dispatches his only son, Tobias, ostensibly on a mission to collect a debt from a relative, but also to visit Sarah. On his travels, Tobias is to be accompanied by his faithful dog, but the boy is so anxious about the perils of the journey that he is allowed by his father to seek out in the marketplace a brawny travelling companion. 'Outside, he found Raphael the angel standing facing him – though he did not guess he was an angel of God.'[28]

Raphael, in disguise, gives his name as Azarias, and says that he, or his people, are known to Tobit from back in the day when things were done in the Temple in Jerusalem in the way they should have been. Once on the road together, Azarias/Raphael helps Tobias to catch a fish, which they eat, but first they cut out and preserve its heart, liver and gall. When they arrive at Sarah's home, Tobias falls in love with this 'thoughtful, courageous and very lovely girl'.[29] With the fish heart and liver the angel drives off the demon that has ruined her previous marriages, and so the two lovers can tie the knot.[30]

Next, in case Raphael's God-given abilities as a healer (and hence, later, as the patron of hospitals and the caring professions) requires any further emphasis, he uses the gall from the same fish to restore Tobit's sight when Tobias and his bride-to-be arrive back in Nineveh. Only then, his work completed, does the angel reveal himself. 'You thought you saw me eating,' he tells Tobias, 'but that was appearance and no more.'[31] One indelible mark of an angel, henceforth, was to be one who does not eat the food placed in front of him.

And the role of an angel? That, Raphael explains to Tobias, was to 'test' his faith (as Job had earlier been tested – in the book that carries his name in the Hebrew Scriptures – by Satan, who is not yet the devil but explicitly a member of the heavenly court, doing God's work), and to reward that faith by bringing healing that reveals the justice and omnipotence of God. 'My presence was not by any decision of mine,' the angel makes plain, 'but by the will of God; it is he whom you must bless throughout your days, he whom you must praise.'[32]

Beyond the heart-warming happy endings all round, the real point about the Book of Tobit is that it was written at a time when the prevailing culture, religious and otherwise, intuitively and effortlessly made no distinction in such holy texts between the actual and metaphorical. They were a seamless garment, so readers would not have wasted energy worrying if they could – in modern terms – 'believe' in Raphael as an angel who manifested himself on earth, or have started resorting to fish gall to test it out as a cure for every illness and affliction. Instead, they were so well attuned to the style that no such separating out of fact and fiction would have been necessary. In these circumstances, the angel Raphael (in Hebrew, the name means 'God heals') in Tobit is a model for how angels work, visible but invisible, in the world to support and assist humanity in the name of a benign, generous, but hidden and sometimes elusive God.

So far, seemingly, so obvious, but another of the enduring joys of Tobit is its ability to speak to different ages, millennia apart. The distinguished British author and psychotherapist Salley Vickers retells it alongside a contemporary story in her bestselling 2001 novel, *Miss Garnet's Angel*. Set in a Venice where nothing is as it seems to be, the book follows a recently retired teacher, Julia Garnet, as she discovers the story of Raphael in an eighteenth-century painting by Gianantonio Guardi in the Chiesa dell'Angelo Raffaele near the city's Maritime Station.

Vickers' take on Tobit is as influenced by twenty-first-century psychological insights as it is by post-Babylonian exile theology. 'Is this so-called archangel in disguise,' she has suggested,

> perhaps just the bundle of qualities which young Tobias needs and will acquire as he makes his testing journey into maturity? Is the story not saying, in an imaginative fashion, that the passage to manhood is a perilous one, and that to make it successfully some more-than-ordinary help may be needed, and if we look for it, is on hand?[33]

One reason for the success of *Miss Garnet's Angel*, then, might be that it chimes with that same modern instinct to turn to angels as a 'more-than-ordinary' way of expressing and allaying our very human existential fears. Raphael's presence gives an imaginative, poetic and dramatic dimension to a story about how to overcome adversity. In that context, the Book of Tobit can thus be read as the initiation story of a young man, Tobias (whose name in Hebrew means 'God is good'), who has to leave home and parents to assert his independence. And, likewise, the demon Asmodeus, who has previously prevented his bride Sarah from consummating seven marriages, becomes an expression of human sexual neurosis.

It should not, though, be a case of one way of reading Tobit being right, and another wrong. Vickers herself recognises the futility of such an approach. Her novel, she has acknowledged, tries to fuse them into one, 'trying to show that angels are not so much other beings, but states of otherness, or states of being other, however you like to put it. They are whatever helps us to rise above what we are, or have been, which in most people's lives is usually accomplished through the agency of other people.'[34]

The Books of Daniel and Tobit are moving us closer to something that looks more like the angels who are part of today's popular culture, imagination and yearning. The next step, in the Book of Enoch, is a mighty leap.

G

G is for British sculptor Antony **Gormley**'s *Angel of the North*, a work of steel, weighing 200 tonnes, which has stood since 1998 close to the Al motorway, near a closed-down colliery, as it enters the industrial northeast of England. The angel is ten times life size and its wings spread fifty-four metres across, dipping slightly as if to embrace all around. Angels often provide a symbol of hope in troubling, even hopeless, times, such as war, plague or famine. Catholic-raised and Benedictine-educated Sir Antony has described his *Angel of the North* in these terms, as a 'focus of hope, at a painful time for the people of the north-east, abandoned in the gap between the industrial and the information age'.

H

H is for the Angel of **Hadley**, credited by a group of English colonists in Massachusetts, in the frontier town of Hadley, with saving them when they came under attack in September of 1675 by Native Americans. As they gathered in their Meeting House to pray for God's help – the townsfolk were among the Puritans who had left Europe for the freedom to practise their religious beliefs – an elderly man with a beard appeared in their midst, bearing a sword. No one knew who he was, but he was so successful in organising the defence of the town that it survived the attack. They therefore attributed their victory to the intervention of the 'Angel of Hadley'. One explanation – much debated and disputed – is that the angel was in fact Major General William Goffe, one of the fifty-nine signatories on the 1649 death warrant for Charles I during the English Civil War, who had fled into hiding in the American colonies when the monarchy was restored in 1660. The imminent danger of attack caused him, now an elderly man, briefly to break cover, and then to 'disappear' again once Hadley had been saved.

4

Enoch and the 'Watchers' of Heaven

'Enoch, a mysterious patriarch ... is the single most crucial figure in the long history of angels, even though he began existence as a man.'

Harold Bloom, *Omens of Millennium* (1996)[1]

The Book of Enoch is sometimes unfathomable but always extraordinary. Parts of its five sections were written around the same time as Daniel and Tobit. If those books had provided a black-and-white outline of the angels of our modern imagination, Enoch suffuses it with colour, identifying the hitherto nameless seven who hover alongside Raphael in Tobit, 'ever ready to enter the presence of the glory of the Lord', and throwing in an abundance of angel names to the so-far very short list of three. In ordering these new recruits, Enoch also suggests for the first time an angelic hierarchy, and – another first – uses the word archangel. Perhaps its greatest significance, though, comes when it adds some menacing shade as well as dazzling light to the ranks of the heavenly host. Daniel had introduced the idea of judgement in death at the gates of heaven. In the pages of Enoch, the angels too come under scrutiny for their actions, and a band of them pay a heavy price for their independence from God, falling into evil ways down on earth, and thereby fuelling the rise of the Christian devil.

As always, literature of a particular period reflects wider changes going on at the time it was written. In the case of the Book of Enoch, the backdrop is largely the same as for Daniel and

Tobit, with the Jewish people becoming ever more fixated on angels as supercharged intercessors at the heavenly court of a distant Yahweh. Enoch (one of three books to bear the name, and therefore usually referred to as First Enoch, to distinguish it from two later texts, which are effectively commentaries on it) belongs to a distinct era stretching from the third century BCE to the first century CE. These four hundred years span the gap between the last books of the Hebrew Scriptures and the earliest texts in the Christian New Testament, and are therefore sometimes referred to as the 'intertestamental' period. Many of the books it produced are now deemed Apocrypha, though Daniel and Tobit are found in many Christian Old Testaments, and Enoch is considered part of the canon in the Ethiopian Orthodox Church.

What marks out this epoch is the renewed turmoil that was causing such self-doubt among the Jewish people. Their sense of abandonment by an inaccessible Yahweh was acute. The trauma of the exile in Babylon could not be forgotten when they were facing once more grave outside threats to their identity and very existence. After the Greek king Antiochus Epiphanes' attempts to Hellenise Jewish rituals and worship had been defeated by the Maccabees, a brief period of independence had followed from 142 BCE. Then in 63 BCE, the Roman general Pompey captured Jerusalem and returned Israel to the status of an outpost of a foreign empire.

Roman rule was resisted, just as Antiochus' decrees had been by the Maccabees, but the new overlords proved harder to defeat. Insurrections in Judea and Galilee were brutally crushed, with the rebels condemned to the Romans' favoured means of keeping order: public crucifixion. In the face of apparently irresistible brute force, the Jews fragmented ever more into squabbling factions, each with their own ideas about how far to co-exist with occupation, or oppose it outright, all in the shared cause of national liberation. In the process, the very idea of a Jewish nation, of a collective fate, a concept that had guided them to their greatest victories, as well as led them into devastating defeats, came under scrutiny as never before. No longer was it only about the destiny of Israel; the fate of each individual was also being debated.

The Pentateuch, the first five books of the Hebrew Scriptures, had described how the Jews collectively deepened their bond with Yahweh by scrupulously observing in their daily lives the laws he had laid out for them, not only in the Ten Commandments given to Moses, but also in the more than six hundred rules – or *mitzvot* – later distilled from those five books. Obedience to the law was, for hundreds of years, the sign of the Jews' special status as a chosen people, the seal on their covenant with Yahweh. Yet it had not saved them in the sixth century BCE from defeat, the destruction of the Temple and exile in Babylon.

On their return home from captivity and subjugation, the law remained, but was subject to constant debate, challenge and reinterpretation. Those passionate arguments continued to spill out in writing, in a manner that Jonathan Sacks, Chief Rabbi in Britain until 2013, has described as distinctly Jewish. 'Judaism is a tradition all of whose canonical texts are anthologies of arguments. In the Bible, Abraham, Moses, Jeremiah and Job argue with God. Rabbinical literature is an almost endless series of Rabbi X says this, and Rabbi Y says that. When one rabbi had the chance of asking God who was right, God said, "They're both right"'.[2]

What gave an edge to those debates and discussions was that it was widely believed that God was no longer sending great prophets to the Jewish people to act as guides. Instead he was leaving them to work it out for themselves. One response was to lean increasingly on something new, an apocalyptic and messianic form of Judaism, articulated clearly in the Books of Daniel and Enoch, that anticipated what was called 'the end of days', a time of the triumph of good over evil, when the absent Yahweh would return in glory to quell the chaos, exalt his chosen Israel, reverse its defeats and smite its enemies. If there were no new prophets with God-given visions to support this myth-making, then Jewish teachers and writers grew adept at resurrecting figures from the recent past (for example, Daniel and Tobit) and from the earliest days (Enoch) as vehicles for their predictions of what was to come.

And in the various accounts they produced (books known to scholars as pseudepigrapha, meaning 'false ascription' in Greek, because they were named after people who hadn't written them) angels were everywhere. It was part of a wider trend. The seventy-two translators – six from each of the twelve tribes of Israel, the legend goes – who worked from the third into the second century BCE to produce the Septuagint (from the Latin *septuaginta*, or 'seventy'), a Greek version of the Hebrew Scriptures, were also busy inserting angels into texts where previously there had been none. So their translation of Deuteronomy 32:8, for instance, gratuitously substituted the words 'sons of God' in the Hebrew original with 'angels of God'. This over-enthusiasm for angels also inevitably produced a reaction in a divided nation. The Sadducees, one of the Jewish factions, held that (contrary to the Essenes' enthusiasm, already reported) there were no angels at all.[3]

Part and parcel of this rise and rise of angels was a new and growing obsession with each individual's contribution to the sum total of evil in the world, and how that might be weighed at the end of their life in the resurrection that Daniel had promised. As the Jews were struggling to decide whether Yahweh could ever really be their mainstay again, one obvious explanation for his neglect was to castigate themselves individually for alienating him by not keeping his law. A more palatable alternative also began to be heard, though, influenced by what had been learnt of Zoroastrianism while in Babylon. It had externalised the blame for bad things in the world away from individuals and onto Angra Mainyu, the Lord of Evil and Destruction. His blandishments

were the source of why people went astray. And so in the messianic myth told in Enoch, the Jews were being tempted away from
God by devilish demons who had once been angels.

Devil – Greek in origin, and meaning slanderer or accuser – is
not a word previously heard in the Old Testament, where the
Satan of the Book of Job, written in the wake of the Babylonian
exile, is explicitly part of God's heavenly court. Except, that is, in
the Book of Wisdom, another work belonging to this intertestamental period, post-dating Daniel, and excluded from the canon
of Hebrew Scriptures, but included by the Catholic Church in the
Old Testament.[4] It is typical of the literature of this time in highlighting the contrast between the fate of righteous individuals –
who will be rewarded by God – and that of the wicked who
embrace evil.

> Yet God did make man imperishable.
> He made him in the image of his own nature;
> it was the devil's envy that brought death into the world,
> as those who are his partners will discover.[5]

It is a glancing reference. What caused 'the devil's envy' is explored
in more detail in the Book of Enoch.

Opening up heaven

According to the Book of Genesis, Enoch was the father of
Methuselah, who lived to be 969 years, and the great-grandfather
of Noah, who survived the flood in his animal-packed ark. Enoch
had one particular distinction that attracted the myth-makers.
Genesis reports that he 'walked with God', only managing a
modest 365 years (compared to his father) before 'he vanished
because God took him'.[6] In the Jewish tradition, this enigmatic
line prompted the belief that Enoch was the only other figure in

the Hebrew Scriptures, apart from the prophet Elijah,[7] who had gone to heaven, rather than to Sheol – the ill-defined, non-judgemental, catch-all place reserved for the dead that symbolised an older approach to the nation's fate after death. By trading under Enoch's name, the writers of the Book of Enoch suggested that it offered a means by which others could join him at God's right hand.

And so these writers provided the first account of the geography of a heaven that potentially awaits not just two extraordinary Old Testament figures, but all those Jews who live their lives with the express purpose of following in God's ways. And for those who don't, Enoch also gives glimpses of 'the pit' that became hell in the Christian imagination.

'Enoch [was] a righteous man,' begins the first of the five sections (dated to between 300 and 150 BCE) that make up the Book of Enoch. '[His] eyes were opened by God, [and] saw the vision of the Holy One in the heavens, which the angels showed [him], and from them [he] heard everything, and from them [he] understood as [he] saw, but not for this generation, but for a remote one which is for to come.'[8]

The text of Enoch raises the roof on the number of angels far above anything hitherto imagined, when it refers to 'thousands and ten thousands of angels without number'.[9] This proved to be one more abiding image among the many it provided. In 200 CE, for example, the rabbinic commentator Jehuda Ben Jechesqel embellished this report of angelic abundance with a striking image, suggesting that there was a different angel set over every individual raindrop. When the drop fell, he ventured, the relevant angel would say, 'praised and glorified be the name of God. He sets thousands upon thousands, myriads upon myriads of angels over every single raindrop that comes down. They take 500 years to get here from the firmament, and yet not one drop is ever mixed with another.'[10] It is a charming thought, but also a pointer to the later obsession in medieval Christianity about how far angels might hold the key to understanding how God has organised the workings of nature, including the weather.

Most of the multitude of angels that the Book of Enoch reports remain anonymous, but this first section takes its title – 'the Book of Watchers' – from how it characterises the activities of seven particular named angels.

> And these are the names of the holy angels who watch. Uriel, one of the holy angels, who is over the world and over Tartarus. Raphael, one of the holy angels, who is over the spirits of men. Raguel, one of the holy angels who takes vengeance on the world of the luminaries. Michael, one of the holy angels, to wit, he that is set over the best part of mankind and over chaos. Saraqâêl, one of the holy angels, who is set over the spirits, who sin in the spirit. Gabriel, one of the holy angels, who is over paradise and the serpents and the cherubim. Remiel, one of the holy angels, whom God set over those who rise.[11]

The references – more resonant for readers at the time than now – pile one on top of the other in this passage. In Greek mythology, Tartarus is the abyss, a hellish dungeon of torment and suffering for the wicked. 'Chaos', part of Michael's portfolio, again would suggest a place of disorder and suffering, while Gabriel is given oversight of both the cherubim at the gate of Eden and the serpent inside its walls who leads Adam and Eve astray. That serpent, in intertestamental Jewish thought, was being increasingly seen as an early manifestation of a separate evil force at work in God's hitherto perfect creation.

The Book of Enoch is notoriously hard to decode and endlessly open to interpretation. Most confusing of all are its references to these seven prominent angels as 'watching' – literally being the 'eyes of God', a benign form of guardianship. Later, though, in the same text the phrase the 'Watcher Angels' indicates those malign angels who fall – even though three of the original list of 'watchers', Michael, Gabriel and Raphael, are sent to vanquish them.

Of the other four named, only Uriel ('God-is-my-light' in Hebrew) plays any principal role thereafter. It is to him, and not to the already-familiar names, that the task is allocated of guiding Enoch through the realms of heaven. Uriel is explicitly the equal of the other three. The text describes Michael, Raphael and Gabriel *and* Uriel as 'the holy angels who are above the heavens'.[12]

In the Christian tradition, similar claims have repeatedly been made since for Uriel – for instance, as the source of one of the 'four winds of heaven' mentioned in the Old Testament Book of Zechariah.[13] Yet, because the Book of Enoch is not part of the canon, official teaching has resolutely limited the roll call of chief angels to Michael, Gabriel and Raphael, all of whom first appear in authorised books.

Meanwhile, in the Jewish tradition, Uriel is, like the other three angels, projected backwards into the earliest appearances in the Hebrew Scriptures of their shadowy forerunners, and is most readily identified with the angel who, in the Book of Genesis, warns Noah of the impending flood that will devastate the earth.[14] In later centuries, among writers and artists, Uriel continued to have his champions who gave him a bigger role than the Church officially allowed. The Puritan poet John Milton celebrates him in *Paradise Lost* as the ultimate 'watcher', the angel who *is* God's eyes, 'the sharpest sighted spirit in all of heav'n'.[15]

In the Book of Enoch, though, it is the biblical patriarch himself whose eyes are out on stalks as he is engulfed in mist and swept up to heaven through the clouds on a breeze. What Enoch sees on Uriel's tour, conjured up in the imagination of the writers of the Book of Enoch, is so powerful in its imagery that it continues to shape our mental picture of the afterlife to this day. There are 'seven magnificent mountains', made of pearl, jacinth and other precious stones. One is of alabaster, topped by sapphire, whereupon sits the throne of God. Then there is a 'garden of the righteous', the sweet-smelling 'tree of life' that grew in Eden (heaven being the new Eden) as a shelter for the meek, plus a mystical vision of the 'blessed place' of Jerusalem as a heaven on earth. The angels Enoch meets as he goes round, busy themselves with teaching him the names of the stars, at the same time as becoming those stars themselves.

> And I saw other lightnings and the stars of heaven, and I saw how [Yahweh] called them all by their names and they harkened unto him. And I saw how they are weighed in a righteous balance according to their proportions of light: [I saw] the width of their spaces and the day of their appearing, and how their revolution produces lightning: and [I saw] their revolution according to the number of the angels, and [how] they keep faith with each other.[16]

In the subsequent follow-on text, the Secrets of Enoch – sometimes referred to as 2 Enoch and a first-century-CE commentary on First Enoch – the writers attempt to bring some sort of order and precision to that original, rambling vision. They divide heaven into ten layers – an approach later also favoured by Dante in his *Paradiso* – and post different groups of angels to each. So, in the second layer, Enoch finds weeping angels whom, he is told, have turned away from the truth. Angels now have something approaching free will.

In the sixth and seventh layers he encounters a band of seven angels brighter than the sun, whom he describes as having command over life in heaven and on earth. They are known as archangels (Greek for 'chief angels'). And in the tenth, still surrounded by angelic companions who are 'shining like the sun', with clothing 'of various kinds in appearance purple, their wings brighter than God, their hands whiter than snow', Enoch achieves the ultimate prize. He is permitted to see God's face – 'ineffable, marvellous and very awful'.[17]

Again there is that element of reworking Genesis. There it was Jacob, after he wrestles with the angel at the ford on the Jabbok, who is permitted to see God's face, though he shares none of the details and mentions only being blessed. Here in 2 Enoch, though, God's face is both wonderful *and* terrifying. Creeping in is some element of God sitting in final judgement, but – through angelic intercession – Enoch achieves in his face-to-face encounter what to Jews of the period, under constant battering by their enemies and feeling utterly abandoned by God, would have been believed impossible. He is in God's presence.

Fallen angels

If you identify the presence of evil as one cause for humankind's alienation from God, then that malign force needs a name and a story. Previously in Judaism, the prevailing orthodoxy had been to think in terms only of an 'evil inclination' – '*yetser hara*' – which lies within each one of us. It required no explanation, no motivation. It was simply part of being human. Now, though, in the Book of Enoch, the source of wickedness is attributed to a band of fallen angels, 200 in total, who come down from heaven to earth to pollute humanity with their wicked ways. In Christianity, these fallen angels grew into the monster that was the devil.

Beyond both heaven and Sheol, the Book of Enoch reports, lies first a wasteland, and then a place of fire that is a prison for those stars that have failed to follow their anointed course. It is also, he is told, the domain of the fallen angels.

And Uriel said to me, 'Here shall stand the angels who have connected themselves with women, and their spirits assuming many different forms are defiling mankind and shall lead them astray into sacrificing to demons. Here shall they stand, till the day of the great judgement in which they shall be judged till they are made an end of. And the women also of the angels who went astray shall become sirens.' And I, Enoch, alone saw the vision, the ends of all things: and no man shall see as I have seen.[18]

The story he is telling has resonated through history ever after. It is, for example, specifically referred to in the Christian New Testament, in the Epistle of Jude, the penultimate book and the preface to the final apocalyptic vision of the Book of Revelation. 'Let me remind you of the angels who had supreme authority, but did not keep it, and left their anointed sphere; he [God] has kept them down in the dark, in spiritual chains, to be judged on the great day.'[19]

Once more, the starting point for the story of the fallen angels in the Book of Enoch is located in Genesis. The writers are reworking the very origins of the Jews. Chapter six of Genesis tells of 'the sons of God' who, looking at 'the daughters of men saw they were pleasing, so they married as many as they chose'. Yahweh, Genesis makes plain, was not pleased. 'My spirit', he says, 'must not forever be disgraced in man, for he is but flesh; his life shall last no more than 120 years.' Then it continues: 'The Nephilim were on earth at that time (and even afterwards) when the sons of God resorted to the daughters of man, and had children by them.'[20] Such was 'the wickedness of man', the text states, that Yahweh decided to send a cleansing flood, sparing only Noah and his family and animals in the ark.

First Enoch embroiders lavishly on this strange passage. The 'sons of God', the writers take for angels who rebel against God. As a result, these angels tumble out of heaven and down to earth where, on Mount Hermon, their treacherous hearts boil over with lust as they fall into the arms of 'daughters of earth'. Pure celestial beings created by God to do good thereby turn into sexualised demons who go on to produce a generation of giants, the curiously named Nephilim – thought to derive from the Hebrew word for fall.

And so, says First Enoch, evil is introduced into the world.

And it came to pass when the children of men had multiplied that in those days were born unto them beautiful and comely daughters. And the angels, the children of the heaven, saw and lusted after them, and said to one another: 'Come, let us choose us wives from among the children of men and beget us children.' And Semjâzâ, who was their leader, said unto them: 'I fear ye will not indeed agree to do this deed, and I alone shall have to pay the penalty of a great sin.' And they all answered him and said: 'Let us all swear an oath, and all bind ourselves by mutual imprecations not to abandon this plan but to do this thing.' Then swore they all together and bound themselves by mutual imprecations upon it. And they were in all 200 who descended on the summit of Mount Hermon.[21]

This platoon of 'fallen angels', Enoch stresses, rebel against God of their own free will, and descend from heaven like stars. The imagery recalls an earlier reference in Isaiah when a tyrant king of the Babylonians is defeated by Yahweh and goes down in Sheol as a 'Daystar' who 'falls from the heavens'.[22] And it is later repeated in the Gospel of Luke in the New Testament, where Jesus describes 'watching' Lucifer (a name used subsequently for the Christian devil) fall 'like lightning from heaven'.[23]

The names of the 200 fallen angels, from Baradiel to Za'amiel, Lailiel to Zi'iel, Galgalliel to Kokabriel, include references to some of the malign individuals, or pagan spirits, referred to in other books of the Hebrew Scriptures, including Belial, mentioned disparagingly as the 'worthless one' in the Book of Deuteronomy,[24] and Azazel, the scapegoat from Leviticus,[25] now apparently an over-enthusiast for weaponry. Among the many forms of wickedness that these fallen angels introduce to earth are sex, warfare and general 'unrighteousness'. Yahweh's response, Enoch tells us, is to dispatch Raphael, Gabriel and Michael to defeat their erstwhile comrades, and their offspring, the generation of giants, and then cast them into 'the pit' – a first description of what became hell in the Christian tradition.

'And to virtuous Gabriel said the Lord, "Proceed against the biters and the reprobates, and against the children of fornication . . . send them one against the other that they may destroy each other in battle: for length of days shall they not have."'

Michael, the warrior angel, is detailed to deal with Semjâzâ 'and his associates who have united themselves with women so as to have defiled themselves with them in all their uncleanness'.[26] He is instructed to show any survivors no mercy and instead to

> bind them fast for seventy generations in the valleys of the earth, till the day of their judgement and of their consummation, till the judgement that is for ever and ever is consummated. In those days they shall be led off to the abyss of fire [and] to the torment and the prison in which they shall be confined forever. And whosoever shall be condemned and destroyed will from thenceforth be bound together with them to the end of all generations.[27]

It is a vivid, vengeful, blood-drenched, apocalyptic and ultimately moral tale, and one that has inspired artists – notably the Flemish painter Rubens, whose 1620 *Fall of the Rebel Angels* is displayed in Munich's Alte Pinakothek. It has the victorious Michael, shield in hand, accompanied by other angels, driving the wicked, a mass of naked flesh and contorted limbs, down into the fires of the pit of hell.

The Flemish artist Peter Paul Rubens, in Fall of the Rebel Angels
*(1620), has the Archangel Michael, shield and sword in hand (top),
banishing his erstwhile companions down into the depths of hell.*

The reference to Nephilim has long intrigued biblical scholars. Among the cache of Dead Sea Scrolls found at Qumran are fragments of a Book of Giants, thought to belong to this same intertestamental period. It makes a link between the giant Nephilim and the giants found in another text the Jews would have come across during their exile in Babylon, the *Epic of Gilgamesh*, said to be the oldest story in the world, first written down around 2100 BCE, and one of the foundation documents on which Babylonian religion, society and politics were built.

Most obviously missing from Enoch's account, though, is any clear explanation of why these angels have fallen. The obvious conclusion, for a modern reader, is to suspect lust. Sex has long been treated in Catholic Christianity as the work of the devil. So here are angels, who may have been created flawlessly pure by God, higher than humans as the Book of Psalms estimates it,[28] yet even they are not immune to wicked human lust, with the consequence that they betray God and themselves. The question of the sexual desires – if any – of angels was to become one of the major debating points between medieval Christian 'angelologists' such as Thomas Aquinas and Bonaventure.

That argument, though, was already underway at the time of the Book of Enoch. The Testament of Reuben, another of the holy books typical of this period, dated around 110 BCE and placed in some Christian Bibles among the Apocrypha, suggests in mitigation that the fallen angels were more sinned against than sinners when it came to sex. It takes the example of Eve's temptation of Adam in the Garden of Eden and extrapolates that it must have been the 'daughters of earth' who seduced naïve, otherworldly angels. Another text found in the Apocrypha, the Book of Jubilees, dated around 130 BCE, also revisits the figure of Enoch, and places him in a discussion with the angels that lasts for 294 years. Again the fallen angels are partially exonerated by suggesting that their original motivation in coming down from heaven to earth was suitably benevolent and angel-like – to help humankind. But it all goes awry when their sexual urges are aroused, which causes them to turn their backs on Yahweh, setting out on a road that can lead only to disaster. Their fate becomes, in part, a metaphor for sinful humanity, but also symbolic of the Jews' wider general failure to obey God's laws.

Nine-tenths of the fallen angels are defeated, but Jubilees leaves one-tenth of them, led by the angel Mastema (in Hebrew meaning 'hostility'), to roam the earth, trying to tempt those they meet into wickedness so as to spite God and avenge the defeat of his comrades. Like Satan in the Book of Job, Mastema is an *agent provocateur* and tester-of-faith who is ultimately under God's control, but Jubilees allows this rogue angel almost unlimited licence to wreak chaos.

He is not quite yet the devil of the New Testament, but does represent a solution to the Jews' anxieties about what had soured their relationship with Yahweh. They could externalise the blame onto a group of rogue angels. Comforting though it may have been, it is an abdication that ultimately raises more questions than it answers. If God has the power to destroy Mastema/the devil/the Jews' enemies, and moreover presumably wishes them to be destroyed since they are such unappealing characters, why then is it necessary to wait until apocalyptic end-of-days for him to intervene?

In its commentary on the fallen angels of First Enoch, 2 Enoch prefers to see their lust as more about power than sex. They feel in competition with Yahweh, it argues, as if they are deities in their own right to rival him. 'One from the order of archangels deviated,' God explains,

> together with the division that was under his authority. He thought up the impossible idea that he might place his throne higher than the clouds, which are above the earth, and that he

might become the equal to my power. And I hurled him out from
the height, together with his angels. And he was flying around in
the air, ceaselessly, above the Bottomless [pit].[29]

Metatron

Angels are hankering after power, too, in the second of the
commentaries on First Enoch. If 2 Enoch in the first century CE
had ended with Enoch becoming an angel, the fifth-century-CE
rabbinical text, the Hebrew Book of Enoch, also known as
3 Enoch, takes that story forward and sees the transformation of
the Old Testament patriarch into an angel himself, named
Metatron, 'the angel of the presence', a competing source of
power in heaven, referred to as 'lesser Yahweh'.

Fittingly, since Enoch is the first human to become an angel, the
physical changes he undergoes are described in detail. He becomes
'the size of the length and width of the world [with] 72 wings, 36
on each side, and each wing was as the whole world; and he [God]
fixed on 365 eyes: each eye was as the great luminary'.[30] He is not
just an archangel but, in 3 Enoch's description, the chief angel
and also heaven's resident scribe.

By the time 3 Enoch was written, however, the intertestamental
period had passed, Christianity was fast becoming established, in
places at the expense of Judaism from which it had emerged, and
many rabbis had come to regard with the deepest suspicion the
apocalyptic tales found in the books of the Apocrypha and
Pseudepigrapha, including the Book of Enoch. The creation story,
the foundation of the Jewish nation in Genesis, had been so over-
worked to accommodate angel-intermediaries, it was said, as to
have become a kind of idolatry on account of the worship of false
angel-gods, given names borrowed from Greek and Roman deities.
Moreover, this distortion had had the opposite effect to what was
intended. Far from strengthening Jewish resolve and bringing

them back under God's protection as they faced down their enemies, it had caused hysteria and a loss of self-belief and collective will in troubled years that had included the destruction of the Second Temple in Jerusalem in 70 CE by the Romans.

And 3 Enoch, for all the mighty claims it makes for Metatron, is careful to insist that he is an angel, not a God. In this respect, it echoes a passage in the Talmud, composed over the first five centuries CE and, after the Hebrew Scriptures, the pillar upon which Judaism continues to rest. In it, the first-century-CE rabbi Elisha ben Abuyah is reported as having described a vision of heaven in which he meets Metatron. Alone among the assembled angels, Metatron is allowed to sit in God's presence, rather than follow the usual rules of showing his respect by standing. Yet even if Metatron is receiving special treatment that places him above the others, his ambitions are very publicly slapped down when he is condemned to sixty strokes from a fiery rod to teach him that, however important he is in the angelic hierarchy, there can be no rival to Yahweh.[31]

The origins of the word Metatron are unclear. The Latin word *metator* means messenger or guide, which would fit with Enoch's experience of angels in heaven. Others associate it, though, with Hebrew roots that suggest it refers to 'keeper of the Watchers', or even with the first- to fourth-century-CE cult of Mithraism, which flourished in the Roman Empire. Its exact nature is clouded in mystery, but it is widely believed to have been an offshoot of Zoroastrianism, which was a rival of early Christianity.

Untangling the myths and legends of Jewish writings from this frenzied period is no easy task, but what Metatron undoubtedly reveals is a wider debate on whether angels could ever be rivals to God. Mainstream Judaism came down firmly against this proposal – and indeed ultimately reverted back from the fifth century CE onwards to its traditional teaching of a *yetser hara*, or evil inclination, in preference to talk of fallen angels. But some more esoteric, less orthodox branches, notably the Kabbalah strain of Jewish mysticism in medieval Europe, remained fascinated by the powers and reach of angels, both for good and for ill.

In the books of the Hebrew Scriptures, the angels had sometimes been bringers of ill-tidings and death,[32] but are not, in most translations, ever referred to specifically as the 'angel of death'. So when Moses in Egypt instructs his fellow Jews on the feast of Passover to mark their doors with animal blood for protection, it is usually either Yahweh himself or the angel 'that brings death' who 'will pass over the door' and leave those inside safe.[33]

Yet the concept – or character – of a specific 'angel of death' was another enduring legacy of the intertestamental period, emerging more strongly in later mainstream Jewish thought, including in the Talmud. It stretched to encompass a twelve-winged creature, who lived in heaven but would attend the death pangs of individuals. As they breathed their last, they would see the 'angel of death' appear. If the shock of its arrival was not enough in itself to polish them off, the angel would let a drop of bitter gall fall from its sword onto the lips of the suffering person and spare them further suffering.

Christians, too, incorporated a similar tradition into their thinking with the 'Grim Reaper', the angel who carries a sickle in the Book of Revelation, the final chapter of the New Testament, taking on the role of announcing impending death.[34] And it is to Christianity that we now must turn. Like Islam after it, Christianity's ideas of angels are inherited from Judaism.

I

I is for **Ishim**, the tenth and lowliest layer of angels proposed by the revered twelfth-century CE Jewish philosopher Moses Maimonides. Others such as Pope Gregory, Pseudo-Dionysius and Thomas Aquinas had produced their own hierarchical tiers of angels to bring order and logic to the world between heaven and earth, but they all stuck at nine. In his *Code of Law* (*Mishneh Torah*), though, Maimonides included Ishim (which means 'men' in Hebrew) as 'the angels who speak with the [Old Testament] prophets and appear to them in prophetic visions. They are therefore called Ishim because their level is close to the level of consciousness of human beings.'

J

J is for **Jegudiel**, one of seven archangels in the Eastern Orthodox Church, said to exercise a special guardianship over Fridays and over those looking for employment. He is regarded in a similar light by the Eastern-rite Churches that are in communion with the Catholic Church. In icons of him, Jegudiel holds a crown and a whip – the equivalent of the carrot and stick – the first symbolising the reward to be had by following God's laws, the second the punishment. The origin of the name is once again believed to be found in the Book of Enoch.

5

Putting Angels in Their Place
– the New Testament

'Angels, saints and nations sing:
"Praise be Jesus Christ Our King." '
Patrick Brennan CSsR, 'Hail, Redeemer, King Divine' (1940)

Christianity begins with an angel. 'I am Gabriel who stands in God's presence,' he announces as he reveals himself at the start of the New Testament's Gospel of Luke. His task is to reveal the coming of Jesus, the Son of God – the role that has since made him the most famous angel in Western culture – but first Gabriel must prepare the ground by appearing to Zechariah, an elderly priest who is burning incense alone in the sanctuary of the rebuilt Temple in Jerusalem.

Luke makes it a low-key affair – or as low key as things can be when an angel appears as you go about your daily work. There is no mention of wings, no sudden burst of light from the heavens, but still the mission of this visitor is a familiar one. Gabriel tells Zechariah that he and his wife Elizabeth, until now childless, are to have a son. The news comes as a shock. Like Abraham and Sarah before them, this is a couple getting on in years.

Gabriel makes certain stipulations: that the boy child should be named John; and that he 'must drink no wine'. In return, Zechariah is told, his son will be 'great in the sight of the Lord', bringing 'many of the sons of Israel to the Lord their God'.[1] And it is a promise that is fulfilled for, in Luke's account, the infant grows up to be John the Baptist, paver of the way for Jesus.

The clearest echo of Isaac, that other late, late baby announced by an angel in Genesis, comes in how the news is received. When ninety-something Sarah overheard at Mamre that she was to have a child, she laughed out loud at the biological impossibility of it all – and was sternly rebuked for her lack of faith by Yahweh. Now, when Zechariah expresses incredulity, the angel is harsher still, punishing him by depriving him of the power of speech until the baby arrives.

The first angel of the New Testament is, then, no cosy companion, but rather a stern task-master. The message for readers may be clear – do not doubt God's word – but it is still a curiously heartless act since this elderly man must now convey life-changing news to his equally elderly wife about their miracle arrival by scribbling notes on a pad.[2]

How, otherwise, to treat this story? There has long been a tendency within mainstream Christianity, particularly encouraged by a traditional or narrow faith education, to downplay its debt to Judaism. It took Catholicism, for example, until 1965 formally to absolve the Jews of killing the Son of God.[3] And so, too often, the Old and New Testaments of the Christian Bible are treated as if separate in time, effectively the 'before' and 'after' of Jesus' birth, even while still accepting that passages in the first are prophesying what will happen in the second. The reality, however, is a great deal of continuity. The later books of the Old Testament and the first books of the New were written in broadly the same period between 300 BCE and 100 CE that is called 'intertestamental' by scholars, somewhat misleadingly since it suggests a gap, not an overlap. Yet overlap there is, since the letters of Saint Paul – the earliest accounts of Jesus in the New Testament, dating from between 50 and 63 CE – and the four authorised Gospels of Mark, Matthew, Luke and John,[4] from roughly 70 CE to 100 CE, all fall within this intertestamental era. They are contemporaries of the outpouring of literature in Judaism, as set out in the previous chapters, where angels were embraced with great enthusiasm as a means of bridging the chasm that appeared to have opened up between Yahweh and his chosen people. And, where Judaism led in giving angels names, greater prominence and enhanced roles, the Christianity that emerged from within the Jewish fold naturally followed suit, as in Luke's portrait of Gabriel at the very start of his Gospel.

There is nuance, though, in the interplay. Yes, Luke names Gabriel, taking his lead seamlessly from the Old Testament Book of Daniel, but the angel's role in relation to Zechariah owes more to the unembellished one of God's messenger, as set out way back in Genesis.

Another factor to weigh is the symbolism that is carried by each and every significant detail in both sections of the Bible. When Christianity was dominant in Western society, there would have been no need to point this out. Hearing the words of the Gospels read aloud from the pulpit, seeing them recreated in religious art and, for that minority in medieval times who were literate, studying the texts, was intuitively understood to be a double process. In the same way that, in the Eucharist, bread and wine were simultaneously the body and blood of Jesus Christ, so episodes recounted by the Gospel writers were both literal and symbolic. One way of understanding why the writer of Luke[5] places at the start of his text such an obvious parallel to the Abraham/Sarah/Isaac story is to see it as a contribution to that debate going on within Judaism about the extent of angels' roles. The writer of Luke is re-asserting the traditional job description of angels, more messenger than mediator, and therefore is pushing back against those Jewish teachers and scribes who were writing at the same time of a looming cosmic battle that would signify end-times, and who were urging that angels be given ever more scope and ever greater influence, to the point where some feared they risked becoming minor deities in their own right.

After visiting Zechariah – who, it is worth noting in passing, when seeing the links between Old and New Testaments, shares a name with the Old Testament prophet who experienced a prolonged vision of an unnamed messenger angel[6] – Gabriel next turns to his main task. He is 'sent by God' to Elizabeth's 'kins-woman', Mary, in the town of Nazareth in Galilee. 'Rejoice, so highly favoured!' he greets her. 'The Lord is with you.'[7] She is, he tells her, to bear a son whom she will call Jesus. He will be the 'Son of the Most High', rule over the House of Jacob, 'and his reign will have no end'. Though initially (and inevitably) 'deeply disturbed' by the news, Mary is more accepting than Zechariah. 'I am the handmaid of the Lord,' she answers Gabriel, 'let what you have said be done to me.'[8]

Along with other Renaissance masters, Fra Angelico
('the angelic friar') made the Annunciation the most
famous appearance of an angel in Western culture
with his Virgin of the Annunciation *(c.1450).*

Again, in the Gospel's description of this extraordinary encounter, there is no suggestion of wings, a halo, an accompany-ing horde of cherubim, or any disturbance in the light (or even

that Mary is little more than a girl, as Christianity has traditionally asserted). Yet this scene, the Annunciation, has become the
most depicted of any biblical episode, and the many artists tack-
ling it, often commissioned by the Church, have included some or
all of these features in their depictions. Fra Angelico, in his *c.*1450
fresco at the monastery of San Marco in the north of Florence,
adds both an unusual degree of intimacy – Mary and Gabriel
incline towards each other as if sharing confidences in a private
conversation – and a rainbow of colours to the angel's wings. In
Sandro Botticelli's 1489 *Annunciation*, for the monastery church
of Cestello in Pinti (but now in Florence's Uffizi Gallery), there is
a white lily in Gabriel's hand, as a symbol of Mary's virginity.
And Lorenzo Lotto in his 1534 *Recanati Annunciation* depicts
not a serene Mary but one who is making as if to leap out of the
picture frame in horror at what the angel is telling her.

Back on the page in Luke's Gospel, Gabriel leaves Elizabeth and
Zechariah to their own devices when it comes to the birth of their
son, and it is the anonymous 'angel of the Lord' who is on hand
when Jesus is born in a stable in Bethlehem, appearing to shepherds
nearby to tell them what is happening. 'And the glory of God,' it is
recorded, 'shone around them'.[9] Here then is that oft-depicted shaft
of heavenly light, though the text can be read as the angel giving off
the light himself, sufficient to 'terrify' the shepherds.

Here, too, is mention of the ranks of angels that today decorate our Christmas cards with their hosannas. 'And suddenly with
the angel, there was a great throng of the heavenly host, praising
God and singing'.[10] The reference is back to Isaiah and 'The Song
of the Angels'.

Angel attendants at the birth of every child was a popular
belief in Judaism at the time. Included in the Talmud is the wider
suggestion that every child ever born was fashioned by God in the
first six days of creation, and thereafter waited for his or her
moment to enter the world, secure in a place called Arabot, the

In his Recanati Annunciation *of 1534, Lorenzo Lotto replaces the usually serene Virgin Mary favoured by the Renaissance with a more surprised, even horrified, figure.*

last of what both the Talmud and later Rabbinic Judaism taught were seven heavens.[11] When the time comes for that unborn child or 'soul' to be implanted in a woman's body at the moment of conception, it is written, God 'commands the angel who is the guardian of the spirits [in Arabot], saying, "bring me such a spirit which is in paradise and hath such a name and such a form".'[12]

As part of that ongoing interchange between emerging Christianity and Judaism, something very similar is also found in the writings of the influential Early Church theologian, and convert to Christianity, Clement of Alexandria. At the end of the second century CE, in his *Prophetic Eclogue*, he describes how the soul enters the body of a baby in its mother's womb after being 'introduced by one of the angels who presides over generations'.[13] Clement goes on to note explicitly the connection between this remark and the stories in the Bible of angels announcing the birth of a child.

It offers another way of thinking about Bronwen Astor's story, told in the prelude to this book, of the angels whom she saw attending the difficult birth of her older daughter. In both Old and New Testaments, the moments when angels are most likely to manifest themselves are at times of strain or crisis – including childbirth. And it also shines a light onto the widespread and enduring belief that everyone has a lifelong guardian angel – something that figured so strongly in my own childhood. Thomas Aquinas, the thirteenth-century Italian widely held as Christianity's greatest ever theologian and its leading angelologist, argued that the guardian angel is there from the very moment every child is born.

If the Annunciation is recounted only in Luke, then he isn't alone among the four Gospel writers in describing what is now routinely known as the Nativity. While Mark and John contain no reference to it at all, Matthew's version – believed by scholars to be, like Luke's, based in part on a now-lost source, referred to as 'Q' (from *quelle*, the German for source), which contained the sayings of Jesus – tells of 'the angel of the Lord' who appears not to Mary but instead to Joseph, the man to whom she is betrothed. Curiously, in Matthew's much briefer account, Mary is left to deal with the news that she is 'with child through the Holy Spirit' unsupported by any heavenly messenger.

In the favoured Old Testament manner, Joseph is visited by the angel in a dream. He is distressed by the news he is given, because he knows his relationship with Mary to be chaste, and therefore wants to divorce her because her baby can't be his. Yet the angel has instructions to impart. 'Do not be afraid to take Mary home as your wife,' Joseph is told, 'because she has conceived what is in her by the Holy Spirit.' Her son will grow up to 'save his people from their sins'. When he wakes, an apparently reassured Joseph does as instructed.[14]

This unnamed angel is about more than words of advice and comfort, though, as is made plain when he greets Mary's betrothed as 'Joseph, son of David'. The author of Matthew was keen from the outset to establish Jesus as part of the distinguished blood line that stretches all the way back through King David to Abraham (even though, of course, Joseph isn't the father). In that way, Matthew calculated, followers of Jesus could claim to be heirs to the special relationship with God that had hitherto belonged only to the Jews. And the text amplifies the symbolism of the angel's presence when it adds an explanatory note to his exchange with Joseph, in case readers had missed it: 'Now all this took place to fulfil the words spoken by the Lord through the prophet.'[15] The reference is to the prophet Isaiah – 'the virgin will conceive and give birth to a son'.[16]

Matthew allocates the angel one additional role. News reaches the Jewish king Herod after Jesus' birth that a child has come into the world who will be 'king of the Jews'.[17] Determined to eliminate any rival, Herod orders the murder of all male children under two years found in the vicinity of Bethlehem. An angel comes to Joseph in another dream, this time to forewarn him of what is called in Christianity 'the massacre of the innocents' and is remembered each year on 28 December. Again Joseph obeys without question and takes his wife and her new-born child, as instructed, to Egypt, where they take refuge until the angel returns – once again in a dream – to tell him that Herod has died and that it is now safe for the family to go back to their home in Nazareth.[18]

The Revelation angels

The New Testament is not short of angels, but few of them have names. Aside from Gabriel, there are only two others: Michael and Abaddon. The first, familiar already from the Book of Daniel, appears in the Epistle of Jude, one of the seven 'Letters to All Christians'. It is dated between 70 and 80 CE, making it a contemporary of the Gospels of Mark and Matthew. The Jude of its title is thought to be a reference to the apostle Jude, sometimes also known as Judas, who is mentioned in Luke's Gospel as one of the twelve in Jesus' inner circle.[19] He is not to be confused with Judas Iscariot, the apostle who betrayed his master for thirty pieces of silver.

Simpler to disentangle is the historical backdrop to the Epistle of Jude, namely the ongoing tension between those followers of Jesus, led by Paul, who after Jesus' resurrection and ascension into heaven wanted to share his message with as many people as possible, Jews and non-Jews alike, by setting off on missionary journeys, and in effect starting a new church, and those others, in and around Jerusalem, who looked for direction to James, brother of Jesus,[20] seeing themselves as a reform movement within Judaism. A council had taken place in Jerusalem around 50 CE between the two factions, at which the first group prevailed,[21] but the argument had yet to subside. The epistle written in the name of Jude contributes to the debate by warning Jews who have embraced Jesus' message to beware of false teachers. Specifically, it draws a parallel between such individuals and the 'Watcher' angels from the Book of Enoch (referenced by name in Jude) who were seduced by false ideas and fell out of heaven.

'Not even the Archangel Michael, when he was engaged in argument with the devil . . . dared to denounce him in the language of abuse; all he said was, "Let the Lord correct you." But these people abuse anything they don't understand.'[22]

The passage is rich in references. The only previous mention in the New Testament of archangels had come in Paul's First Letter to the Thessalonians (which predates the Epistle of Jude), where it is foretold – in terms similar to those found in Jewish apocalyptic writings – that an unnamed archangel will herald the Second Coming of the Lord as he descends from heaven in judgement. The Epistle of Jude, though, awards the archangel title specifically to Michael, in a way that Luke does not to Gabriel.

The Archangel Michael's prowess in battle, already hinted at in the Book of Daniel, is taken up with gusto in the final, dramatic – and to modern readers bizarre and beguiling – section of the New Testament, the Book of Revelation, which is again steeped in the sort of apocalyptic, end-time speculation that figured so prominently in Jewish literature and debate in this period. There are other outbreaks of the same in the New Testament. The Gospel of Mark, for instance, contains a section known as the 'Markan Apocalypse', which employs imagery, taken from the Book of Enoch's description about the Watcher Angels, of 'stars coming falling down from heaven', without ever quite naming them.[23] But Revelation, usually dated somewhere between 70 and 95 CE, outdoes all the rest in its account – while Christians on earth are undergoing persecution – of a parallel cosmic clash that accompanies the Last Judgement, the end of the world, and the victory of God's kingdom on earth ever after.

As in the Book of Daniel, Michael is in command of the heavenly host as it fights the good fight against its erstwhile colleague, the devil.

And now war broke out in heaven, when Michael with his angels attacked the dragon. The dragon fought back with his [Watcher] angels, but they were defeated and driven out of heaven. The great dragon, the primeval serpent [who tricked Eve in the Garden of Eden²⁴], known as the devil or Satan, who had deceived all the world, was hurled down to the earth and his angels were hurled down with him. Then I heard a voice shout out from heaven, 'Victory and power and empire for ever have been won by our God, and all authority for his Christ.'²⁵

It is a lively dispatch from the frontline, so much so that it inspired the engraving on the back of an English coin, first introduced in 1465 in the reign of Edward IV, and therefore popularly known as an 'angel'. And that name is still used in the Isle of Man, the British Crown dependency and tax haven in the Irish Sea, where Michael's fight with the devil features on the reverse of small gold coins minted for investors and known as 'angels'.²⁶ Perhaps the most resonant reminder of the scene, though, comes in Milton's *Paradise Lost*:

> but the sword
> Of Michael from the Armorie of God
> Was giv'n him temperd so, that neither keen
> Nor solid might resist that edge.²⁷

It is also on Revelation's battleground that the other named angel of the New Testament appears. Abaddon is described as 'the angel of the Abyss'.²⁸ The word Abaddon in the Hebrew Scriptures had referred to a place or state of mind, part of the bottomless pit of Sheol, the resting place of all the dead in Judaism before notions of judgement in death had crept into the Book of Daniel.²⁹ Here in Revelation, though, the name is allocated to a hard-to-place angel who has been interpreted variously as being on God's side in the battle – bringing about the destruction that is a necessary apocalyptic prelude to the Last Judgement – or as another disguise for the devil.

In Revelation, this 'angel of the abyss' leads an army of locusts, with 'gold crowns on their heads and faces that seemed human and hair like women's hair and teeth like lions' teeth . . . The noise of their wings sounded like a great charge of horses and chariots into battle.'[30] The overall impression recalls those winged gods and demons of Egypt, Canaan, Greece and Babylon described in Chapter 1. From a historical and contextual perspective, the locusts could also be serving as a metaphor for the Roman legion that laid siege to Jerusalem for five months in 70 CE before finally defeating it and destroying the Second Temple.

In the battlefield running order of Revelation, Abaddon appears in that section about the seven angels with seven trumpets 'who stand in the presence of God', a passage that loudly echoes the description of Raphael and the seven other nameless angels and their closeness to God in the Book of Tobit.[31] 'Another angel,' Revelation continues, 'who had a golden censer, came and stood at the altar.' A censer, as any former altar boy will recall, is the ornate container in which incense is burnt during religious ceremonies. 'A large quantity of incense was given to him to offer with the prayers of all the saints on the golden altar that stood in front of the throne; and so from the angel's hand the smoke of the incense went up in the presence of God and with it the prayers of the saints.'[32]

This mingling of angels and saints was to become more pronounced in Christianity once it grew into a formidable institution, fusing heavenly with human heroes, but next in the Revelation narrative the angels take turns to blow their trumpets in accompaniment to the peals of thunder and flashes of lightning as the earth is shaken to its very core. They are heralds of the coming of the new kingdom of God. The first angel – taken in the Judeo-Christian tradition to be Gabriel, hence portraits often showing him holding a horn or trumpet – is announcing the dawn of

Judgement Day in which 'a third of the earth was burnt up'.[33] By the time it gets to angel number seven, heaven and earth have merged into one as an eternal paradise for the righteous, symbolised by the return of the lost Ark of the Covenant.[34]

The imagery in Revelation is strange, full of dream sequences and notoriously difficult to decode. As befits a dreamscape, it is a world crammed with angels – 'ten thousand times ten thousand of them'[35] – whose every twist and turn endows them with more skills and characteristics. Some control the winds, standing at the four corners of the earth,[36] others bring death and destruction by various means, but those that emerge in the cleansed and new age at the end of the book are benign. They speak God's words and bring a message of hope to their hearers.

'[The angel] took me,' relates John, the narrator of Revelation, traditionally said to be the apostle John, 'to the top of an enormous high mountain and showed me Jerusalem, the holy city, coming down from God out of heaven. It had all the radiant glory of God and glittered like some precious jewel of crystal-clear diamond. The walls of it were of a great height, and had twelve gates; at each of the twelve gates there was an angel.'[37] The Bible, which begins in Genesis with cherubim at the gates of Eden, draws to a close in Revelation with angels at the gates of the heavenly city of Jerusalem.

Paul's warning

Nowhere is it clearer that the debate within Judaism about the proper role of angels was spilling over into the emerging Christian Church than in the letters of Saint Paul. The influences on Paul – previously Saul – were many. His family was Jewish, and tent-making, we are told in the Acts of the Apostles, was their trade.[38] He was educated as a Pharisee, one of the several factions in Judaism at the time, and the one that went on, after the destruction of the Second Temple by the Romans in 70 CE, to dominate

Rabbinic Judaism. Yet he had grown up among Greek-speakers in Tarsus in the Roman municipality of Cilicia, today on the south-eastern coast of Turkey, opposite the island of Cyprus.

A zealous persecutor of Jesus' followers before the risen Lord appeared to him on the road to Damascus,[39] Paul thereafter dedicated himself to spreading the 'Good News' that, by his death and resurrection, Jesus had proved he was the Messiah who would save Jew and Gentile alike. His letters, written in Greek, were communications with the fledgling Christian communities that were springing up, and date from 50 to 67 CE, the year – again according to an ancient Christian tradition – that he and Saint Peter were crucified upside down in Rome. The last of the texts ascribed to him, the Letter to the Hebrews, is thought to have been put together by those who had been influenced by Paul, anxious on this occasion to show the continuity between Paul's teaching and the Old Testament.

There are certainly angels in Paul's writing, reflecting the influences on him. When he was shipwrecked en route for Rome, and his fellow travellers were in fear of their lives, the Acts of the Apostles recounts how he was visited by 'an angel of the God to whom I belong and whom I serve'. The angel gives him a message that 'God grants you the safety of all who are sailing with you'.[40]

So far, very much in line with the messenger angels of the past. Yet Paul did not write the Acts of the Apostles. By contrast, in his own letters, he is at best equivocal about angels. 'Do not be taken in', goes his siren warning in his Letter to the Colossians,

> by people who like grovelling to angels and worshipping them; people like that are always going on about some vision they have had, inflating themselves to a false importance with their worldly outlook. A man of this sort is not united to the head, and it is the head that adds strength and holds the whole body together, with all its joints and sinews, and this is the only way in which it can reach its full growth in God.[41]

By decrying in such strong terms dreams, angels and those who claim to see them, Paul is also, by association, decrying those then dominant strands of Judaism that placed so much hope in angels.

This letter, it is thought, was written around 61 CE when Paul was under arrest in Rome – 'a prisoner of Christ Jesus for the sake of you pagans' as he puts it in his Letter to the Church at Ephesus, produced at the same time. This second text explores in greater detail those warning words about angels being the playthings of those 'not united to the head' that are found in the Letter to the Colossians.[42] In Ephesians (and the Letter to Philemon, also believed to have been written from his prison cell), Paul confronts the growing belief he has observed in Christians and Jews alike in celestial and cosmic powers, part of the fashionable and comforting apocalyptic speculations of the day. While he accepts angels as part of the Jewish tradition, referenced repeatedly in the Hebrew Scriptures, he makes plain that – unlike the writers of Daniel, Tobit and Enoch, and later of Jude and Revelation in the New Testament – their role is merely to prepare the way for Jesus. Why this downgrading? Because Paul's principal argument is that Jesus, by his death and resurrection, has created a whole new order, a new covenant as it were, to replace the old one between Yahweh and the Jewish people.

So angels should be esteemed, he writes in his First Letter to the Church at Corinth, with women covering their heads at public services 'out of respect for the angels' – though men needn't bother, he adds, fuelling his reputation for misogyny. Since men are the equals of angels, he explains, Adam having been created, like the angels, by God, in his image and as a reflection of his glory, they require no head covering. Women, though, he goes on (in terms that do little to endear him to a modern audience), were created for men and reflect men's glory, and so must show due respect to angels and men.[43]

Beyond the now unappealing details, the bigger picture that Paul was trying to paint about angels was that they still had their part to play, but it was henceforth on the edge of the canvas. If believers wanted a way of connecting with God, they had it in Jesus Christ. As Harold Bloom puts it in his *Omens of Millennium*, 'there is clearly an opposition between the Incarnation [God made human in Jesus] and any exuberant angelology, an opposition that finds its classical statement in Saint Paul'.[44]

There is one phrase that Paul uses in Ephesians of angels, however, which was subsequently much picked over by Christian theologians. He refers to them as 'Sovereignties and Powers'.[45] If he is seeking to downplay their role, it is, at first glance, odd language to employ. Yet he is a man of his times and is taking his cue from the Book of Enoch, in particular its efforts to organise angels into ranks of importance. Cherubim, seraphim and ofanim we have come across already, but Enoch had added four more: angels of power, principalities, the Messiah and the elemental powers.[46]

It is only now, Paul writes in Ephesians, through the 'special grace' that he has been given to proclaim 'the infinite treasure of Christ [and] . . . how [that] mystery is to be dispensed' that these 'Sovereignties and Powers' can 'learn, through the Church, how comprehensive God's wisdom really is, exactly according to the plan which he had had from all eternity in Christ Jesus our Lord'.[47]

Paul is hijacking Enoch's classifications of angels and then debunking them. In Ephesians, he is insisting that the angels – who, elsewhere simultaneously, are being elevated as playing a leading role in the end-times and the coming of the kingdom of God on earth – are now largely redundant as intermediaries. Because of the revelation in Jesus of God's plan, he writes, 'we are bold enough to approach God in complete confidence, through our faith in him; so, I beg you, never lose confidence just because of the trials I go through on your account: they are your glory'.[48]

At the end of Ephesians, he goes further. The Sovereignties and Powers are not just angels, he suggests, but fallen angels, in league with the devil. 'Put God's armour on so as to be able to resist the devil's tactics. For it is not against human enemies that we have to struggle, but against the Sovereignties and the Powers who originate in the darkness in this world, the spiritual army of evil in the heavens.'[49] Every angel, he appears to be warning, is potentially fallen unless proven otherwise. The best course, therefore, is to avoid them altogether.

In other letters, he may seem to go along with notions of an angelic/heavenly hierarchy. In his Second Letter to the Corinthians, for instance, he writes of God's knowledge stretching 'right into the third heaven'.[50] But his overall approach is to belittle such talk. In Romans, Paul writes: 'For I am certain of this: neither death nor life, no angel, no prince, nothing that exists, nothing still to come, not any power, or height or depth [i.e. in heaven or hell], nor any created thing, can ever come between us and the love of God made visible in Christ Jesus our Lord.'[51]

Equally forceful are the formal instructions he gives at the start of his Letter to the Church at Colossae. Christ, he writes, is 'the image of the unseen God' and therefore paramount. In him were created 'all things in heaven and on earth . . . visible and invisible', including 'Thrones, Dominations, Sovereignties, Powers'.[52] If there is a heavenly hierarchy – as suggested by this final list of four – then it is as nothing compared with Christ.

And, lest Paul sound like a lone voice in pouring cold water on speculation about angels, in his first letter the apostle Peter chips in in the same vein. It is baptism, he says, that will save people come Judgement Day, because of the resurrection of Christ, 'who has entered heaven and is at God's right hand, now that he has made the angels and Dominations and Powers his subjects'.[53] Angels are, in other words, just details, while Jesus is the way to God, and his Church – being established by Paul, Peter and others – the means of following that way.

Just in case anyone has missed this point, those who produced the Letter to the Hebrews as if from Paul's pen – 'A Letter

Addressed to a Jewish-Christian Community' as it introduces itself in its subtitle – spell it out with a phrase that has become familiar to those who know their Bibles. God, they state, 'did not appoint angels to be rulers of the world to come'. Though God's son came to earth in human form, and submitted himself to a human death on the cross so as to atone for human sin, his resurrection in glory establishes his pre-eminent role, including over angels. God's concern, moreover, is not with angels, but with those who have 'descent from Abraham' – in other words, human beings.[54] They are, in a reversal of the pecking order laid down in the Book of Psalms, higher on his list of priorities than angels.

In the same spirit of clarifying what the Old Testament books do and do not say, Hebrews opens with a lengthy section that quotes from the Psalms, the Second Book of Samuel, and Deuteronomy, all key Old Testament texts for those Jewish teachers who have been giving angels such emphasis, to show instead the limitations on angels' activities when compared with those of the Son of God, the new Messiah. 'The truth', Hebrews concludes about angels, 'is they are all spirits whose work is service, sent to help those who will be the heirs of salvation.'[55] Which sounds remarkably like a promise of guardian angels.

Jesus the Great Angel

Reinforcing Paul's downgrading of angels, the Jesus of the Gospels – all four written after Paul's letters, though they precede them in the standard running order of the New Testament – tends to *talk* of angels rather than detail encounters with them. In Matthew's Gospel, there is the occasion when Jesus is challenged by his disciples over exactly who is 'the greatest in the kingdom of heaven'. Jesus answers that only those who make themselves like little children will get to heaven, and so 'the one who makes himself as little as little child is the greatest in the kingdom of heaven'. As he speaks, he has brought a small child into the gathered group. 'See that you never despise any of these little ones,' he continues, 'for I tell you that their angels in heaven are continually in the presence of my Father.'[56] Here is reinforcement of the notion, already popular, that each individual has a guardian angel from the moment of their birth, perhaps even of their conception.

Later in Matthew, Jesus is challenged once more about heaven. If a widow has remarried, he is asked, which of her husbands will be waiting for her in eternal life? His questioners are trying to put him on the spot, but he dismisses their question as too earthbound a view of heaven. 'At resurrection men and women do not marry; no, they are like the angels in heaven.'[57]

Angels, long since established as male in Judaism, are now therefore also to be regarded by Christians as chaste, since by the moral codes of the time marriage would be the only context for sexual relationships. Jesus is painting their role as close to the 'spirits whose work is service' already described in the Letter to the Hebrews.[58]

There are also angels at Jesus' resurrection, but in the Gospel accounts they appear only after he has left behind an empty tomb, their role being to announce, as messengers, what has happened. Mark, the earliest Gospel, doesn't even use the word angel, instead referring to 'a young man in a white robe'.[59] Matthew, often an expanded version of Mark, does refer to an angel and adds to the picture. 'His face was like lightning and his robe white as snow.'[60] The first detail has largely been ignored in subsequent centuries when the scene was reproduced by artists, on the basis that the angel should surely be looking benign, but mention of that white robe has helped provide Christian angels with their standard uniform, while the vigilant angel, sitting by the tomb, has inspired many millions of copies as memorials on the graves of Christians.

All four Gospels include angels, and indeed in one enduring Christian tradition each of their four writers is equated with angels. An exact contemporary of mine, raised a few miles away in a Catholic home in another part of Liverpool, remembers that she would use a different wording from the one I recited for her bedtime prayer to the angels. 'There are four corners to my bed / There are four angels at my head / Matthew, Mark, Luke and John / Bless the bed that I lie on.'

In places, the Gospels give voice to Paul's new orthodoxy about the reduced role of angels. There is the account in John of the healing pool at Bethesda in Jerusalem. Here the sick gather, we are told, 'for at intervals the angel of the Lord came down into the pool, and the water was disturbed, and the first person to enter the water after this disturbance was cured of any ailment he suffered from'. But now Jesus comes to the pool and requires no help to cure a man who tells him that he has been sick for thirty-eight years but has never been able to find anyone to lift him into the pool. Healing, the story says, is for Jesus, not angels.[61]

Yet, one consequence of including in the New Testament four different Gospels – rather than just one – written over a span of thirty-plus years, is that the mass of detail contains conflicting perspectives. So, elsewhere, Jesus is shown not replacing angels as Paul had set out, but rather requiring their assistance. As he prays, Luke reports, hours before his night-time arrest in the Garden of Gethsemane, he is let down by his apostles, who fall asleep on him. It is an angel who steps in to comfort him. ' "Father," he [Jesus] said, "if you are willing, take this cup away from me. Nevertheless let your will be done, not mine." Then an angel appeared to him, coming from heaven to give him strength. In his anguish, he prayed even more earnestly, and his sweat fell to the ground like great drops of blood.'[62] Likewise, in Matthew, when Jesus is in the wilderness, being tempted by the devil for forty days and forty nights, it is angels who come to 'look after him', albeit only once he has resisted the devil's promises.[63]

This second episode pits the good angels against the ultimate bad, or fallen, angel, the devil, and so builds on the narrative first heard in the Book of Enoch. Paul has already expanded on that in his letters, casting the devil as the obstacle to human salvation (obstruction being one meaning of the Hebrew word *stn*, or Satan, in the Old Testament), rather than the figure who subsequently does battle with the Archangel Michael in the Book of Revelation. The forty days and forty nights see Jesus fight his own battle with the devil. He doesn't need angels to do it for him. They only come to him once victory is complete.

Because Paul replaced angels with Jesus, there arose a tradition in the early Christian Church that presented Jesus as the ultimate or 'great' angel, both the message and the messenger. He is, as John's Gospel begins, the word of God made flesh.[64] The origins of the Jesus-as-Great-Angel school of thought take us back once more to the Book of Isaiah, and in particular to the passage promising the birth of a son that Christians take to be a reference to Jesus.

> For there is a child born for us,
> a son given to us
> and dominion is laid on his shoulders;
> and this is the name they give him:
> Wonder-Counsellor, Mighty-God,
> Eternal-Father, Prince-of-Peace.[65]

In the Septuagint, sometimes referred to as the Greek Old Testament, and the earliest surviving Greek translation from the original Hebrew, completed between the mid-third and second centuries BCE, the Jewish compilers, apparently caught up in the general enthusiasm for angels in those times, rendered 'Wonder-Counsellor' as 'Angel of Great Counsellor'.[66]

Since the Septuagint was treated with great reverence by the early Christians, this description of Jesus as an angel, the Great Angel, had an immediate resonance. It is seen, for example, in the writings of the influential early Christian Justin Martyr (*c.*100–165 CE), but, ultimately, it could not endure in the mainstream beyond those first centuries because, by referring to Jesus as an angel, there was an implicit denial of his humanity. The emerging Church decided at the Council of Chalcedon in 451 CE that he was both fully human and fully God. To refer to him as the Great Angel compromised these twin claims. Angels were neither gods nor flesh-and-blood humans.

It may sound an arcane debate now, but it exercised many minds in those early centuries of the Church because it went to the heart of the objections of dissenters who stressed the spiritual, mystical aspect of Jesus, and rejected the authority of those teachings of Christianity that sought to emphasise his humanity. Notable among these groups were the Docetists, who insisted that Jesus only *seemed* to be human, but was in reality spirit not flesh, and therefore an angel. The Church Fathers refused to allow what to them was downgrading his sacrifice on the cross and his resurrection to the level of an illusion. The Docetists were condemned as heretics at the First Council of Nicaea in 325 CE.

Liberating prisoners

The Acts of the Apostles were written around 90 CE after Mark, Matthew and Luke, but before John, and are positioned in the New Testament narrative after all four Gospels. They are believed to have been produced by the same hand responsible for Luke. And, as we have seen, that hand liked to add in angels. So when the resurrected Jesus ascends into heaven – 'a cloud took him from their sight' – the apostles are comforted by what are referred to in some translations as 'two men in white', in others as two angels, who tell them: 'This same Jesus will come back in the same way as you have seen him go there.' They are making an unambiguous promise of a Second Coming, though without any of the destruction that accompanies the Day of Judgement in the Book of Revelation.[67]

Acts also has an angel intervene to open the gates of the 'common jail' where the apostles have been detained by the Jewish authorities, and free them so they can preach at the Temple.[68] Later, when Peter is imprisoned (after James, brother of Jesus, has been beheaded by King Herod), he is guarded by 'four squads of four soldiers'. They are, though, no match for the angel of the Lord, who comes in a familiar Old Testament role as rescuer. 'The cell was filled with light', and the shackles on Peter's wrists fall away.[69]

There then follows a dream passage. 'The angel next said, "Wrap your cloak round you and follow me." Peter followed him but had no idea that what the angel did was all happening in reality; he thought he was seeing a vision.' After slipping past two guards, the prison gates open 'of their own accord' and the angel and Peter escape onto the street, whereupon the angel departs. 'It was only then that Peter came to himself. "Now I know it is all true," he said. "The Lord really did send his angel and has saved me from Herod and from all that the Jewish people were so certain would happen to me." '[70]

And it is Acts, as already mentioned, that details the clash between the 'Jewish' faction of Jesus' followers and those, led by Peter and Paul, who want to start a new Church for everyone. In this account of Peter's escape from prison, the real purpose could be read as invoking angelic protection for one of the main figures in the new Church as proof that this faction has God on its side – in other words, using an angel as crude propaganda. It was a habit the Early Church was to develop.

K

K is for **Kushner's angels** in Tony Kushner's multi-award-winning, watershed 1991 play, *Angels in America*, about the AIDS pandemic. It features a group of angels, collectively the 'Continental Principalities', harking back to a word used to rank angels in the Early Church. Each has steel-grey wings, and is an all-powerful bureaucrat, representing America, Africa, Asia, Australia, Oceania and Antarctica. Made up of *fluor* (minerals), *phospor*, *lumen* (light) and candle, they sit around a table covered with ancient and broken astronomical, astrological, mathematical and nautical objects of measurement and calculation, listening to a 1940s wireless, their role, 'in this time of crisis and confusion', being to represent heaven as it 'reaches down to disaster and in touching you, touches all of earth'.

L

L is for **Loki,** one of two fallen angels who have been expelled from heaven for insubordination in Kevin Smith's whimsical 1999 comedy *Dogma*. They find themselves stuck in Wisconsin. Behind the jokes, and the sending up of religion (the Catholic League in the US condemned the film as blasphemous), there is a surprising amount of theology. Loki (Matt Damon) and Bartleby (Ben Affleck) hope to recover their lost status in heaven by purchasing an indulgence – the sort of free pass into paradise that began Martin Luther's rebellion against Catholicism and hence the Reformation – but if they succeed they will reveal God as fallible for expelling them in the first place. So Alan Rickman, playing a mighty seraph called Metatron, tries to block them at every turn in what becomes a road movie, with the ultimate destination being a reunion with God, played by rock star Alanis Morissette.

The Recording Angels of Islam

'[Muhammad] taught the Arabs no new doctrines about God: most . . . were already convinced that Allah had created the world and would judge humanity in the Last Days, as Jews and Christians believed.'

Karen Armstrong, *Islam: A Short History* (2000)[1]

Muhammad was sleeping in a cave near the summit of Mount Hira, just outside Mecca. It was 610 CE and, as in previous years, this devout forty-year-old family man and respected merchant had removed himself from the hustle and bustle of everyday life to go to this remote location to pray, meditate and fast. What is known to Muslims as 'The Night of Destiny' ('*Laylat al-Qadr*'), and commemorated each year during the holy month of Ramadan, began when Muhammad felt a grip tightening around his body, squeezing out all of his breath. He was terrified and convinced himself he was under attack from jinni.

The name comes from the Arabic word for 'hidden', and these jinni were believed to be fiery, capricious and deeply unreliable spirits, part of the religious tradition that was followed by Muhammad, many others in the Quraysh trading community in Mecca to which he belonged, and, more broadly, many in the Arabian Peninsula.

Next he heard a voice. 'Recite in the name of your Lord who created . . . man from a clinging form.'[2] Only later was Muhammad able to identify that voice as belonging to the Angel Gabriel, or (in Arabic) Jibr'il. But recite he did, and so the first words of a new Arabic scripture, the Qur'an (or 'Recitation'), handed down by Allah, the high god of Arabia, to Muhammad his messenger, came pouring out.

This was the birth of Islam, and the presence of two angels at that birth, Gabriel and Michael, Jibr'il and Mikha'il, is recorded in the Qur'an.

> Say [Muhammad], 'If anyone is an enemy of Gabriel – who by God's leave brought down the Qur'an to your heart, confirming previous scriptures, as a guide and good news for the faithful – if anybody is an enemy of God, his angels and messengers, of Gabriel and Michael, then God is certainly the enemy of such disbelievers.'[3]

Jibr'il is not identical, though, to those other messenger angels of the Hebrew Scriptures and New Testament. Rather, it is Muhammad who in Islam is the messenger and what he recites – God's revelation – that is the message. Jibr'il's role is somewhere between messenger, guide, encourager and protector of the messenger. Yet a similar list might be compiled for the Old Testament angels who speak God's word to Jacob, Abraham, Ezekiel and Daniel, all of whom then go on as prophets to share what they have heard with their people.

In Islam, the role of angels (or *malaa'ikah* in Arabic) is best defined by their position – between Allah and the Qur'an – in its six 'Articles of Faith', based on a verse early in the Qur'an. 'The messenger believes in what has been sent down to him from his Lord, as do the faithful. They all believe in God, his angels, his scriptures and his messengers.'[4] The messengers come after the angels, as does the message – i.e. the scriptures – though this may be more a reflection of the chronology of events than of their importance.

Emerging Judaism had developed its ideas about angels from the belief systems that had gone before it. And then Christianity had fashioned its angels, influenced by the debates going on in Judaism about them around the time of Jesus. Now Islam's angels grew out of the essentially Judeo-Christian tradition in which Muhammad was raised. Like many of his fellow Arabs, he was familiar with the stories of Abraham, Lot, Jacob and Jesus. His people, the Quraysh, were great traders – Mecca being a commercial city – and their caravans headed south to Yemen, where there was a thriving Christian community, and west to what we call Syria, where over the intervening centuries the missionary work of Paul and others had borne fruit in a well-established Church. And there were plenty of Jews, too, who had been living in Arabia for over a millennium, originally migrating there after the Babylonian exile, or during the subsequent invasions of Israel, maintaining their beliefs in their new home, but integrating and intermarrying with local people.

It is explicit in Allah's revelations to Muhammad that they build on existing traditions, with Abraham as the shared starting point. 'People of the Book, why do you argue about Abraham when the Torah and the Gospels were not revealed until after his time?' says the Qur'an. 'Abraham was neither a Jew nor a Christian. He was upright and devoted to God . . . and the people who are closest to him are those who truly follow his ways, this prophet, and [true] believers – God is close to [true] believers.'[5]

Where Judaism (and hence Christianity) traces its line back to Abraham via his son with Sarah, Isaac, saved by an angel when his father was about to sacrifice him, Islam looks instead to Ishmael, the child Abraham had previously fathered with the servant girl, Hagar.[6] In the Hebrew Scriptures, when Isaac is born, Sarah demands that Hagar and her child be banished. God tells Abraham to do as his wife demands, but promises that he will 'make' this other child 'into a nation'.[7] And that promise is repeated again shortly afterwards, when a rescuing guardian angel finds Hagar and Ishmael, lost and despairing in the 'wilderness of Beersheba', after their banishment.[8]

In the Qur'an, Allah appears in a dream to Abraham/Ibrahim to demand he sacrifice not Isaac but Ishmael/Isma'il.[9] Islamic tradition accuses the devil in disguise of being the real and malign source of the dream, prompting Allah to intervene directly to stop the sacrifice. When Hagar/Hajarah and her son are lost and thirsty in the wilderness, Islam teaches that it is the angel Jibr'il who intervenes to save them, causing a spring to open where they stood (known as the Well of Zamzam and part of the pilgrimage route in Mecca). Later Abraham/Ibrahim and Ishmael/Isma'il are reunited and together build the cube-shaped sanctuary in Mecca, the Ka'bah, which remains one of its most holy sites.

Among those like Muhammad who, at the time of the Night of Destiny, lived in towns and cities – what might be referred to as the settled Arabs, rather than nomadic Bedouin – Allah was generally regarded as the most important god, and the creator of the world, though essentially a distant figure. Some even claimed he was the same as the God worshipped by Jews and Christians, but there were also other lesser deities in the Arabic pantheon, a whole spirit world that was seen as more connected with everyday life than Allah.

Some of Muhammad's contemporaries also nurtured a hope, perhaps even for a few an expectation, that just as prophets had been sent by God to the Jews and Christians, one day an Arab prophet would come to them. The ground might therefore have been prepared for Muhammad but, after his experience in the cave, his sense of his own profound unworthiness made it hard for him to believe that he could be that prophet, the 'final prophet', as Muslims believe. He had hurried back down Mount Hira, home to his wife Khadijah, mother of his six children, and told her what had happened, and of his fears that he was somehow being tricked by jinni.

While there were more revelations in the days that followed, shortly afterwards they ceased, to Muhammad's great dismay. The silence only increased his suspicions that he had been tricked by jinni rather than brought into God's presence by an angel. Still, though, he persevered, kept faith, and eventually, after two years, the revelations resumed. Thus emboldened to embark on his public ministry, Muhammad would, at first, speak to individuals and small groups, people who had noticed the change in him and wanted to find out what had caused it. He told them of the message he had received of submission (the meaning of 'Islam') to Allah. As his reputation grew, though, he attracted larger crowds.

Whenever he addressed them, he would now refer confidently to the role of the Angel Jibr'il in Allah's continuing revelations to him, which were to last until his death in 632 CE. The angel, Muhammad said, took on many different forms. Sometimes he was big enough to fill the sky – 'with mighty powers and great strength who stood on the highest horizon and then approached, coming down until he was two bow-lengths away or even closer, and revealed to God's servant what he revealed'.[10] At others, all Muhammad could see were Jibr'il's eyes.

His arrival was unpredictable. He was just as likely to come when Muhammad was deep in prayer, or asleep, as he was when the Prophet was going about his work. The angelic visits weren't confined, as they had been for many before him, to dreams. And the voice Muhammad heard could also vary, one day sounding as clear as day, and next like muffled bells that gave him a headache.

Sometimes, recalling the Book of Genesis, Jibr'il would take the form of a man.

Umar[11] related that a man once came to a gathering of the Prophet and his companions – nobody knew who he was. He was extremely white with white clothing, and jet black hair. He proceeded to sit very close to the Prophet and questioned him in detail about Islam. When the Prophet replied, the strange man told the Prophet that he had answered correctly. It was only after he left that the Prophet told his companions that this was the Angel Jibr'il who had come to question and teach them about their faith.[12]

Others who were present when Muhammad received a new revelation described him as sweating and swept up in a trance-like state. For the Prophet, the appearance of Jibr'il signalled not the reassuring presence that is today associated with angels. It was a time of pain. 'Never once', he said, 'did I receive a revelation without thinking my soul had been torn away from me.'[13]

Jibr'il, as described, has unmistakable echoes of the Jewish and Christian scriptures, while his part in revealing the Qur'an to Muhammad most obviously recalls those angels who revealed knowledge to Enoch. Such connections are freely acknowledged in the Qur'an, with references back, for example, to Gabriel's mission in the opening sections of Luke's Gospel. 'Remember Zachariah, when he cried to his Lord, "My Lord, do not leave me childless, though you are the best of heirs." We answered him. We gave him John [the Baptist], curing his wife.'[14] And the Annunciation, too. 'We sent Our Spirit [Gabriel/Jibr'il] to appear before her in the form of a normal human . . . he said, "I am but a messenger from your Lord, [come] to announce the gift of a pure son." '[15]

That son, Jesus, or Isa in Arabic, is revered in Islam as a great prophet, but in January 624, during prayers, Muhammad told the congregation assembled with him to turn so that they no longer faced Jerusalem, as had been their habit until then, but instead to reorientate themselves to Mecca, where Allah had revealed himself through Jibr'il. The symbolism was clear. Islam would henceforth direct itself to God alone.

What Islam believes about angels

It wasn't until around 650 CE that the first version of the Qur'an was compiled, its language subsequently coming to be regarded as a masterpiece of Arabic prose and poetry. It took a further eighty years for scholars to begin collecting details of Muhammad's teachings and sayings in the Hadith and the Sunnah (the life and example of the Prophet). By that time, the followers of Islam had expanded way beyond Arabia, occupying Jerusalem in 638 CE and, by 732 CE, ruling an empire that stretched from the Himalayas to the Pyrenees.

The text of the Qur'an is clear about its own origins. It is described as a 'glorious' version of an original written 'on a preserved tablet'[16] and residing in heaven. It was Jibr'il's task to accompany it to earth when it was 'sent down from the Lord of all being'.[17] In Christianity the word of God becomes flesh in Jesus. In Islam, the word of God becomes a book that – like the Torah for Jews – is the way, the truth and the life.

There are many angels in the pages of the Qur'an, but their roles are practical rather than mystical or opaque. This was in keeping with the overall tone of the revelations Muhammad shared. They were about doing rather than being. The imperative was to get on with building a community based on compassion and the fair distribution of wealth. Indeed, the sort of complex, imaginative theological speculation that had so marked the literature of the intertestamental period in Judaism and Christianity was sidelined by Islam as '*zannah*' – a sort of whimsy about matters that should and will always remain a mystery.

The practical angels of Islam act, first and foremost, as guardians – 'we are your allies in this world, and in the world to come'.[18] They can, on occasion, dispense God's justice, as had happened at Sodom and Gomorrah in the Hebrew Scriptures. 'We send down the angels only to bring justice.'[19] And, once more with resonances of what has gone before, they join in earthbound battles. In a rare historical reference, the Qur'an mentions how angels contributed to Muhammad's victory at the Battle of Badr in 624 CE against a larger force of those Quraysh from Mecca who opposed him. 'Will you [too] be satisfied if your Lord reinforces you by sending down 3,000 angels? Well, if you are steadfast and mindful of God, your Lord will reinforce you with 5,000 swooping angels if the enemy should suddenly attack you.'[20]

Elsewhere Islam's angels undertake the familiar task of surrounding Allah's throne and singing, as they do in Ezekiel and Tobit. 'Those [angels] who carry the throne and those who surround it celebrate the praise of their Lord and have faith in him.'[21] They have wings. 'Praise be to God, creator of the heavens and earth who made angels messengers with two, three, four [pairs of] wings.'[22] They gather in great numbers. 'By those [angels] ranged in rows, who rebuke reproachfully and recite God's words.'[23] And, they are definitely male.

'Now [Muhammad], ask the disbelievers: is it true that your Lord has daughters, while they chose sons for themselves? Did we create the angels as females while they were watching? No, indeed. It is one of their lies.'[24] This passage appears to have its roots in the conflicts of the time, a riposte to those Arabs who had rejected Allah and referred to his daughters – in their eyes a slur, since they themselves were anxious to have only sons.

Over angels, as with much else about Judaism, Christianity and Islam, what is shared in common is far greater than what divides. Yet there are significant developments in the story of angels in what the Qur'an teaches. Some arise from questions of emphasis. For example, as well as them watching over humankind, the Qur'an describes angels as acting explicitly as advocates for us in heaven, a role that Christianity came largely to ascribe to saints (though the line is blurred because some of its angels were also regarded as saints). 'They beg forgiveness for the believers: "Our Lord, you embrace all things in mercy and knowledge, so forgive those who turn to you and follow your path. Save them from the pains of Hell." '[25]

Other shared details are magnified many times in Islam. In the Hadith, there is talk of Jibr'il having not six wings like Isaiah's seraphim, but six hundred, decorated with emeralds, pearls and rubies, each one so powerful that it takes only a touch from its tip to destroy a whole city. More intriguing is the consensus among most Muslim scholars that the Qur'anic passage that talks of '*ruh*' or 'the Holy Spirit' bringing 'the revelation with the truth step by step from your Lord to strengthen the believers and as guidance and good news to the devout' can only refer to Jibr'il.[26] Given that Christianity regards the Holy Spirit as one of the three-persons-in-one-God, alongside God the Father and Jesus, God's son, this is one area of significant theological divergence.

More tangible, though, is the Qur'an's description of a new breed of 'recording' angels. Each individual has, it says, not one but two guardian angels, one in front and one behind. 'It makes no difference whether any of you speak secretly or aloud, whether you are hiding under cover of night, or walking about in the day: each person has angels before him and behind, watching him by God's command.'[27]

In a later passage, those two guardians are referred to as 'watchers', a description heard for good and for ill in the Book of Enoch, but these angels are, the Qur'an makes plain, 'noble recorders, who know what you do'.[28] They are literally watching, both protecting and keeping a chart on each person's virtuous and bad deeds. The same is implied, but not quite said, in another verse. 'We created man – we know what his soul whispers to him: we are closer to him than his jugular vein – with two receptors set to record, one on his right side and one on his left: he does not utter a single word without an ever-present watcher.'[29]

There is just a hint of menace in this, with the guardian/recorder/receptor angels less the one who looks out for you when, for example, you leave your empty wheelchair unattended on the driveway, and more the inspector, compiling a lifelong school report to share with a heavenly parent. In Islamic tradition these two angels have names – Raqib and Atid, collectively the '*kiraman katibin*' (or 'noble recorders') – but it is stressed that, while their final score cards are consulted at the gates to heaven, Allah's judgement on who to admit is not dependent on them.

In some versions of the tale of Raqib and Atid, one is presented as good and the other as bad. That approach echoes an idea already developed in the Talmud. 'Rabbi Yosi, son of Rabbi Yehudah said', it is recorded,

> [that] two ministering angels accompany a person home on Friday night from the synagogue. One is the angel of good and one is the angel of evil. When the person arrives home to find the Sabbath candles lit [as tradition demands], the table set and the beds made, the angel of good says, 'May it be the divine will that the next Sabbath should be the same.' And against his will, the angel of evil answers, 'Amen.' If not [unlit candles and unmade beds], then the angel of evil says, 'May it be the Divine will that the next Sabbath should be the same.' And against his will, the angel of good answers, 'Amen.'[30]

The setting is domestic, and therefore essentially about private deeds, not public actions, but the two angelic figures are delighting in, respectively, good and bad deeds. What is striking, though, here as in the Qur'an, is the impotence of the angels to do more than watch and record. They cannot influence events directly, cannot intervene, cannot make their charge do good or evil.

Christianity, too, toyed during its development with what might be called the two-angel solution as part of a recognition of humankind's essentially fallen, sinful nature. This is reflected, notably, in the influential writings of Gregory of Nyssa in the fourth century. This bishop from Cappadocia (in today's central Turkey), who in the 380s was sent on a mission to Arabia by the First Council of Constantinople, described the human condition as being forever torn between two angels – one offering the virtuous path of God's limitless goodness, and the other the time-limited temptations of earthly life that could lead to eternal damnation.[31]

Gregory does not give names to his good twin/bad twin angels. Islam, however, is far more relaxed about identifying particular angels who exist, it says, in that much larger part of the iceberg-like universe that is unseen (known as '*al-Ghayb*'). Raqib and Atid are two among many new names added to the angelic ranks, though almost all of them exist in Islamic writings other than in the Qur'an itself. This abundance may be because Islam gives much less emphasis to sainthood than is accorded in the strictly regimented processes of beatification and canonisation that are associated above all with Catholic Christianity's eagerness to offer flesh-and-blood role models. Certainly later works on Islamic spirituality would advocate being more like angels as one means for human beings to improve and even perfect themselves. It was, suggested Rumi, the popular thirteenth-century-CE Persian poet and mystic (from the Sufi tradition in Islam), like seeking out the right rather than the wrong companions in life. 'Man's situation is compatible to an angel's wing that has been attached to a donkey's tail, so that perhaps, through the angel's radiance and companionship, the donkey may itself become an angel.'[32]

This theme was also explored in a more visionary context by the noted ninth-century Persian Qur'anic scholar, polymath and ascetic, Al-Tabari, who described an 'Earth of Emerald Cities', which he names as Jabarsa, Jabalqa and Hurqalya (the significance of which has stumped scholars ever after). In these places, heaven and earth mingle, and angels accommodate humans, who live among them as if they are angels too, in a spirit of perfection and wholeness. They are bathed in light from the mountain, eat only vegetables, and wear no clothes, because there is no distinction made between genders and no instinct to sexual intimacy.[33] Islam's angels are, as in Jesus' description in the Gospels, chaste.

The Hadith extends Mikha'il's brief beyond his mention in the Qur'an, giving him the care of plants and rain as well as a general responsibility to nourish humankind – quite a task in the dry, inhospitable conditions of Arabia. Angelic stewardship of nature, in particular, was to become a central tenet of later studies that sought to invoke angels to reconcile religion and science.

Then there is Munkar and Nakir, far removed from any modern notions of an angel. In the Islamic tradition, they inhabit the domain of al-Barzakh (literally 'barrier'). Roughly the equivalent of Christian purgatory, where the dead wait for the final Day of Judgement, al-Barzakh is referred to in the Qur'an as 'a barrier [that] stands behind such people [the dead] until the very day they are resurrected'.[34] What is not mentioned in the text is the part played by Munkar and Nakir – 'the Denied' and 'the Denier' in Arabic. Their roles are, though, filled out in the Hadith and elsewhere.

They have solid black eyes, and shoulders so broad they stretch for miles, and they carry hammers, which they use on the dead. Everyone placed in a grave is forced to sit up by them and answer three questions: about their God, their faith and the Prophet. If they give the right answers, they are left in peace to await final judgement on their ascent to *Jannah* (heaven) or their descent into hell where 'the fire will scorch their faces and their lips will be twisted in pain'.[35] But if they get their replies wrong, they are beaten every day except Friday by Munkar and Nakir until Allah tells them to stop. Scholars have pointed out some parallels between these two unlikeable angels, and figures in the pantheon of Zoroastrianism (which was largely wiped out by the spread of Islam).

Unlike Zoroastrianism, Islam is monotheist – it believes in one supreme, omnipotent god. Munkar and Nakir are therefore doing Allah's work and are under his command. The Qur'an describes another pair of provocateur angels, Harut and Marut, tempters both, again under Allah's control, who are schooled in the magic and sorcery that is said to have suffused the pre-existing religions of Babylon. They know 'what can cause discord between man and wife, although they harm no one with it except by God's leave'.[36]

In this account Harut and Marut (whose names have been linked with Zoroastrian Haruvatat and Ameretat, two of the 'divine sparks' or prototype archangels discussed earlier) are intimately acquainted with evil and cause people to sell their souls. In the Islamic tradition, that confusion about their motivation was resolved with a fuller telling of their tale that gives them a wider context. The two are part of a group of angels sent to earth to test human weakness, but who get involved with women. When one of their number spots these liaisons and rebukes the others, they kill him, but they cannot escape Allah's all-seeing eye. In atonement for their sins, they are given the choice of hell or being suspended by their feet down a well in Babylon until the Day of Judgement. They choose the latter, for the glimmer of hope it gives them.

Hell is part of Islamic beliefs, as is a devil-like figure. There were, of course, the jinni, who Muhammad had suspected at first were tricking him in the cave on Mount Hira. The Qur'an explains their place. 'We created man out of dried clay formed from dark mud,' Allah recounts; 'the jinn we created before, from the fire of scorching wind.'[37] Next Allah talks to the angels. 'Your Lord said to the angels, "I will create a mortal out of dried clay, formed from dark mud. When I have fashioned him and breathed my spirit into him, bow down before him", and the angels did so.'[38]

But, it continues, one angel among them would not bow down to man as Allah commanded. 'Not Iblis: he refused to bow down like the others.'³⁹ Where angels usually have no free will – a key concept in the mainstream of all three religions – and have to do as God commands, Iblis is able to make a choice to refuse to do as he is told. So, was Iblis – mentioned eleven times in the Qur'an – a defiant, even fallen angel, or a jinn? Or an angel who by his refusal becomes as much God's opponent as the jinni – who in some ways came to represent in the Qur'an all those who refused to accept Muhammad's revelation? Another of Iblis's names – Shaytan – is a word used to describe jinni in pre-Muslim Arabia.

The distinction is, in many ways, irrelevant, since the net result of defying God is the same. 'God said, "Iblis, why did you not bow down like the others?" And he answered, "I will not bow to a mortal you created from dried clay, formed from dark mud." "Get out of here!" said God. "You are an outcast, rejected until the Day of Judgement." '⁴⁰ What then follows is a description of Iblis's fate and it sounds very much like that of Harut and Marut. Iblis promises to 'lure mankind on earth and put them in the wrong, all except your devoted servants'. God responds that Iblis will have no power over devoted servants, and those who go astray will end up in hell, while the righteous will enter heaven – 'gardens with springs – enter them in peace and safety'.⁴¹

The fate of Iblis becomes wrapped up with both that of Harut and Marut, and that of the jinni. Sometimes Iblis is even referred to as the 'chief of jinni'. All deny or defy God, and all must wait until the Day of Judgement, where good will inevitably triumph over evil. In other words, their defiance is pointless. Though it borrowed concepts and even names from Zoroastrianism, Islam rejected its dualism – as Judaism and Christianity had also done. Whether they be bad angels or bad spirits, who spend their energy tempting humankind away from Allah, they had no power ulti-mately to rival his.

Night journey

'Glory to him who made his servant travel by night from the sacred place of worship to the furthest place of worship, whose surroundings we have blessed, to show him some of our signs.'[42] This brief description in the Qur'an is the basis for an event that is the second-most important in the Islamic calendar – The Night of Ascent ('*Laylat ul-Miraj*').

Said in Islamic tradition to have taken place in 621 CE, most of the details that are given come from the Hadith (including one version by Anas ibn Malik, who was a young boy when Muhammad was alive) and other writings. The beginning is the usual one when it comes to angels. Muhammad is asleep in Mecca ('the sacred place of worship' as the Qur'anic verse puts it) when he is disturbed by the angel Jibr'il. As with Jacob in the Old Testament, there are those who see the whole episode as a dream (the Prophet's then wife, Aisha, was later reported to have said that his body was in his bed the whole night), others who view it as a spiritual journey, and still more who insist that it literally took place.

Jibr'il directs Muhammad to mount a mystical white creature, Buraq – often referred to as smaller than a mule and bigger than a donkey – who then flies him through the night sky to Jerusalem ('the furthest place of worship') with Jibr'il in attendance.[43] This section of the journey is referred to as '*al-isra*', after the title of the Qur'anic surah or verse that hints at it. Once there, Muhammad tethers Buraq on the Temple Mount, site of the Second Temple that had been destroyed 550 years earlier by the Romans. What is reputed to be the exact spot is now part of the complex of the al-Aqsa mosque, the third holiest site in Islam. The angel asks Muhammad to choose between wine, water and milk to drink. The Prophet chooses milk – evidently the right answer because it is 'the natural instinct' ('*fitrah*') and opens the way to the second stage of his journey.

This part is known as the '*mi'raj*', or 'ladder', in another nod to Jacob, and Muhammad next explores the seven layers of heaven. If the calibration recalls Jewish and Christian literature, so too do those figures that Jibr'il introduces to Muhammad in each tier. Jesus (Isa) is in the third heaven, Moses (Musa) in the sixth. In the seventh, highest stage, the Angel Jibr'il as Muhammad's guide, and more significant than any of the other figures on previous levels, is only permitted to accompany the Prophet as far as the holy trees of Sidrat al-Muntaha, the boundary beyond which no created being can pass.

Muhammad goes forward alone to find himself in the presence of God and is told that he and all Muslims must recite their ritual prayers fifty times a day. The Prophet accepts this commandment, but on his way back through the layers is stopped by Moses/Musa, who suggests (with typical Islamic practicality) that fifty times a day may leave time for very little else in everyday life. After a series of as many as nine returns by the Prophet to the seventh heaven to negotiate a reduction, Allah agrees on five times a day, henceforth to be observed as the '*salat*', the keystone, of Muslim life.

The observations attributed to Muhammad on his Night Journey by later writers are part of the Islamic tradition and they provide angels in Islam with their particular characters. Principal among them is a saying attributed to Muhammad that Jibr'il had revealed to him that every day 70,000 angels enter the seventh heaven for the first time. If multiplied by the number of days in a year, it suggests a vast heavenly host ready for service.

How this might work itself out is addressed elsewhere in the tradition, where the '*Baitul Ma'mur*', or the 'Frequented House', is referred to, situated in the seventh heaven. This means that it is in the skies directly above its earthly replica, the Ka'bah in Mecca. Just as Muslims made the hajj or pilgrimage to Mecca and the Ka'bah as a once-in-a-lifetime religious obligation, it is taught, so the angels also make a one-off hajj to '*Baitul Ma'mur*'. The parallels between the two draw angels and humans closer together in a single endeavour.

Numbers of angels are sustained at 70,000 daily because Jibr'il goes each day to the fourth heaven and dips his wings in the River of Life. When he shakes them dry afterwards, 70,000 drops fall, and each is a new angel, a process that will continue until Israf'il's trumpet sounds a second time to indicate that the Day of Resurrection has arrived.

Israf'il

If Jibr'il and Mikha'il equate to Gabriel and Michael, then Israf'il is linked with Raphael, though he more specifically recalls the trumpet-blowing angels of the Book of Revelation. It is Israf'il who calls souls on Judgement Day. The Qur'an says only that 'the trumpet will be sounded',[44] but the Hadith is more specific in identifying Israf'il as the one doing the blowing. At his first blast, from the holy rock in Jerusalem (of which more later), everything will be destroyed. At his second, it will be the Day of Resurrection.

For much of its history Islam has eschewed portrayals of heavenly (and human) beings as a distraction, in marked contrast with Christian attitudes, particularly in the West. Figurative art, generally, is seen as diverting believers from transcendence, which cannot be adequately expressed in human imagery, though calligraphy is highly prized. There have, though, been periods when wealthy Muslim sultans did commission illustrated texts. In a fourteenth-century miniature, from a manuscript called 'The Wonder of Creation', made in Baghdad and now in Washington's Smithsonian Institution, Israf'il is seen blowing his trumpet for all his might, with his red and green wings and his voluminous matching robe, tied by a snake-like sash that appears to have a life of its own.

Islam eschews figurative art, but a fourteenth-century miniature from the 'Wonder of Creation' manuscript, made in Baghdad, depicts the Angel Israf'il summoning souls on Judgement Day with his trumpet.

If such images are few and far between, outside Islam Israf'il inspired the nineteenth-century American poet, short-story writer and critic Edgar Allan Poe to produce a memorable portrait of him in verse in 1831. Poe seized upon another tradition in Islam – that Israf'il's heartstrings were a lute.

> In Heaven a spirit doth dwell
> Whose heartstrings are a lute;
>
> None sing so wildly well
> As the angel Israfel,
> And the giddy stars (so legends tell),
> Ceasing their hymns, attend the spell
> Of his voice, all mute.[45]

From the anonymous figures in a heavenly choir who produce 'The Song of Angels' in Isaiah, we have reached a place where named angels, across the three great monotheistic religions, now have not only instruments to play on, but heartstrings as well. How these distinctive, recognisable, often very human angels go on to play a part in shaping the world around us is the second part of this story.

Part Two

The Enduring Influence of Angels

'There are many more things in heaven and earth, Horatio,
Than are dreamt of in our philosophies.'

Hamlet, by William Shakespeare (1.5.167–8)

M

M is for **Moloch**, who ranks second only to Beelzebub in John Milton's list of the fallen angels in *Paradise Lost* (1667). Milton's angel names were often borrowed from those the Hebrew Scriptures deemed enemies, including Moloch, who in the Second Book of Kings is part of the Ammonite pagan deity. Milton turns him into a bloodthirsty monster who requires the sacrifice of young human souls: 'horrid king besmirched with blood / Of human sacrifice and parents' tears'.

N

N is for **Nephi**, the name used by the founder of Mormonism, Joseph Smith, in his earliest accounts, for the angel that visited him in 1823. Nephi was, Mormons believe, the son of the prophet Lehi, and remains as the narrator of the first two sections of the Book of Mormon. By 1838, though, Smith was identifying the angel as Moroni, the name that has stuck. Nephi, however, remains a popular name for Mormons to give their children. Its origins have been much debated. One avenue of exploration has been to look for a link between Nephi and the Nephilim, the race of giants who appear in chapter six of the Book of Genesis, where in the Christian tradition the fallen angels come down to earth and get involved with the daughters of earth.

7

How Angels Helped the Early Church to Grow

'If a man is not rising upwards to be an angel, depend upon it, he
is sinking downwards to be a devil.'

Samuel Taylor Coleridge, *Table Talk* (1833)

For a few short months between 1256 and 1257, the two leading
medieval angelologists were teaching side by side at the
University of Paris. The Dominican Thomas Aquinas – known
as 'the Angelic Doctor' – and his great friend and contemporary,
the Franciscan Bonaventure – called the 'Seraphic Doctor' by his
admirers, together made the study of angels an integral and
required part of the theology curriculum at the university.

Both Italians, they had risen to the rank of *magister* – master
or professor – in what had become the intellectual powerhouse of
Catholic Europe. Though Bologna was the continent's first
university, Paris, which received its royal charter in 1200 after
emerging from the cathedral school of Notre Dame, had come to
overshadow it, attracting all the greatest thinkers in the Church.
There were faculties of law, medicine and the arts, but theology
was the leading academic discipline.

Aquinas and Bonaventure had both been sent there as young
men to study by their religious orders, singled out for this honour
because of their precocious intellectual abilities. After completing
their studies, both had then been directed to serve their orders in
other places – Aquinas in Cologne as secretary to fellow
Dominican Albert the Great, known as 'Doctor Universalis' on

account of the breadth of his learning, and Bonaventure to various places in Italy. But in 1253 Bonaventure returned to Paris to take up his prestigious teaching position. Three years later Aquinas joined him.

The two were contrasting characters, Bonaventure a smiling, genial figure who drew people to him, Aquinas more austere, driven and lacking in social graces. Outside the classroom, Aquinas's life was one of prayer, study, writing, reading and more prayer. In Cologne, the story goes, Dominican students had referred to him as a 'dumb ox', allegedly on account of how little he said when among them, rather than for any lack of intellect. When Albert heard the nickname, he is said to have rebuked them: 'this dumb ox will one day bellow so loud the whole world will hear him'.[1] His words proved prophetic. Aquinas's *Summa Theologica*, his greatest achievement, a compendium or digest (as was the fashion then) of all the Church's major theological teachings, though unfinished at the time of his death in 1274, remains a standard text in schools of theology to this day.

Whatever their differences in personality, and on the great theological debates of the age, together Aquinas and Bonaventure were as one in placing angelology, the study of angels, at the top of the academic tree in the Faculty of Theology, inspiring those they taught to pore over every detail that could conceivably be known about them, down to whether they had bodies, ate food, smelt, had eyes or had sex.

With its various strange-sounding spin-offs of angelomachy (the study of the battles between angels), angelographia (the nature and power of angels) and angelocracy (government by angels),[2] angelology was a subject that provoked the same sort of buzz around continual innovation that today characterises computer science.

At the heart of angelology, though, certainly as studied in

Paris, was not a fascination with the minutiae of angels' lives, bodies and functions for their own sake, but instead an all-embracing ambition to understand the workings of the cosmos – and by association the mind of God – through the lens of his heavenly creatures. It was an endeavour that would continue in theological faculties on and off through to the eighteenth century (though by then the word angelology had been discarded as toxic). Initially, it had a strong connection with – and influence on – popular belief, ritual and religious practice, but increasingly over the centuries it became detached in its ivory tower from this more everyday world of believing and belonging, so much so that it ended up being treated by most as an irrelevance, long since superseded everywhere else by a scientific approach that sidelined God.

In their time, though, the angelologists were convinced that, through debate, discussion, and the careful ordering and measurement of arguments around angels, the intuition of belief and the rational basis of science could advance hand in hand. Hitherto, angels had been the ladder that connected heaven and earth. Now they were the means of bringing together all human knowledge, and placing it within the wider sphere of the divine.

Aquinas's speculations about angels can, seven hundred and fifty years later, sound like the bizarre whimsy of some strange disengaged New Age cult. And the systems he so painstakingly built around angels to connect with, and explain, a God-created universe appear as redundant in the light of subsequent scientific progress as the typewriter did after the advent of the laptop. Yet Aquinas was, by common consent, one of the most extraordinary intellects of his own and any time. His devotion to angels cannot be caricatured or lightly cast aside. Instead, what has to be addressed is the 'why'. Why was this clever man so obsessed with what seem to us ludicrous details about angels?

The answer requires a proper understanding of two things. The first is how the Catholic Church grew in the first millennium since the death and resurrection of Jesus to become the dominant force in European religion, politics, culture and society. Accompanying that rise was the regular invocation of angels, in almost every situation of life, from liturgy to the longing for afterlife, as a way of the Church asserting a divinely derived authority over those in the pews.

And the second is a grasp of how, for Aquinas, Bonaventure and most believers at the time, angels were neither abstract theory nor literal fact, but rather an integral and everyday part of their world, visible to some, but real in the sense that they were available to all as helpers and role models of the sort of perfection that was required to achieve salvation and eternal life in heaven.

To a medieval mindset convinced that the universe contained 'thousands and ten thousands of angels without number', as promised in the Book of Enoch, it was entirely logical that Christians should pray to angels for assistance as they worked in fields, fought in armies, saw their children die in infancy and tried to scrape a living. After all, they heard about them often enough in sermons and readings from the scriptures, and saw them all around in carvings and frescoes in their churches. Angels were there, too, bewinged and benign, in the growing number of elaborate plays, pageants and processions that were staged under church auspices on the streets of their villages, towns and cities on religious feast days.

In its medieval setting, angelology was almost a form of anthropology. The academics at the University of Paris spent a great deal of time focusing on the creation story as told in Genesis. Since angels, they argued, were created before humans, they must therefore offer clues as to why God made Adam and, by association, the rest of the human race. By scrutinising angels, Aquinas and his colleagues believed, they were ultimately finding out more about themselves and their origins, rather as today's anthropologists go back to primates to find the roots of human evolution.

A final thought, before we turn our attention to the build-up to the golden age of angelology: it may be helpful to clear the decks in advance of a phrase in regard of Aquinas's interest in angels that continues to dog his reputation. He is regularly credited – and derided – as the source of the question, how many angels can dance on a pinhead? The attribution is usually made to indicate that he (and by association the Church) wasted time on tedious, pointless detail – which is precisely what 'angels dancing on pinheads' has come to mean in everyday parlance.

Yet, on this, Aquinas surely stands unjustly accused. Nowhere in his writings does he mention pinheads. The earliest verifiable reference to Aquinas's making the remark is instead found in the seventeenth century, with most fingers pointing at the English Protestant polemicist William Chillingworth, in his 1637 attack on medieval Catholicism, *Religion of Protestants*. Chillingworth, though, was the first of many. In their hugely popular fantasy novel *Good Omens*, about the birth of the devil's son and the end of life as we know it, the contemporary English authors Neil Gaiman and Terry Pratchett include an angel called Aziraphale, based on the cherub who once guarded the gates of Eden. They list among his accomplishments being the only angel who could dance the gavotte on a pinhead.[3]

There is, though, in the accusation no smoke without fire. For what Aquinas certainly did question, as part of applying reason to the existence of angels, was whether more than one of them could be active at the same time at the same point in the universe – where, among other things, I suppose they might conceivably dance on a pinhead, not that this thought entered his head. His conclusion was that they couldn't. While a modern physicist might disagree with his answer, they would also recognise the essential scientific dilemma that he was grappling with – namely, whether two forces could act at the same point at the same time. This wasn't, then, just some obtuse religious speculation. In trying to quantify the sublime nature of angels, Aquinas and his like were probing at what seemed to them nothing less than the fabric of reality. In other words, they were doing what scientists do to this day.

Invisible husbandmen

One of the greatest challenges confronting emerging early Christianity was that of authority. At the end of Matthew's Gospel, the risen Christ meets his closest followers on a mountain in Galilee and tells them to 'go [and] make disciples of all the nations'.[4] That is what they did. As a result of the missionary journeys of Paul, Peter and others, Christian communities sprang up in the first and second centuries all across the Middle East, along the southern shores of the Mediterranean, and up through Greece into Rome, the imperial capital.

The expansion was rapid, remarkable and fiercely resisted by the authorities. The Romans persecuted the 'new' religion on and off right up to the start of the fourth century, accusing Christians of incest, orgies and cannibalism.[5] When such slurs failed to dent the rise in Christian numbers, the Empire became ever more furious at the challenge posed to its official policy of one 'national' religion to bind its far-flung domains together. Often Christians found themselves treated as the scapegoats for all and anything that was going wrong. As late as 303, a hard-pressed Emperor Diocletian was ordering all Christian places of worship to be destroyed and all holy books burnt, in an attempt to improve his popularity.

For the leaders of this burgeoning but besieged Church – known to history as the Early Church Fathers – the blood of those martyred in the Roman persecutions was one focus of unity for geographically distant Christian communities that were otherwise prone to heading off in their own directions. Angels provided another. For the early Christians, faced with a merciless onslaught designed to wipe them out, the 'angel of the Lord' was an inspiring figure. In the Acts of the Apostles, he had come to free Peter when he was locked in jail, and so he might also, they hoped, become their liberator, or at least comforter, as they too suffered imprisonment, torture and death.[6] And in the Book of Revelation, written towards the end of the first century when the persecutions were well underway, the same besieged early Christians were equally drawn to those avenging angels, notably the Archangel Michael, who see off God's opponents and herald the imminent arrival of the kingdom of heaven on earth.

Such spirited resilience, though, was not sufficient on its own to create the robust ties that were required if a growing cult was to be transformed into a church. So a clerical hierarchy started to develop from as early as 160. Ordained men were appointed as regional bishops and local priests, replacing the lay men and women who had hitherto been elected by their congregations as leaders. The new structure wasn't always a welcome imposition, and so proved hard to enforce. As late as 492, Pope Gelasius I was writing to churches in southern Italy, rebuking them for allowing women to 'officiate at sacred altars and all matters reserved for the male sex'.[7]

Even arguments for the elevation of the office of pope (from the Latin for father) to supreme authority within the Church were only first properly heard in the late second century when Saint Peter began, posthumously, to be described as the first Bishop of Rome. For those more modestly titled clerics with aspirations to lead a church that was already claiming to be 'Catholic' (meaning universal),[8] the day-to-day challenge was how to avoid their rulings being ignored by their flocks in favour of a series of local and tangential interpretations of Jesus' message and example.

To impose a sort of unity, the Early Church Fathers mobilised on several other fronts. First, a standard set of texts was decreed, starting with Paul's letters and the four Gospels, and rejecting other documents that had followed them but were now judged heretical. Again, it was a process that was often fraught with difficulty, and dragged on into the fifth century before a definitive Latin translation of the Bible, known as the Vulgate, was compiled by Saint Jerome.

Then there was the protracted struggle to agree a common set of basic beliefs, teachings and rituals for the whole Church. It was here that angels came into their own, providing a reference point in internal debates, and bolstering the authority of those in leadership positions. For example, Athenagoras (c.133–c.190), an Athenian philosopher who converted to Christianity, was one of several among the Early Church Fathers to refer in his widely disseminated writings to the 'office' of angels. His choice of word suggests that the heavenly hosts were now somehow attached to and approving of the new earthly hierarchical structure of 'office holders' that was being imposed from the centre on the Church. 'The office of angels', Athenagoras wrote in *A Plea for Christians*, 'is to exercise providence for God over the things created and ordered by him.' God, he argued, exercises a 'universal and general providence of the whole' – in other words, he oversees the world he created – but the micromanaging of 'the particular parts . . . are provided for by the angels appointed over them'.[9]

It was an early attempt to champion a tiered hierarchy, with allocated functions, that was pictured not only as linking the Church in Rome horizontally to local Christian communities, but also as stretching vertically by means of angels from God in his heaven to humankind on earth. This was to become an abiding model in the Christian Church, with ultimate authority being delegated down by God to the angels, and from the angels to the clerical caste.

Origen, a revered Greek scholar and ascetic based in Alexandria in the first half of the third century, was one of the most significant among the early Christian theologians. In his treatise *Against Celsus* (written to clamp down on heresies within Christianity) he embraces the concept that the angels are, effectively, regional managers in the universe, taking orders from the managing director in heaven, and then overseeing local bosses in the shape of popes, bishops and priests. Everything, he wrote, from streams to the purity of the air, was under 'the agency and control of certain beings, whom we may call invisible husbandmen and guardians'.[10] In other words, angels. They were in charge of the stars and the meteors as well as the plants and animals. They were directing the whole economy of the universe, combining both terrestrial and extra-terrestrial. As ever, these angels were operating in the space between heaven and earth.

Athenagoras, for his part, put it this way: '[As] creator of the world, God, through the medium of his word, has apportioned and ordained the angels to occupy the elements, the heavens, the world, and whatever is in the world.'[11] Again the language is significant. Take 'ordained'. The select few men who were being ordained to become the new caste of leaders of the Church were, he suggests, like the angels who had been 'ordained' by God to minister to the universe.

In enlisting angels as a force for unity and authority in the emerging Church, some among the Early Fathers extended the idea further still by giving the three named archangels – Michael, Gabriel and Raphael – geographically specific responsibilities. 'The presiding powers of the angels', wrote Clement of

Alexandria (150–215), theologian and missionary, in his *Stromateis* (or *Miscellanies*), a trilogy of texts on the Christian life, 'have been distributed according to the nations and the cities.'[12] The concept of places as well as individuals having a guardian angel was taking off. Basil of Caesarea (329–79), a bishop fierce in his pursuit of heresy, confirms the trend. 'There are some angels set at the head of entire nations ... each of whom has been set up to protect and watch over the nation which is placed under his authority.'[13]

Guardianship, one of the tasks allotted to angels in the Old and New Testaments, was here being applied to sustaining cities and whole nations, and into the bargain binding them into one, holy apostolic Church. In this regard, the warrior Michael was much in demand. Over the centuries his patronage was claimed by Brussels, France, Portugal and even (though he was later eclipsed by Saint George) England.[14]

Yet guardian angels' concern for individuals remained unwavering. 'All the faithful in Christ, no matter how small, are helped by an angel,' wrote Origen,[15] drawing directly on Jesus' words in Matthew's Gospel.[16] But, for the Early Church, they were also examples of how perfection could be achieved by falling in line with God's word (as interpreted through the rules of the Church and its leadership). And they served as a sobering reminder of the terrifying consequences of flouting that authority. The cautionary tales of the fallen Watcher Angels from the Book of Enoch, and of the ultimate fallen angel to be found in the New Testament in the shape of the devil, quickly also became mainstays of early Christianity.

The generous view would be that, by placing so much emphasis on the risks abroad in the world in the shape of the devil and his demons for the unwary, inattentive or plain ungodly, the Early Church Fathers were being good shepherds, showing an active and appropriate pastoral concern for the eternal fate of their flocks. The Church, in this scenario, was all that stood on earth between fair-weather or flawed believers and the fires of hell. Yet, somewhere in there too, amid all this talking up of the good angel/bad angel dichotomy, was the drive to bring order and control through fear to a disparate Christian community. Unless you model yourself on the good angels, stick to church rules, and respect authority, those in the pews were told, you run the risk of going the way of the fallen angels. It was to prove an effective tool in defeating heresy.

'Just as with men who have freedom of choice as to both virtue and vice,' wrote Athenagoras in *A Plea for Christians*, 'so it is among the angels . . . Some free agents, you will observe, such as they were created by God, continued in those things for which God had made and over which he had ordained them [i.e. the good angels]; but some [fallen angels] outraged both the constitution of their nature and the government entrusted to them.'[17]

Angels, then, were designed for heaven, but could go awry. They were not always perfect creations. The same, of course, was true of humanity. God had given angels and human beings alike the freedom to choose, it was taught, and some had chosen badly. It was this freedom therefore, that was the real source of evil in the world, because the devil could only thrive if angels or human beings used their freedom to fall into his clutches. While the good angels – the vast majority – were there to keep the universe in balance, the bad angels were the ones who upset the apple cart.

The point was made forcefully in *Against Heresies* by Irenaeus (130–202), another leader among the Early Church Fathers. 'In man, as well as in angels, [God] has placed the power of choice (for angels are rational beings), so that those who had yielded obedience might justly possess what is good, given indeed by God, but preserved by themselves.' To the already extensive list of angels' attributes, Bishop Irenaeus was now adding reason.

A time-slot in creation

Discussion of the freedom to choose – or free will – in both angels and humans emerged out of a broader debate that went on from the earliest days of the Christian Church around God's creation of the world. In the Book of Genesis' account of the fashioning of Adam and Eve, God gives them free will, which they then abuse and so are ejected from the Garden of Eden. Where, though, did angels fit in those six days that Genesis tells it took God to create the world, stopping to rest only on the seventh? Well, to judge by the text, absolutely nowhere, since there is no specific mention of them.

That puzzled the Early Church theologians keen to define angels' status in the universe, and their relationship with God. By contrast, the Talmud and, later, the Qur'an were clear. In the first, the angels ask Yahweh what he is doing as they observe him making Adam, so it is plain that they predate humankind. And in the Qur'an,[18] the angels, it is stated explicitly, were created first, and then assisted in creation of the first human.

If this is beginning to sound a little like one of those questions about angels dancing on pinheads, then think again. This was much more than an abstract theological debate. One of the greatest threats to church unity, to the authority of the Church Fathers, indeed to their whole understanding of Christianity, came from a broad movement known as Gnosticism (which included the Docetists, already mentioned as having been condemned for heresy). It spanned both Christianity and Judaism, and was especially prominent from the first to the third centuries CE, teaching of an interior, mystical knowledge of the divine (gnosis is the Greek noun for knowledge), practising asceticism, and rejecting the sort of hierarchical and institutional structures that the Early Church Fathers were building. Though vigorously rejected by writers such as Irenaeus as a heresy, Gnosticism nonetheless thrived all around the Mediterranean, especially in the first and second centuries.

At the core of Gnosticism was a rejection of everything to do with this world as the work of the devil, and therefore evil – and that included the whole creation narrative. So efforts to define the place of angels – who were highly prized by Gnostics – inevitably caused more conflict with the Early Church Fathers. The only angels involved in creation, said the Gnostics, were fallen angels.

In texts such as *The Secret Revelation of John* (dated to the first or second century), Gnostic writers reordered the Book of Genesis. The fall of angels, which comes in chapter six of Genesis, is shifted back by them to the very start. They were the angels who were around when God created Adam, and hence the earth was poisoned at the outset. In *The Secret Revelation of John*, no fewer than seventy-four fallen angels were reported to have been present to install Adam's various limbs and vital organs, while a further five were responsible for each of his senses.[19] They were assisting not God, but rather Yaldabaoth, the central devil-like figure in the Gnostic credo.

The Early Church Fathers' insistence that angels were a positive part of creation, even if not mentioned explicitly in Genesis, was then, in part, one element in their fight-back against the Gnostic threat. The place of angels went to the heart of a dispute over the future of the Church. So important was it deemed to make this point about angels that they were referred to in the prescribed words of the Nicene Creed, a basic, unifying statement of faith for the whole Church – approved in 325 (and still in use today) – to be recited by congregations. 'God, the Father Almighty' was 'maker of heaven and earth, of all things visible and invisible' – that is, angels.

For some, even this formula of words did not provide sufficient clarity. Were angels, they asked, part of the general material creation, as described in the opening verses of Genesis, or did their absence from this narrative mean they somehow predated creation? Into such troubled waters stepped Augustine of Hippo (354–430), bishop, theologian and as influential a figure in Western Christianity as Aquinas (with whom he shared a fascination about angels).

Augustine argued for locating the creation of angels right at the start of the creation process. They were formed, he insisted, directly after God had created heaven and earth, specifically at the moment when he announces, 'Let there be light' and calls into existence the sun, the moon and the stars.[20] 'It is not plainly said [in Genesis] whether or when the angels were created,' Augustine conceded in his classic philosophical treatise, *The City of God*, 'but . . . it is implicitly under the name "heaven" . . . or perhaps under the name of "light".'[21]

Such a thesis – which ultimately carried the day – fitted neatly with angels' accepted role in linking heaven and earth. It also aimed to settle another question troubling the early Christians: what were angels made of? The answer, according to Augustine, was that they were spirits made of light. As intermediaries, he proposed, angels' entire being was so designed as to allow God's light to shine through them onto humanity.

His insistence that angels could not have bodies – in the human understanding of the word – did, however, mark a partial retreat from earlier generations of Christian teachers who, in the heat of persecution, had seen angels as being so close and attentive to humans that, in some intangible, ill-defined way, they had what at least appeared to be a body. Origen, for example, described them as having an almost translucent form, taking his cue from Saint Paul's words in his First Letter to the Corinthians that, while the soul has its own embodiment, 'so does the spirit have its own embodiment'.[22]

There was another more practical dimension to Augustine insisting that angels could not have anything approaching a body.

He regarded the body as intrinsically sinful. Though raised by a devoutly Christian mother, Monica, later Saint Monica, as a young man he had travelled and strayed far from the ideals she had taught him about relationships between men and women. Once he had repented of his own sexual licence, though, and returned to the faith, Augustine's horror at his past excesses led him to take a particularly negative and pessimistic view of the body, and its sexual urges and appetites. Angels could not be burdened down with such things.

His description, then, is of angels made of light, without bodies and all the urges that go with bodies. It contributed to a developing cult of virginity that had been part of the Church from its earliest days. Those who promoted it – and this was in centuries, it should be noted, when priests were allowed to marry, in imitation of Saint Peter who, the Gospels tell us, had a wife[23] – pointed to angels as compelling models of the benefits to be derived from chastity in allowing them to draw ever closer to God. Such a line of argument could, though, on occasion give rise to some awkward questions, and answers. When challenged to explain how, exactly, the virginal Mary had fallen pregnant with Jesus, Origen – overeager to rebut even the faintest stain of impropriety on the good name of her visitor, Gabriel – insisted that angels could not be bound as humans were by mere biology. Mary had been impregnated, he explained, by Gabriel speaking God's words into her ear.[24]

Angels abounding

The status of Christianity changed dramatically when, in 312, the Roman emperor Constantine lifted the ban on the Church, ending centuries of persecution. There were a few hiccups in the subsequent years but, by 380, Christianity was the official religion of empire. Such a seismic shift inevitably pushed the Church further down the road it was already travelling – towards uniformity and conformity.

The process was further accelerated by the collapse of the Western part of the Roman Empire in the fifth century. Under exceptional leaders such as Pope Gregory the Great (590–604), the Church that was based in Rome began, quite consciously, to assume the mantle of empire, which included asserting the quasi-monarchical authority of the papacy in all aspects of faith, and increasingly of life, spiritual and temporal, thereby ultimately laying the basis for a whole new Christian civilisation in the West.

As part of that drive to what by the Middle Ages had become Europe-wide dominance, angels were regularly and variously deployed more than ever to enhance the institutional Church's authority over its members. It was, in many ways, the opposite of the situation now. Those who reject religious institutions today turn to angels as representatives of a freer sort of spirituality, devoid of the chains of 'official' religion; but in the first millennium of Christianity angels were very much bound up with head office strategy.

In 529, Benedict of Nursia, a former hermit, established his first monastic community at Monte Cassino, eighty miles south of Rome. The governing document of his new Benedictine order, *The Rule of Saint Benedict*, makes explicit reference to the angels. 'Hence, brethren,' Benedict writes,

> if we wish to reach the very highest point of humility and to arrive speedily at that heavenly exaltation to which ascent is made through the humility of this present life, we must by our ascending actions erect the ladder Jacob saw in his dream, on which angels appeared to him descending and ascending. By that descent and ascent, we must surely understand nothing else than this, that we descend by self-exaltation and ascend by humility.[25]

Humility was the default position of angels and, for Benedict, the key virtue in monastic life. As his experiment at Monte Cassino was repeated elsewhere many times over, with the strong encouragement of the papacy, angels came to represent for those who felt called to the cloistered monastic life a route to understanding God's ability to know everything about each and every one of them. There could be, Benedict stressed, no secrets from God – or, in practical terms, divergence from or dissent from the *Rule* – because angels were there reporting all deeds and misdeeds back to God.

In organisational terms, the concept made for a virtuous circle. When the monks gathered to sing the Divine Office, an integral part of the structure of their day and the rhythm of their lives, they were, Benedict told them, singing with the angels, who should be their models, not just in their music and worship, but also in obedience, chastity and contemplation of the divine. 'Monastery' comes from the Latin word *monos*, meaning to be alone, so though his monks were a community, each one was also – like the angels – alone before God.

Such angelic guardianship promoted in monks an ethos of individual vigilance, and that vigilance in its turn encouraged the discipline and the avoidance of sin and corruption that made monasteries in the early medieval period beacons of good practice in a Church that otherwise was struggling with the rackety lives of parish clergy and worldly bishops.

The life of another revered monk, Abbot Columba, reveals a different aspect of angels' service within monastic communities. In the sixth century, Columba brought Christianity from Ireland to the Scottish island of Iona, thence forward in various waves into mainland Britain. His own authority over his brethren rested on his saintliness, of which one outward sign was said to be his strong relationship with angels. Members of the Iona community would describe seeing Columba standing on a particular grassy knoll on the island talking to strangers. If they tried to approach, though, his angelic visitors would disappear. In his *Life of Columba*, Adomnán, one of his successors as head of the Iona community as well as his first biographer, tells of the day when Columba had a vision of a monk in one of the Irish monasteries that were under his control. The man was falling to his death, but so close was Columba to the heavenly hosts that he was able immediately to summon up an angel who, the very next instant, was there to scoop up the tumbling figure before he hit the ground.[26]

With such an example from those in high office, it is little wonder that in daily life outside of the cloister, or of the precincts of the local church, believers became convinced that hosts of angels were in attendance. In a fourth-century hymn attributed to Saint Ambrose, Bishop of Milan, the second verse of what is now known to those in the pews as 'Holy God, We Praise Thy Name' is positively awash with them.

> Hark! the loud celestial hymn
> Angel choirs above are raising.
> Cherubim and seraphim,
> In unceasing chorus praising;
> Fill the heavens with sweet accord:
> Holy, holy, holy Lord.

Congregations at this time were overwhelmingly illiterate. The writings of Origen, Augustine and others would have gone straight over their heads. When the essence of their teaching was distilled into ritual and worship, however, it had a profound impact on the way they imagined the world around them to be. Ambrose is credited with being a pioneer in the use of choral music in churches and he clearly understood the power of lyrics, regularly sung or heard, in fixing ideas in the minds of those present. The Early Church had a Latin motto to describe the process – '*Lex orandi, lex credendi*'. First heard in the fifth century,[27] it roughly translates as, 'The law of prayer is the law of belief'. The constant repetition of words, said or sung out loud in the liturgy, was, it suggested, an effective means of instilling doctrine.

As were the sacraments, especially those of baptism and eucharist, the first the anchor at the start of a Christian's life that fastens him or her in God's Church, and the second the 'daily bread of life', offered in memory of Jesus' sacrifice of his body and blood in the form of bread and wine at the Last Supper, that sustains believers through the trials and torments of life. Here, too, angels were present. In baptism, wrote Tertullian (160–220), another North African Christian theologian, credited with making Latin the unifying official language of the expanding Church, angels were at the very heart of the ritual. 'Cleansed in the water by the action of the angel, we are prepared for the Holy Spirit . . . thus the angel set in charge of baptism makes ready for the coming of the Holy Spirit by the washing away of sins.'[28]

A specific 'angel of baptism' is not referred to quite so explicitly by any other Early Church Father, yet baptismal fonts found in ancient churches are routinely decorated with angels. Saint Mark's Basilica in Venice, for example, built in the middle of the eleventh century, has a cupola in the ceiling of its baptistry that is magnificently adorned with hosts of angels looking down to carry the new-born into the bosom of the Church.

The significance of incorporating angels in the sacraments and the liturgy as symbols of God's blessing on the Church's authority and organisation was well understood. Angels, wrote John Chrysostom (347–407), theologian, Archbishop of Constantinople and one so renowned as an orator that he earned the name Chrysostom, meaning 'golden-mouthed', were a sign of that mystical connection being made at such moments between earth and heaven.

> The Church's worship is not that of a human religious society whose liturgy is tied to a temple. Rather, it is a worship that permeates the entire cosmos, in which sun, moon, and all the stars take part ... The heaven of the angels is ... the most central, the most spiritual part of the cosmos ... the singing of the angels would never be permitted to disappear from the Church's worship, for that is what first gives the Church's praise the depth and transcendence that are called for by the character of Christian revelation.[29]

Again, it is worth stressing that these were not just fine words to portray the Church as indispensable, like angels, in connecting humankind with God. They were also sincerely believed. Senior churchmen often had a deep devotion to particular angels. Men such as Pope Gregory the Great.

Gregory and his angels

Gregory had been elected to the papacy in 590 after the incumbent, Pelagius II, had fallen victim to a deadly plague that spread quickly through Rome when the River Tiber burst its banks. The Roman emperor was still in theory in charge of the city, but was now based thousands of miles away in Constantinople, while his troops were occupied elsewhere in the Italian peninsula repelling various invaders. So the pope was, for all practical purposes, the civic as well as religious head of a city in crisis. Gregory, therefore, led a religious procession through the streets, praying for the lifting of the threat posed by the plague to life and limb.

As many as eighty participants were said to have died as they followed him through the streets, but when the despairing throng reached the Tiber, Gregory was greeted by a vision of the Archangel Michael, poised over the mausoleum of the Roman emperor Hadrian. He had his sword unsheathed and was, the pope said, busy banishing the plague as he had once banished the devil in the Book of Revelation.

If it sounds fanciful to modern ears, within days the deadly infection had gone and the suffering ended. Gregory declared it a miracle and ascribed it to Michael. He celebrated by placing a statue of him on top of the mausoleum, which was renamed as the Castel Sant'Angelo – Castle of the Holy Angel – today standing at the start of the avenue that runs up from the Tiber to Saint Peter's.

Gregory's devotion to angels, though, went deeper than that single moment of deliverance. The Venerable Bede in his late eighth-century *Ecclesiastical History of the English People* tells an enduringly popular story of how Gregory once saw some fair-haired, fair-skinned young men in the slave market in Rome. When told they were Angles from northern Europe, he replied, inspired by their pale countenance, '*non Angli sed angeli*' ('not Angles but angels').[30]

The pun probably works better in Latin, and the story is surely so neat as to be invented, but Gregory was undeniably preoccupied in his writings by angels – blond-haired or not. In his four volumes of *Dialogues*, story-like sermons which he intended – as part of his push for conformity across the Church – that local priests should read aloud from the pulpit instead of their own potentially off-message musings, Gregory urges his listeners in a reflection on the Nativity, 'Let us be worthy of their [angels'] respect and fellowship.'[31]

Elsewhere, he pictures himself in imagined exchanges with Saint Peter, in which the apostle whom Jesus chose to lead the Church confirms to his successor that angels have no bodies. And Gregory tells, too, of being able to see otherwise-invisible angels at the deathbeds of those who have lived good, Christian lives, where they wait to carry the dead to the bosom of Abraham, as promised in Luke's Gospel.[32]

The angels are also there in large numbers, Gregory writes, at each and every eucharistic celebration, just at the moment when the priest recalls Jesus' words over the bread and wine at the Last Supper. 'At the words of the priest, the heavens be opened, and the quires [choirs] of angels are present in that mystery of Jesus Christ; that high things are accompanied with low, and earthly joined to heavenly, and that one thing is made of visible and invisible.'[33]

Gregory was far from alone in his devotion to Michael. In the devil-obsessed early and medieval Church, there were plenty of places where the archangel's prowess in seeing off the devil was remembered and celebrated. In fourth-century Egypt, for example, it was written that richly decorated shrines dedicated to Michael and Gabriel could be found 'not only in the towns but also in private lanes, houses and fields'.[34] At Monte Gargano in southern Italy, from the end of the fifth century, there had stood what is said to be the oldest surviving shrine in Europe to Michael,[35] built to commemorate a reported appearance when he promised the local bishop that he would defend the town from pagan invaders and was then credited as its deliverer when it emerged from the battle unscathed.

Later, what were purported to be relics of the Archangel Michael (in reality, fragments of the altar at Monte Gargano, where he is said to have stood when addressing the bishop) became popular and caused pilgrims to visit the shrine. Since officially angels did not have tangible bodies, it was in pure theological terms a strange outbreak of piety, but in the lived world of the medieval Church the boundary between angels and saints was becoming blurred. It was around the sixth century, too, that the Archangel Michael first began to be referred to as Saint

Michael the Archangel, in which form he was allocated a feast day on 29 September.[36]

Celestial hierarchy

As an archangel, Michael certainly had one up on those now officially nameless angels, but did his special status on earth mean he was equally important among the heavenly hosts? Trying to bring order to heaven preoccupied writers and theologians in these early centuries of the Church. Once more, it is tempting to see their motivation as oddly abstract, making a neat pattern out of something bound forever to be invisible, but an increasingly hierarchical Church had an obvious interest in shaping and endorsing a heavenly hierarchy, especially if it then reinforced what was happening on earth.

And such speculation was nothing new. It had been going on in Jewish and Christian circles since the Book of Enoch first produced an angel map of the heavens. The definitive study had to wait, though, until the fifth century. *Celestial Hierarchy* was the work of an anonymous Syrian monk, known to history by the strange-sounding name of Pseudo-Dionysius. It went on to become one of the set texts of medieval angelology.

As had long been the way in both Judaism and Christianity, the writer of *Celestial Hierarchy* assumed the disguise of a biblical figure, in this case Dionysius the Areopagite, who makes a fleeting appearance in the Acts of the Apostles when he is convinced to convert by Saint Paul, who was on a mission in Athens.[37] The choice, albeit of such a minor character, was intended to give the text a patina of New Testament authority, all the more so since Dionysius the Areopagite was usually referred to as a judge. And it reflected, too, the increasing cachet of anything even remotely associated with the philosophical tradition in Greece; the same tradition, moreover, that had helped shape Pseudo-Dionysius' ideas.

Plato and Aristotle in particular had both concerned themselves with trying to order and explain the cosmos. Christianity
took up the quest and now Pseudo-Dionysius was attempting to
arrange the angels. His proposal was a nine-rung hierarchical
ladder, with (unadorned) angels at the very bottom, followed in
ascending order by archangels, principalities (sometimes called
sovereignties), powers, virtues, dominations (dominions), thrones,
cherubim and, at the very top, the seraphim, those extraordinary,
intimidating six-winged creatures from the Book of Isaiah with
whom we started this story. 'The appellation of seraphim',
Pseudo-Dionysius writes, 'plainly teaches their ever moving
around things divine, and constancy, and warmth, and keenness,
and the seething of that persistent, indomitable, and inflexible
perpetual motion.'[38]

It is, at first glance, an unexpected list because it relegates those
familiar names of Michael, Gabriel and Raphael to the lowliest
positions, and leaves the designations already mentioned in the
writings of Saint Paul – sovereignties and powers – in mid-table.
Yet the formulation has its own revealing logic. What Pseudo-
Dionysius wanted to emphasise was the superiority of the contemplative task of angels, and so he gave it the top six of his nine
rungs. His agenda was to promote a more distant view of angels,
as belonging in the faraway realm of heaven, closest to God. He
was, therefore, reversing what had until then been popular in the
Early Church, namely the idea that the main business of angels
and archangels was conducted on earth. Such concerns were
'manifested and mundane things' according to Pseudo-Dionysius'
damning judgement.[39]

It is another step-change in the history of angels. Pseudo-
Dionysius was pushing them further away from the human
sphere, and from human lives, to a place where the needs and
requirements of men and women were trivial compared to the
sight of the unimaginable majesty of God. Only a pale

ninth-hand version of that dazzling, celestial luminescence could filter down through the rungs and reach the faithful through their guardian angels.

Pope Gregory approved of this shift. Before his election, he had served in Constantinople as a papal representative and had learnt there of the philosophical and theological teachings of Pseudo-Dionysius. In his own *Moralia in Job*, the pope follows the anonymous monk in giving pride of place to those angels who contemplate over and above their helping-hand/guardian colleagues. 'They refresh us on earth with their ministry and help, because they become fertile in heaven by the dew of contemplation.'[40]

Pseudo-Dionysius, though, did not only propose a one-to-nine hierarchy. He also bunched the angel categories into three distinct tiers (three, like seven, being a sacred number in Christianity, and beyond it in other faiths too). Those in the highest group of three, the seraphim, cherubim and thrones, were the 'primal perfections ... invariable and firmly fixed, settling around the very Highest'.[41] All represented the ultimate calling of angels: to be utterly absorbed in God's love.

This description of angels who could gaze on the face of God in all its glory held a special appeal for subsequent generations of Christian mystics, who were engaged in their own quest for spiritual perfection and oneness with God. Among those who drew heavily on Pseudo-Dionysius' formulation was the German philosopher and mystic Meister Eckhart (1260–1328). 'The soul at its highest is formed like God,' he suggested, 'but an angel gives a closer idea of Him. That is all an angel is: an idea of God.'[42]

Where Pope Gregory varied Pseudo-Dionysius' grand design, however, was in the middle tier, often referred to as that of governors, and including those angels who sat halfway between God in his heaven and the Church down on earth. These were the dominions, virtues and powers. Virtues, though, had referred in Jewish thought in the early centuries CE to miracle-workers, a quality that, for Gregory, made them a superior kind of guardian angel, and therefore fitted better in the bottom tier of 'working' angels.[43] Gregory demoted them.

Francesco Botticini's 1475 The Assumption of the Virgin *offers a vision of heaven where the angels are placed in ascending order of importance as they get closer to God.*

Perhaps the best-known artist's representation of the angelic ranks – or choirs, as they were routinely referred to – was commissioned in 1475 from the Italian early Renaissance master Francesco Botticini, a close ally of the city's ruling Medici dynasty. It was an altarpiece for a Florentine church but is now in the collection of the National Gallery in London. *The Assumption of the Virgin* is dominated by a vision of heaven, bathed in the most dazzlingly golden light and presented as if it is the dome of a church. In it, three tiers of angels are gathered round God, each one consisting of three ranks, all of them ready to welcome Jesus' mother. In the second and third tiers, the angels have wings (though Pseudo-Dionysius had not given them any). In the lower levels, the angels are mixing with saints, earthly bodies with heavenly beings, but in the top tier, there are no wings, no interlopers, but simply the all-consuming presence of God.[44]

O

O is for Clarence **Odbody**, the guardian angel in Frank Capra's ever-green 1946 classic film, *It's a Wonderful Life*, played by Henry Travers. An 'AS2' – a second-class angel, who is still waiting after 200 years to be given his wings – this hapless trainee is drafted in when there is a short-age of first-class guardian angels, and sent to assist George Bailey (James Stewart) as he contemplates suicide as the only way out of his financial problems. Odbody ends up throwing himself off the bridge first, causing Bailey to jump in to rescue him. As they dry off once out of the water, Odbody manages to persuade Bailey of all the good things he has done in life, and why it is worth going on.

P

P is for **Panchiel**, described in the *Durham Collectar* or *Ritual*, a collec-tion of prayers and rituals from tenth-century Northumbria that is now kept in the Durham Cathedral library. The name comes in a section of 'prayers for the field', designed to keep away birds, vermin and demons from attacking crops and livestock. One is addressed to the Archangel Panchiel, 'who is over all the fruits of the earth and over seed'. It is a rare reference and may be a corruption of another angel's name, which it has been speculated was brought to Britain from Ireland by the monastic communities that spread from Iona in Scotland to Lindisfarne or Holy Island off the coast of Northumbria.

Francis, Avicenna and Aquinas – When and Why Angelology Was Taken Seriously

'The greatest among the saints and men of God, from Saint Augustine to John Henry Newman, have always lived on familiar terms with angels.'

Jean Danielou SJ, *The Angels and Their Mission* (1953)[1]

As Christianity moved into its second millennium, the veneration of saints became ever more a feature of the daily life of the Church and of believers – and had a knock-on effect on how angels were perceived. Shrines dotted across Europe, housing and displaying the relics of saints, acted as a magnet for pilgrims. Great basilicas and wayside chapels were regularly named after them. Elaborate devotions and processions took place on their feast days, and a regular round of miraculous cures was popularly ascribed to them. They became as integral a part of the lives of the faithful as *de facto* family members.

Saints were protectors, intercessors, role models and patrons rolled into one, their names honoured when taken by sons and daughters and added to their own as they received the sacrament of confirmation. From the thirteenth century onwards, this took place at the point when children were judged old enough to make their own commitment to the Church – rather than have it done for them at baptism by their parents. It was a step on the road to adulthood, and those being confirmed showed their maturity by selecting a saint as their guide in life.

You had to be dead to be declared a saint. Christianity has long been wary of 'living saints', and so these human examples of outstanding virtue were, in the teachings and practice of the Church, assumed to be residents of heaven, like the angels. Yet they differed from the heavenly host because they offered something more tangible as an object of devotion. They all had names, for one thing. More than that, they had life-stories whose twists and turns, crises and moments of disbelief, were all-too-recognisable for those in the pews. Their virtue may have made them feel distant, and hard to emulate, but their humanity counter-balanced it. Identifying with saints, the Church intended, would increase each individual believer's sense of belonging in the church community.

Paul had been the first to write of saints,[2] but referred to them as a group of the virtuous who served God devotedly rather than as individuals. His saints were living, but the word was subsequently taken up by the Early Church and used for celebrating the memory of those who had died 'in the Lord', notably those who had been martyred for their faith. Paul and Peter were early members of those raised to the 'company' of saints. Once the persecution had ended, the appellation of 'saint' evolved into a more general means of honouring the dead who had lived distinguished lives within the Church.

Saint-making, as practised in early medieval times, entailed nothing of the formal, bureaucratic canonisation process that Catholicism now operates. That only came about in 1234 when Rome took control of what previously had often been more spontaneous and localised, with saints created as the consequence of popular acclaim.

The medieval Church directed its members to share their troubles in prayers and intercessions to both angels and saints. Since angels, by their very spiritual, non-bodily nature, didn't tend to leave any trace behind that could be venerated in a shrine, they lost out. The reason was as earthly as it was heavenly. Those pilgrims who visited shrines to glimpse the relics of saints were encouraged to make donations. It was offerings at the shrine of the murdered archbishop Saint Thomas Becket in Canterbury that enabled the cathedral to be rebuilt after a fire in 1174. Later, pilgrims would be encouraged to buy 'indulgences', pieces of parchment that in theory wiped away their sins and guaranteed them a place in heaven.

In other ways, too, saints, with their full life-stories, were simply more adaptable than nameless angels to playing required roles in a Church that now dominated all aspects of life in Europe. They could be formally attached as the front-line patrons to various needy groups – whether they be professions (Augustine for printers, for example), those suffering particular health problems, or those experiencing hard times, such as prisoners.

Gradually angels were – intentionally or not – replaced as intercessors in what had hitherto been one of their prime roles. Even the three named archangels were sometimes so eclipsed by saints that they were reported to have resorted to stealing their rivals' clothing to get noticed. In the ninth century, at a shrine to Saints Peter and Marcellinus – both early martyrs who died at the hands of the Romans – it was told that Marcellinus once appeared to a blind man in a dream. 'It is not as you think,' he announced himself. 'I am the Archangel Gabriel but have taken the form of Marcellinus because God has committed to me all the affairs of the martyrs.'[3]

Running alongside this shift from angels to saints was a debate within the Church over extending the list of angels who could officially be honoured and invoked. The various Books of Enoch in particular had provided an endless list of named angels, many of them with specific roles. Yet any moves to incorporate even a handful of them in the devotional life of the Church was resisted. In 363, a synod of Church Fathers gathering at Laodicea (named in the Book of Revelation as one of the 'Seven Churches of Asia'[4]) considered the matter. Anxiety about encouraging so great an attachment to angels that it could border on idolatry scotched the proposal.

Like many other regulations in a Europe-wide Church in an age when no report could be carried faster than a horse could gallop, the restriction to just a trio of named angels proved in practice hard to enforce. In eighth-century Germany, Boniface, the Anglo-Saxon church leader credited with bringing Christianity to its hitherto pagan peoples, publicly rebuked one of his bishops, Aldebert, after the latter had composed and already widely circulated a prayer of supplication to be used by believers that named a total of eight angels. Michael was there – and so was permitted by Boniface – but the other seven (Adinus, Raguel, Sabaoc, Simmiel, Tubuas, Tubuel and Uriel – all names found in versions of Enoch or other Jewish literature of the second to fourth centuries CE) were not only disallowed but condemned as demons.

Even the 'Apostle of the Germans', however, did not have sufficient authority completely to banish such characters. In the ninth-century *Book of Cerne*, an illustrated Anglo-Saxon compilation of prayers and devotions, now in the collection of Cambridge University, these six angels-who-must-not-be-named are again referenced, along with new additions such as Rumihel and Phannihel, the latter reportedly having a special way with healing the sick.

None was ever to be given the imprimatur, the Church's official stamp of approval, much less allowed to stray across the invisible boundary into sainthood as first Michael, then Raphael and Gabriel had done. If archangels could become saints, however, the Church was clear that saints did not become angels, though in some depictions – such as Botticini's *The Assumption of the Virgin*, already mentioned – they are seen mingling with the heavenly choirs. And if saints instinctively felt closer to humankind, then angels maintained their edge when it came to expressing that fundamental human yearning to gaze upon the face of God. It was angels, not saints, who had the front-row seats in heaven. Increasingly, though, as a consequence in the medieval period angels came to be regarded as essentially ethereal beings, creatures of contemplation, not action – as Pseudo-Dionysius had argued with his nine tiers – more concerned with the things of heaven than the things of earth.

Francis of Assisi and the seraph

Some monks and clerics continued to have a close friendship with angels. That they were frequented by angels, not saints, singled them out as if it were a mark of their exceptional calling. Already, as we've seen, angels enjoyed a special place in the contemplative life of monasteries and abbeys. It was something that fed into that sense abroad in the Church that those with vocations to the religious life were one step closer to heaven than those in the pews. Now that same bond was being extended to include the mendicants, a new form of religious life that arose at the start of the thirteenth century.

The mendicants lived not in great abbeys on the produce of monastic lands but shoulder to shoulder with the poor whom they set out to serve, begging alongside them on the streets. To vows of obedience, chastity and worshipping God was added a new one – of poverty. In angels, who had neither material needs nor wants, the mendicants found particular inspiration. First among this new group in the life of the Church were the followers of Francis of Assisi. The Franciscans were also among the most passionate angelologists of the Middle Ages.

Francis, the son of a wealthy merchant, had in 1210 turned his back on rank, worldly goods and the frivolous pleasures of his privileged youth after he had heard God's voice telling him to 'repair my falling house'. That year, he and a small group of companions embraced poverty and humility as Friars Minor, 'Lesser Brothers', and began a great reform of religious life in the Church by taking it out onto the streets. Francis is still often referred to by Christians as the human being who came closest to the perfection of Jesus. That judgement is based mainly on the radical choices he made about how to live his life – turning on their head the values of a world where, especially in his own part of Italy, the new capitalist, money economy was replacing old systems of barter. But it also picks up on an episode towards the end of his life.

Like many others at the time, Francis had a particular devotion to the Archangel Michael, especially to another of his growing portfolio of roles as the 'presenter' of the souls of the dead. Michael would, it was believed, transport them from their death-bed to heaven, where their eternal fate would be decided.

Again, a little context helps. This was a time when life was felt to be much more fragile than now, and hence death, judgement and the fate of souls was a much more immediate and ongoing concern. The cult of Michael was one focus in assuaging those fears, as it was believed he would use his mighty, protective wings to carry the dead up before God's throne. Those who wanted to offer prayers for the dead would, therefore, climb the highest mountain they could find. From its summit, they hoped, their prayers might just have a better chance of bridging the gap between earth and heaven and joining with those of the Archangel Michael in persuading God to grant their departed loved ones a place in paradise. It may now sound like an ill-founded ritual, but in its day faith in its effectiveness was widespread.

In the summer of 1224, therefore, Francis and his group ascended to a high point on Mount La Verna in Tuscany to begin forty days of prayer and fasting up in the clouds (just as Jesus had spent forty days in the wilderness in the Gospels). They were preparing for Michael's feast day on 29 September. The journey was intended as both physical and spiritual. As well as the 'active' ministry of the Friars Minor – sharing the daily realities of the lives of the marginalised and sick by joining them – prayer and meditation were also strongly emphasised. Indeed, it is said that Francis spent up to a third of his waking hours on his knees in prayer.

Already, since Francis had embraced his new life of radical poverty, there had been visions, trances and ecstasies, but early one morning, towards the end of the forty days, he found himself on a cliff top on Mount La Verna, perched on the edge of a precipice, suspended between earth and sky, this world and the next. It was here that he saw a vision of a six-winged seraph straight from the pages of Isaiah. Afterwards, Francis gave a detailed account of what happened to Leo and Angelo, two among his companions.

> There appeared to him a seraph in the beautiful figure of a crucified man, having his hands and feet extended as though on a cross, and clearly showing the face of Jesus Christ. Two wings met above his head, two covered the rest of his body to his feet, and two were opened as in flight. When the vision passed, the soul of Francis was afire with love; and on his body there appeared the wonderful impression of the wounds of our Lord Jesus Christ.[5]

The central, potent image of Christianity, the suffering Jesus on the cross, there to relieve the suffering of humankind, was in effect framed in Francis's vision by the wings of the mighty seraph, who was both his pall-bearer and his attendant. It has been reproduced many times, most memorably by the Florentine artist Giotto (1267–1337). In the fresco cycle that adorns the upper level of the Basilica of Saint Francis in Assisi, he captures the moment with that psychological intensity that is his hallmark. Two of the seraph's wings are stretched out to suggest the bar of the crucifix on Calvary.

The risen Christ appears within a seraph's six wings in Giotto di Bondone's 1295 Saint Francis Receiving the Stigmata. *The rays transmit the marks of Jesus' crucifixion onto the body of the ecstatic saint.*

There has been much debate among art historians as to whether the traditional attribution of most of this remarkable cycle of frescoes to Giotto can be relied upon, but with another of his works, *Saint Francis Receiving the Stigmata*, dated around 1295 and now in the Louvre in Paris, there is no such doubt. Again the curious, dark, slightly menacing shape of the seraph, half bird, half children's aeroplane to modern eyes, is set against a golden backdrop, as rays of angelic light travel as physical messages from the wounds on Jesus' body to make their marks on an ecstatic Francis, praying on the mountainside.

Francis was by no means alone in encountering angels. They were, Christians were convinced, everywhere in the world in great numbers for those specially chosen to have eyes to see them. And neither was he unique in coming, apparently miraculously, to bear the stigmata, or the five wounds of Christ's crucifixion, on his hands, feet and side. Later, too, the same claim would be made of Catherine of Siena, the Cure d'Ars and Padre Pio.[6] He was, though, the first in Christian history to live out in this respect the words of Saint Paul in his Letter to the Galatians: 'the marks on my body are those of Jesus'.[7]

No other contemporary report of the appearance of an angel in medieval times made such an impact as that of the seraph who answered Francis's prayers that September morning. This moment on Mount La Verna has been part of the cult of Francis ever after. His glimpse of Christ, held by the seraph, is presented as lending divine endorsement to the saintliness that was perceived during his lifetime in his works, words and deeds.

Two years afterwards, Francis was dead, leaving behind a network of friaries that had in a few short years spread as far afield as England, Portugal, Scandinavia and the Middle East. And two years after that, with lightning speed by church standards, an admiring Pope Gregory IX declared him a saint, with the spot where the seraph appeared marked by the construction of the Chapel of the Stigmata, today a popular place of pilgrimage.

The Franciscans became known as the 'Seraphic Order', as if they were earthly guardian angels. And every story about Francis, in the numerous biographies and hagiographies that followed, was adorned with angels, artists taking their cue from Bonaventure, the 'Seraphic Doctor', who after his time teaching at the University of Paris became the seventh leader of the Franciscans. He told of how, when Francis was ill, angels would fill the sick room and play heavenly music on their lutes and harps to soothe him back to health (a scene captured by the Spanish painter Francisco Ribalta in 1620, in a work now in Madrid's Prado). When Francis begged for his food as part of his vow to 'wed Lady Poverty', everything he then received was deemed by his admirers as 'the food of angels'. And whenever he meditated on the crucifix, as was his habit, he was again pictured as surrounded by angels (again the subject of a famous work, complete with stigmata, by the Italian master Sandro Botticelli, in 1475). When Francis was praying, Bonaventure taught, he would speak directly to angels.[8]

Bonaventure even devised a six-step path – based on the seraph's six wings – to help believers who sought to follow the example of Francis and draw closer to the face of God. Here, once again, is that drive, so commonplace in the period and so often seen in efforts of the academic discipline of angelology, to construct rituals and make patterns out of the actions of angels. So for Bonaventure, the two seraph wings that cover Jesus' legs represent those things that are below humanity – the natural world, the animals and plants. The two that cover his body are those things that believers can change – matters of this world. And the third set, hovering above, indicate the immutable things of God.[9]

For Bonaventure, in the prologue to *Legenda Maior*, his account of the saint's life, Francis was not simply a saint, but literally and figuratively something higher than that, something the Church taught could not be possible: an angel. He was, Bonaventure argued, a divine messenger in every sense. 'He [Francis] was joined by a chain of inseparable love to the angels.'[10]

Bonaventure also saw visions of his own, including of heaven, and described once how, in a mystical trance, he had seen Francis occupy a seat, decorated with precious stones and radiating glory, that had previously been occupied by an angel. Francis was sitting among the angels, looking into the face of God.[11]

The claim that human beings, if absolutely exceptional, could become angels introduced a hitherto unimaginable aspiration among the faithful. While they did not expect themselves to be able to match Francis's level of holiness, the idea of his transformation to join the heavenly host gave them, in their daily lives and sufferings, a more secure sense that God and his angels were on hand to protect them.

Avicenna and Maimonides

The symbolic power of angels was one thing, but what about their purpose in heaven, on earth and in the cosmos? How to define exactly what they were created for? It was this sacred geometry that enthralled and excited the medieval angelologists. To examine their labours, though, means looking at a larger, robust and rational system of belief that neither started in nor belonged exclusively to medieval Europe, or even to Christianity. The revival in interest in the teachings of ancient Greece and, in particular, the pagan philosopher, Aristotle (384–322 BCE), had gathered pace in the works of Augustine, Pseudo-Dionysius and others to become central to the debates within Christianity. But it also reverberated around the Middle East and included Islam and Judaism.

Aristotle's influence, in the early centuries of Christianity, had been minor compared to that of his master, Plato, whose approach was regarded as potentially more accommodating of religion. The Church Fathers therefore had concentrated above all on Plato's idea of the immortal soul that pre-exists the body, and is separate from it, in preference to the more material speculations of his pupil, Aristotle, who had contended that the soul only made sense as part of a living body. Yet Aristotle and Plato shared a belief in the existence of eternal and uncreated cosmic spirits, which they called variously 'Intelligences' or 'Necessary Beings', and who were part of a chain of cause-and-effect that shaped and animated the universe. They derived ultimately from – in Aristotle's description – a 'Prime Mover'.

We have already seen how Jewish philosophers such as Philo of Alexandria, in the time of Jesus, and the third-century Early Church Father Origen had seized upon Plato's notion of the soul, including his talk of daimons, to connect it with angels – and demons. Adding to this, Augustine had, in his turn, been heavily influenced by Origen's thinking, but nevertheless rejected his contention that angels could have anything that approximated to a body (for reasons already discussed). They were pure spirit, he insisted, consisting of light. As forces shaping God's creation, they were unseen, known only by the effects of their labours.

Yet Augustine had also been drawn to Aristotle's efforts to explain the workings of the material universe and so had attempted some sort of synthesis between the Greek philosophers' views on the one side, and the claims of religion on the other, between the material and the divine, between God and science.

Such an undertaking was not restricted to the Early Church Fathers, nor to the Christian West. Abu Ali al-Husain ibn Sina, better known as Avicenna, was the most influential of the philosopher-scientists of what is known as Islam's 'Golden Age' of scholarship from the ninth to the thirteenth century. Born in northern Iran in 980, the son of a government official, Avicenna was a child prodigy. He is said to have memorised the entire

Qur'an by the age of ten and mastered medicine by sixteen, accomplishments that won him preferment as a court physician to various members of the ruling Samanid dynasty in Iran and Uzbekistan.

His repute stretched beyond these realms, though, with his *Canon of Medicine* (*Al-Qanun fi al-tibb*), in translation, a standard textbook for European medical students until the early years of the seventeenth century on account of its precocious insights into the nature of fever and disease. Avicenna was also a philosopher, using his privileged access to royal libraries to fuel a lifelong quest to reconcile the rational deliberation and reasoning he found there in volumes on Aristotle and Plato with the Islamic theology of his day-to-day world, a discipline that – like Judaism and Christianity – allocated an elevated place to angels.

For Avicenna, as for others before and after him, the challenge of reconciling religion with science, faith with reason, came to be characterised by how to find a way to fit Aristotle and Plato neatly alongside the accounts offered in the holy books of the creation of the world. When did spirits/souls/angels come into existence? Were they divinely created, or were they intrinsic to the universe? What was their role in an ordered cosmos and in the natural world?

His answer consisted of a series of ten stages, roughly akin to the seven days suggested by Genesis. A 'First Cause' (akin to a creator God) had put in place a hierarchy of spirits and angels that largely followed the speculations of Pseudo-Dionysius and his *Celestial Hierarchy*, and, beyond him, Plato and Aristotle with their 'Intelligences', 'Necessary Beings' and 'Prime Mover'. It was, Avicenna argued, the activity of the angels on the rungs of the celestial ladder as they climbed up to be as close as possible to the First Cause (in Christian terms, the face of God) that was creating the movement and momentum in the natural world of stars and planets. Angel activity, in other words, was behind the functions of the universe.

In *Kitab al-shifa*, his four-volume encyclopaedia that aimed to collect, classify and create a kind of conformity between all human knowledge – scientific, philosophical and religious – he designed a complicated cosmic structure that slotted angels into astronomy, a field of study that was thriving at this time in the Islamic world. Planets were, he said, part of a tiered hierarchy that spread out across the universe from the First Cause, running in parallel with the layers of spirits and angels, and intensifying the work of bringing order as well as closing the gap between the heavens and the earth.

There were, Avicenna proposed, seven layers, each associated with the seven planets then known to astronomers. In order of descent from heaven to earth, he listed Saturn, Jupiter, Mars, the Sun, Venus, Mercury and the Moon.[12] Each had its own 'Intellect' that either created angels or was itself an angel. So Gabriel, in this scheme of things, was the Angel of the Moon, on the basis that it was the nearest planet to earth, and this archangel had the strongest connection with humanity because, in the Christian Gospels and Qur'an alike, he was the one who had carried the message from God that his son was to be born to Mary. Gabriel reflected the divine light of God, and that light was then in its turn passed down to illuminate the intellects of humans. The most illuminated among them might even, he suggested, be able to see visions of angels.[13]

One of Avicenna's most enduring contributions to the pursuit, in the centuries that followed, of a fusion of science and religion that could make sense of the universe came with his 'thought-experiment', known to history as the 'Floating' or 'Flying Man'. What he was trying to do was resolve the different interpretations around concepts of body and soul. To that end, he described a man, wearing a blindfold, unable to hear, floating in silence in space where there was no wind. His arms were outstretched so that they were not touching any other part of his body. Would he still be aware of his own existence, Avicenna asked, even though, deprived of all five senses, he couldn't know that he had a body?

His answer was an unambiguous yes, because human beings, he argued, have an intimate awareness of their own existence that means they can conceive of themselves over and above knowledge of their own body. Each one possessed something intuitive that might be called a soul, and which, he proposed, was illuminated by God's light via the angels.[14]

These were speculations that had a direct influence, when translated for Western readers in the thirteenth century, on the angelologists in the University of Paris. Thomas Aquinas, the 'Angelic Doctor', certainly studied Avicenna. Before that, however, this Islamic physician-philosopher had come to the notice of another significant thinker whose ideas were to spread beyond his religious group, geography and time to reach the ears of the angelologists. Rabbi Moses ben Maimon, usually referred to as Maimonides, remains one of the most significant authorities on Jewish law and ethics.

A polymath like Avicenna, with whom he also shared an interest in astronomy, Maimonides was born in Cordoba around 1135 in a Spain under Moorish (Muslim) rule, but ended up as the *Naqid* (leader) of the Jewish community in Egypt. His fourteen-volume *Mishneh Torah* codifies Talmudic law and remains influential in Judaism to this day. Yet equally significant, certainly for the story we are exploring, are his philosophical writings, notably *The Guide for the Perplexed*, an essay on the Jewish law.

Here Maimonides attempts, like Avicenna before him, to reconcile the Greek philosophers with the Hebrew Scriptures and Jewish law. And that undertaking led him straight to the subject of angels, creations which he describes in *Mishneh Torah* as having 'a form but no matter at all' and 'no bodies, but they are forms that are separate one from another'.[15]

In his '13 Fundamental Principles' (*Shloshah Asar Ikkarim*) of the Jewish faith, Maimonides spelt out a new and different vision of angels from the dominant view of the intertestamental period. God is, he stressed, the creator of all that exists, without any sort of physical entity or manifestation, and must be worshipped exclusively. No longer, he argued, could or should angels be treated as akin to minor deities; similarly, descriptions of them in the front line of apocalyptic, physical battles in heaven were misguided.

So how better to re-imagine them? At the same time as downgrading angels' influence on earth, Maimonides (like Avicenna and Pseudo-Dionysius before him) offered in *Mishneh Torah* an angelic hierarchy, this time of ten ranks, heavily weighted towards their role in heaven. They were contemplative rather than active figures, but he added another dimension. Like Avicenna, he saw his tiers of angels as invisibly influencing the movements of the stars and planets.

'The books of the prophets', he conceded in *The Guide for the Perplexed*, 'contain statements whose external sense can be understood as signifying that angels are corporeal, that they move, that they have human form.'[16] But angels are, he insisted, without bodies or physical forms. 'This agrees', he wrote,

> with the opinion of Aristotle: there is only this difference in the names employed – he uses the term 'Intelligences', and we say instead 'angels' . . . When we assert that scripture teaches that God rules this world through angels, we mean such angels are identical with the Intelligences . . . His [Aristotle's] theory is that the Intelligences are intermediate beings between the Prime Cause and existing things, and that they effect the motion of the spheres, on which motion the existence of all things depends. This is also the view we meet with in all parts of scripture: every act of God is described as being performed by angels. But 'angel'

means, 'messenger'; hence every one that is entrusted with a certain mission is an angel. Even the movements of the brute creation are sometimes due to the action of an angel, when such movements serve the purpose of the creator, who endowed it with the power of performing that movement.[17]

Aquinas – 'the Angelic Doctor'

Among those much taken by this passage from Maimonides was Thomas Aquinas. He quotes it directly and at length in his *Summa Theologica* as he laboured to make sense of the world through angels. Some of his fellow believers may have insisted that God was beyond the reach of reason, and that his intentions must necessarily remain a mystery to weak, pitiful humanity, but Aquinas and his fellow angelologists could accept no such constraint. The mind of God may be impossible to grasp directly, they conceded, but its workings could be revealed by observing the natural world, and then exploring through debate and discussion those observations using logic and reason.

This thirst for knowledge, and conviction that all would become clear, was much more assertive than what had gone before. Pseudo-Dionysius and Maimonides, for instance, had insisted that God could be known only by what he wasn't – an approach known in theology as the Via Negativa.[18] Aquinas, however, believed you could make a positive case for God – the Via Positiva – which was supported by reason as well as faith. The challenge was to ask the right questions. And in his search for those questions – and answers – he turned his attention to both Aristotle and angels.

The best example of Aquinas's theorising is his five 'proofs' for God that are found in his *Summa Theologica*, whose purpose was to guide students, seminarians, academics and his fellow Dominicans, as well as – a radical ambition for the time – that tiny minority of lay people who were literate. The five proofs for God took those things that humans can see or experience in nature – for example, the change from night to day, or a river running into the sea – and then searched out what must be causing them to happen. There was, Aquinas suggested, a chain of causes that ran through the universe, in which angels played an integral role.

It was a chain, not a circle. There was, he insisted, an 'Unmoved Mover' as the 'first cause', and that was God. Everything came from God, but was filtered down by angels into the natural world, and to humankind. Their activity, for Aquinas, represented proof of God in the world.

It may not fit with today's scientific approach to proof of concept, but this method of arriving at eternal truths exemplified Scholasticism, the dominant theological approach in Christianity from the twelfth century right through to the Protestant Reformation. Aquinas was one of its leading lights. Taking inspiration from ancient Greece, most notably from Aristotle, whatever his lack of religion, Scholasticism relied heavily on discourse and debate, among academics and theologians, as the best means of re-imagining Christianity, not as an intuitive, emotional belief, but rather as a coherent, water-tight system built on irrefutable proofs to fundamental questions. Angels are today usually associated with intuition, with emotions, but Aquinas strove instead to encompass them in a thoroughly and painstakingly rational approach to the universe. For his admirers, his work on angels was where, in the words of the twentieth-century Jesuit historian Jean Danieliou, 'the most subtle questions concerning nature and grace, intellect and their love, are solved with an admirable mastery'.[19]

Angelology was, undeniably, a complex academic discipline, too complicated it would seem to have much relevance outside the bookish world of universities or cloisters. That, though, is to ignore how much its findings (if not its methodology) chimed with the continuing appetite for angels in the daily lives of believers across Europe and beyond. These were the figures that gazed down benignly from the hammerbeam ceilings of medieval churches and cathedrals, or out of their stained-glass windows, and in every Gothic detail of their elaborate stone spandrels. As members of the congregation walked in through the great, bronze, tenth-century Bernward Doors at Hildesheim Cathedral in Saxony for services, they were greeted in the panel nearest the ornate handles by the raised, sculpted figure of a mighty winged angel seeing Adam and Eve out of the Garden of Eden. It was both warning and comfort. To turn your back on the Church was to be ejected from a kind of Eden. But to enter in through those doors was to come under its guardianship.

And in his own life, Aquinas is reputed to have seen angels. The youngest son of minor Italian aristocrats, as a young man he had to resist family pressure to take up a career in the law or church bureaucracy, and instead he joined the Order of Preachers, the Dominicans, founded around the same time as the Franciscans, with a similar commitment to living shoulder to shoulder with the poor. In an attempt to dissuade him, the story goes, Aquinas was locked in the family home for a year. One of his brothers even tried to tempt him to abandon his commitment to chastity by sending a prostitute into his bedroom. Aquinas, though, sent her away, and was so angry that he branded a cross on his door to warn his siblings against trying anything similar again. That night, various accounts of his life report, he was visited in his dream by two angels, who tied a cord of fire round his waist, which caused him terrible pain, yet also gave him a fierce strength, so much so that he awoke with a great cry in the darkness of his bedroom.[20] Sigmund Freud would have had a field day with this account – the burning cord is suggestive both of the cord on a Dominican friar's robe, and of a chastity belt that inhibits its wearer – but whether Aquinas himself ever reported any such dream is disputed by his biographers.

What is easier to verify is his commitment to the academic discipline of Scholasticism, something far removed from everyday lives. Yet the reverberations of the angelology it led him to develop were manifold. Angel-adorned liturgies were conducted in angel-adorned churches (in Paris's medieval Notre Dame Cathedral, one stained-glass panel shows angels swinging ornate thuribles, to fill the air with incense). Each and every day was regulated by the chiming of the Angelus – or angel – Bell that recalled Gabriel telling Mary she was with child. It had begun as a feature of monastic life – sounding at six in the morning, noon and six at night – but by the thirteenth century it had spread so that the parish church in every village would ring out with three sets of three peals, corresponding to the three ranks within each tier of the celestial hierarchy of angels. It was an invitation to those who heard it, whatever they were doing, to stop and recite the Angelus prayer, a series of questions and responses based on the New Testament account of Gabriel's visit to Mary.

Then there were the elaborate angel costumes, often worn by young boys as they took part in the cycles of scripturally based religious plays, pageants and processions that spilled out of churches and into public spaces in the 1300s in cities such as York and Wakefield, with scaled-down versions in towns. In this medieval world the Bible was not just a devotional text or a historical document, something read aloud only on a Sunday. It was the primary source for understanding life as it was lived. Christians saw themselves – and were encouraged from the pulpit to do so – as participants rather than observers in the narrative that began in the Book of Genesis, addressed head-on the great questions of life (suffering, fate, death and salvation) and would only move to another stage with the yet-to-arrive apocalypse on Judgement Day described so luridly in the Book of Revelation.

The angelologists, then, were not going about their work in isolation or abstraction, intent solely on their own academic or spiritual satisfaction. In medieval Europe, faith was something as much felt as reasoned out and taught. And in that regard, angels had as much significance with the public as with theologians.

Yet the real world can still seem far removed from the question-and-answer format – typical of Scholasticism – that Aquinas uses in the *Summa*, including questions 50 to 64, known as his 'Treatise on Angels'. His method in each instance is to highlight an issue, examine scripture for guidance, repeat current church teaching, address any contradictory or dissenting views on the matter, and then give his judgement.

On angels' bodies, he is solidly with Augustine. Angels are spiritual creations, as is necessary for the perfection of the universe. They have intellect and free will, but no physical form. We may, he acknowledges, *think* of angels as having bodies when our minds turn to them, but that doesn't mean they do, because thoughts are not material.

Yet scripture – as some of those he debated with over this point no doubt told him – can be tricky on this question. The angels who come to Abraham and Sarah at Mamre share food with them. So they must logically have bodies. Aquinas, though, redirects the line of enquiry with a typically vivid and inventive flourish. Angels *can* take on a body, if absolutely required, he says, but it is made of condensed air. 'Although air, as long as it is in a state of rarefaction, has neither shape nor colour, when condensed, it can both be shaped and coloured, as appears in the clouds. Just so angels assume bodies of air, condensing it by divine power in so far as is needed for forming the assumed body.'

So it is all 'assumed'. Angels, therefore, only appear to eat. If this sounds suspiciously like he is making it up as he goes along – where, after all, does the Bible refer to condensed air? – then he quotes the Book of Tobit, in his defence. The Archangel Raphael has just revealed himself as an angel to Tobit. 'You thought you saw me eating,' he explains, 'but that was appearance and no more . . . And he rose in the air. When they stood up, he was no longer visible.'[21] The change, Aquinas argued, was down to condensed air, or rather the release of it as Raphael arose.

Within the realm of reason and logic, Aquinas was quite prepared to go further than any modern scientist would and include metaphor – speaking imaginatively rather than literally, in order to understand more deeply. 'When scripture speaks of the arm of God,' he writes, 'the literal sense is not that he has a physical limb, but that he has what it signifies, namely the power of doing and making.'[22] But for Aquinas, to be real was not the same as to be physical. The latter was the lot of humans, not angels. Likewise angels do not do the things humans do – like eating, being born and dying, forming emotional bonds, or having sex.

Yet if they are not like humans, neither are they like God. Aquinas placed them somewhere in between in the chain he identified. And since they are not like God, he insisted that they cannot know the future. 'The mind of an angel, and every created intellect, falls far short of God's eternity; hence the future as it is in itself cannot be known by any created intellect.'

In positioning angels firmly between God and humankind Aquinas rules out the possibility that they can have the sort of debates among themselves that took place in the angelology faculty of the University of Paris. That would be too human.

The lower, namely, the human, intellects obtain their perfection in the knowledge of truth by a kind of movement and discursive intellectual operation; that is to say, as they advance from one known thing to another. But, if from the knowledge of a known principle they were straightway to perceive as known all its consequent conclusions, then there would be no discursive process at all. Such is the condition of the angels, because in the truths which they know naturally, they at once behold all things whatsoever that can be known in them.

And, since they are not human, angels don't get it wrong. 'No falsehood, error, or deception can exist of itself in the mind of any angel.' Except, of course, in the case of the fallen angels. They get everything wrong, Aquinas emphasises, and from the very beginning. While he follows Augustine in having God introduce angels at the start of the creation cycle, he also moves the origin of the fallen angels back to this point from its more conventional location in chapter six of the Book of Genesis. Rather than the fallen angels coming down to earth, as is suggested there, Aquinas describes them as those who, when given the choice in the very first moment of their existence to embrace God, opted not to do so. They exercised their free will, he says, but for the bad. Yet, unlike humans, who also have free will, fallen angels are never redeemable. And they will never change, he judges.

But why, to follow his own attachment to logic, is there no mention of the creation of angels in Genesis? Aquinas has an answer for everything, some more plausible than others. To spell it out, he explains, would have confused those who read the Genesis account. Asked why someone as significant as Moses does not speak of angels, he once answered that it was because he was 'addressing an undeveloped people, as yet incapable of understanding an incorporeal nature' and therefore 'inclined to idolatry'.[23]

Beyond the detail, though, the significance of Aquinas's 'Treatise on Angels' is twofold. First, his descriptions of what angels are and aren't, and can and can't do, are based not on the requirements of certain specific circumstances, nor on doctrine. Neither does he simply allow his imagination to run wild. He tests each claim forensically according to his rules of logic and reason and so builds the most complete system yet in which to fit the role of angels in the cosmos. Second, and as a consequence of the first, he completes the move away from the Early Church belief that angels and human are close, and instead takes the position that had been adopted by Pseudo-Dionysius (who is quoted over and over again by Aquinas), which places angels further from the earth and its inhabitants, and closer than ever to God. 'Among other creatures,' Aquinas writes, 'the angels are nearest to God, and resemble him most; hence they share more fully and more perfectly in the divine goodness.' If God is pure intelligence – the highest compliment to Aquinas's enquiring mind – he must have created clever angels, since they are the ones closest to him. Humans, by contrast, are further away in the chain and so were created with many more limitations.

If angels were most at home in heaven, Aquinas does allow that those on the lower rungs of the celestial ladder, near to earth, can influence human behaviour in ways that go beyond ill-defined guardianship. These lesser angels can, he says, illuminate or enlighten, as messengers from God, but they cannot compel a change in any individual's beliefs or 'will'. That is down solely to God, who 'alone can change the will, because he gives the power of such an inclination to the intellectual nature'.

Influential as he was, however, some of the theories Aquinas advanced were not widely taken up in the medieval Church. One example is his idea that each angel is a distinct species all of its own rather than, as had been thought hitherto, one of the larger angel species. Here he was replying to the question of how one angel interacts with another. The two 'love one another with natural affection – in so far as [they are] one with nature', he answers, but one angel does not love another 'with natural love'. Neither do they feel sorrow, he adds. That would be too human. Moreover, he continues, 'in every angel there was impressed the form of his own species according to both its natural and its intelligible condition, so that he should subsist in the nature of his species, and understand himself by it'.

Humans, he explains, all have a mother and father, and many go on to be mothers and fathers themselves. They are linked one generation to the next, and so are all essentially from the same species. Angels, though, are different. One generation does not give way to the next. They have all served God since their creation and will go on serving him. That doesn't mean they are eternal, in the sense that God is eternal – that would make them too God-like and raise the spectre of idolatry – yet he proposes that they do inhabit somewhere called 'aeviternity', sometimes rendered as 'aevum', or 'everlasting time'.[24] It is effectively eternity, but without any guarantee that it will last forever.

That means, Aquinas says, there must be as many species of angel as there are angels. And since by his own description there is a guardian angel for each individual, there must also be as many species of angels as there are humans, or as Aquinas puts it, 'far beyond all material multitude' in numbers. Angels were everywhere, yet invisible to most except by their deeds. For those who could only believe if they were given a visible form, the onus therefore fell on artists to bring them to life.

Q

Q is for '**Queen** of Angels', another of the titles that Catholicism has bestowed on Mary, Jesus' mother. Many of Mary's accolades have a teaching purpose, and by describing her as 'Queen of Angels', the twelfth-century Church was emphasising her proximity to God in heaven. She was, this title was saying, closer to him even than the angels, and therefore the supreme intercessor with God on behalf of humanity. This was the role that had originally belonged only to angels, but over the centuries Christianity added first saints as intercessors, and then Mary.

R

R is for **Ridwan** (also spelt Ridhwan, Rizwan, Rizvan, Ridvan or Redouane), who in the Hadith – the Prophet Muhammad's sayings that first appeared in the eighth century CE – is the archangel in charge of Jannah (heaven). Muslims hoping for an afterlife in heaven direct their prayers to him. In some versions of his story, he is a gatekeeper, like Saint Peter in Christianity. The Qur'an describes (in 13:23–4) how the angels that Ridwan leads in paradise will welcome believers as they arrive: 'Gardens of perpetual bliss: they shall enter there, as well as the righteous among their fathers, their spouses, and their offspring: and angels shall enter unto them from every gate (with the salutation): "Peace unto you for that ye persevered in patience! Now how excellent is the final home!"'

9

From Invisible to Visible –
Bringing Angels to Life

'The golden moments in the stream of life rush past us, and we see nothing but sand; the angels come to visit us, and we only know them when they are gone.'

George Eliot, *Scenes of Clerical Life* (1857)

The Hebrew Scriptures emphatically outlaw 'graven images' of 'anything in heaven'.[1] Since angels were deemed by theologians and believers alike to reside in heaven, even if only as their base when they are travelling through the cosmos, that scriptural injunction should rule out any officially sanctioned depictions of them. Yet it is a prohibition that has never been consistently enforced in Judaism and Islam, and hardly ever in Christianity. Nor for that matter in the Hebrew Scriptures themselves. Within pages of forbidding talk of 'graven images' in the Book of Exodus, the carved cherubim of the mercy seat are described.

In Islam, as we have seen, the Angel Jibr'il was depicted in the manuscripts of medieval Persia. For its part, Judaism has run hot and cold on the subject, though its default position has been one of restraint. Angels abound, though, in the wall-paintings in the Jewish catacombs at Vigna Randanini in Rome, used as a refuge between the second and fifth centuries CE when the city's Jewish community was being persecuted by the authorities for their refusal to conform to the religion of empire. And angels are strikingly there, too, in the remarkable frescoes in one of the world's oldest surviving synagogues, dating back to the second century CE, at Dura-Europos, once a city on the eastern border of the Roman Empire in what is today Syria. When it was rediscovered in the 1930s, archaeologists at first assumed it must be a Greek temple because there were just so many winged, god-like figures in the well-preserved wall-paintings. On closer examination, however, they realised that the scenes came from the Hebrew Scriptures, including Ezekiel's vision of an angel-thronged heaven.

Christianity, too, has not been without those literal-minded folk who follow the letter of the law on graven images. The Synod of Elvira in the early 300s agreed a ban on all images in churches, but most opposition to the practice came much later – notably among some of the Reformed Churches that followed Martin Luther in the sixteenth century in breaking with Catholic Rome (though Luther, it should be added, was keen on retaining certain images in churches).

The wider Protestant rejection, though, remains a minority viewpoint in Christianity. Representational art of 'anything in heaven' has thrived in the Western Church throughout its history, giving tangible form to the yearning for faith in something 'other'. Painting has developed a way of exploring a scriptural narrative, and connecting it directly with areas of human experience, that is sometimes beyond the power of words.

Among its favourite subjects have been angels. The same images of angels that continue to fill our imaginations, and enjoy enduring popularity in the world outside institutional religion, were first created to be shown inside churches, convents, monasteries and basilicas. Or in graveyards, where angels' wings beat the path to eternal life on many a memorial.

The earliest of all Christian depictions of angels – albeit wingless – were on sarcophagi, the decorated stone coffins used to bury the dead in ancient Rome. Those of the rich were housed in necropolii, located outside the city walls, like the one on the

Vatican Hill, then a pleasure ground, across the River Tiber from the imperial capital. For those of more modest means, there were the catacombs, vast subterranean warehouses of the dead, an idea inherited from the Etruscans.[2]

It was here also that the persecuted early Christians would secretly conduct their liturgies out of sight of the authorities. And so, when it came to burying their martyrs who had died at the hands of their Roman persecutors, they copied the sarcophagi around them, but with one important difference. The Romans had decorated theirs with carvings of any number of gods and goddesses, from their own and others' pantheons. A particular favourite was Ariadne, who, legend tells, was abandoned by her lover Theseus on the island of Naxos while in a deep sleep and only much later was found and awakened by Dionysus. The parallels between Ariadne's lengthy slumber and death as 'just' a long sleep were reassuring to the bereaved, especially when her story promised a happy ending.

The early Christians, though, substituted angels for gods and goddesses, exchanging Greek myths and legends for scenes from the Bible to invoke a different sort of immortality. Their sarcophagi, often housed in the catacombs cheek by jowl with improvised gathering places for Christian liturgies, became a focus of inspiration for the living. They told how those who had died for their faith were now enjoying their eternal reward with the angels in heaven.

As if to emphasise the point, the naturalistic style employed in such decorations made no great distinction between humans and angels. The latter – as exemplified by a mid-second-century Gabriel in the Cubicolo dell'Annunciazione in the Catacomb of Priscilla – were therefore without wings. Likewise the elaborate marble sarcophagus of the fourth-century Roman senator and Christian convert Junius Bassus, today housed in the Museum of Saint Peter's Basilica, features among its many carvings the sacrifice of Isaac by his father Abraham. The angel of the Lord who halts the filicide is a young, beardless, short-haired figure, almost impossible to distinguish physically from the other two present.

It wasn't just the Old Testament angels who inspired Christian artists who carved these stone coffins. As well as gods and goddesses, Romans and Greeks had both used as decorations on sarcophagi what to our eyes are angel-like characters. The Romans called them *putti* – from the Latin word for boy – while the Greeks preferred *spiritelli,* or 'sprites'. The latter denoted – as Plato had taught – that the soul was distinct from the body and had departed after death. The symbolism of the *putti* was more of a mishmash that included debts to both the god of wine, Bacchus (the *putti* on Junius Bassus' sarcophagus are eating grapes), and Cupid (in Greece, Eros), the winged god of love, with his bow and arrow, and his assistants called Erotes or Cupids.

These winged lesser gods were usually found on the sarcophagi of children, and their influence on early Christian artists became more marked when they started to give their angels wings. The obvious connection was love that endured beyond life – that the *putti/spiritelli* represented a love that was simultaneously divine and earthly. Much later, when the Renaissance revived interest in classical art, the Roman *putti* came back into vogue once more as child-like angels, while later still, in the Baroque and Rococo periods of the seventeenth and eighteenth centuries, the *putti* were conflated with the cherubim, who were given an infant's sexless body, but an adult face.

We are, however, flying ahead. The Greek and Roman influence when it came to wings was felt much more immediately. As the Early Church Fathers in their speculations and writings slowly began to distance angels from humans, so too did artists. From the fourth century onwards, as Augustine and others focused on what distinguished angels from those over whom they exercised guardianship, wings started to appear as the outward sign of that separation. An angel could no longer be confused with a human being.

Among the oldest images of angels on the walls of a Christian church are early-fifth-century mosaics in the Roman Basilica of Santa Maria Maggiore, celebrating the birth of Jesus. In this version of the Nativity, there are angels everywhere, as the New Testament describes. Their pure white gowns owe much to the standard Roman toga, but they are set apart by their wings – and also by their haloes.

The early-fifth-century mosaics in the Roman Basilica of Santa Maria Maggiore feature some of the earliest surviving representations of angels in Christianity.

This last detail – also applied in the Santa Maria Maggiore mosaics to Jesus, but not Mary or Joseph – was once again taken from the iconography of Greece and Rome, where the halo was a band of divine light placed around the head of gods. So are the angels being treated here as if they are gods, on a par with Jesus? That would be at odds with the message of Saint Paul, who saw Jesus as superseding the angels as God's messenger (as well as being the incarnation of God's message). And the mosaic would have troubled Saint Augustine, too. While the symbolism of the halo fitted with his insistence that angels were wholly made of light, here they are given physical bodies, in direct defiance of his teachings that they had no such thing. The main point that the mosaic seems to be trying to convey, however, is more in keeping with the changing mood: that angels are not the same as Mary and Joseph and are on a higher level than humanity.

Later, the convention changed as the symbolism of haloes was adjusted to reflect subsequent theological shifts. The three persons of the Holy Trinity, God the Father, God the Son (Jesus) and God the Holy Spirit, were allocated their own distinctive triangular haloes. Mary, the mother of Jesus, got a circle of stars, while saints, as well as angels, received the standard band of light. The distinction between the once-living-but-now-dead (saints) and heavenly creatures (angels) was maintained only by the latter always being depicted bare-footed (since they could fly rather than needing to walk) whereas saints wore sandals.

Such codification was partly to provide an education in the teachings of the Church – most of those who saw the images would not have been able to read – and partly, too, concerned that drive from the fifth century onwards to bring order and system to everything on earth, as in the heavens. The various rules around haloes, though, were as nothing compared to the dispute that boiled over in the eighth and ninth centuries around all and any religious images. The Byzantine Empire – formerly the eastern section of the Roman Empire – was thrown into chaos in the Iconoclasm Dispute over religious images (including angels) becoming objects of worship. So much so that in 726 the Byzantine emperor Leo III banned images altogether. His decree, though, caused such consternation that, in 787, the empress Irene summoned the Second Council of Nicaea to reconsider the whole question. It decided that images could be allowed, as long as they were only venerated and adored but never worshipped, which sounded good on paper, but proved hard to enforce.

The Council was attended by delegates of Pope Adrian I, who had travelled there on his behalf from Rome. Yet the concerns expressed at Nicaea were never as strongly felt anywhere in the Western part of what was still at the time a single Christian Church. There, angels remained all the rage, though the company they kept was evolving.

The biggest shift came as part of the rise, in the eleventh and twelfth centuries, of the cult of the Virgin Mary, based on a version of Jesus' mother that insisted she was pure and chaste throughout her life – though the Gospel accounts give her other children. In these same accounts, especially after Jesus' birth and childhood, she is a marginal figure. Only John places her at the foot of the cross.[3] Yet in a medieval Church devoid of women in its upper echelons, with an all-male clerical elite that had signed up for (even if it didn't always practise) celibacy, the focus fell increasingly on Mary as both the perfect woman and the surest route to God's mercy. Just as she had interceded with her son at the Wedding Feast of Cana in John's Gospel and over-come his initial reluctance ('Woman, my time has not yet come'[4]) to perform a miracle by turning water into wine,[5] so she would now – from the lofty perch the Church attributed to her in newly popular hymns such as '*Regina Caeli*' ('Queen of Heaven')[6] and '*Ave Regina Caelorum*' ('Hail, Queen of Heaven')[7] – receive human cries of anguish and pass them on to her son in the hope of another miracle. She was, as the saints had done before her, encroaching on what had been the sole prerogative of angels. And, ultimately, she surpassed them as the celestial intercessor-in-chief, being hailed by Bonaventure as 'mistress of all the choirs of angels'.[8]

The choir-mistress required her angels to act as her backing singers. Angels became little more than heralds of her apparitions, often simply her attendants, as in Filippo Lippi's mid-fifteenth-century *Madonna della Cintola*, where she descends from the skies in an almond-shaped seat, carried by two angels, to give the apostle Thomas her girdle, or 'holy belt'. The painting was for a monastery in the town of Prato, near Florence, where a relic, claimed to be Mary's actual girdle, had become a popular item of devotion with pilgrims, especially pregnant women.

Such regal airs and graces represented a turnabout in Mary's fortunes. In Luke's Gospel, she is the humble recipient of the message the Archangel Gabriel has come to deliver.[9] Now, in popular re-creations of that scene in many medieval churches, Gabriel was the one humbling himself to her. The shift in power had been underway as early as the eighth century, when a six-foot-high icon of 'Maria Regina' was installed in the Basilica of Santa Maria in Trastevere in Rome, showing even the pope (John VII) prostrating himself before Jesus' mother, with the angels standing at her side, holding spears, this time relegated to ceremonial guard duty. The Latin inscription reads: 'As God himself made himself from thy womb, the princes among the angels stand by and marvel at thee, who carried in thy womb the child who is born.'

Mary's new-found prominence did, however, raise the profile of Gabriel above that of his fellow archangel, Michael, hitherto the most often depicted by Christians. Among the popular images of the Virgin Mary cult was, naturally, that of the Annunciation, and it was Gabriel's words from that encounter, as recorded in Luke,[10] that were taken as the opening lines of her special prayer, the 'Hail Mary'. While it was known in the seventh century, the 'Hail Mary' became ubiquitous only after it was championed in the eleventh century by Peter Damian, Benedictine monk,

The medieval cult of Christ's mother elevated her to the status of 'Queen of Angels' and made angels her attendants, as here in Filippo Lippi's mid-fifteenth-century Madonna della Cintola.

philosopher and adviser to popes and emperors, who described it as the 'angelic vesicle'. A late twelfth-century synod placed the 'Hail Mary' on a par with the 'Our Father' and the 'Credo' in Christian worship.[11]

Their close association with Mary also led to angels becoming less obviously masculine. As the cult of Mary as perpetual virgin flourished, it came to be regarded as inappropriate in any depiction of the Annunciation that Gabriel should be too male, lest it impinged on the essential purity that the Church insisted was at the heart of this meeting. It was a far cry from earlier speculation about how Gabriel might have facilitated Mary's impregnation by the Holy Spirit.

Elsewhere, too, that tendency to make angels androgynous when around Mary was gathering pace. The two bearing her down to earth in Lippi's *Madonna della Cintola* are, when compared to images of the martial and aggressively male Michael with his sword and battle armour that had been so familiar in the first millennium of Christianity, decidedly girlie, with their golden locks and loose-fitting, cover-all smocks, even if the task they were performing – bearing an ornate throne – might have been deemed traditionally a more masculine job.

One more contributing factor to angels becoming less male came with the growing theological consensus that their principal residence was heaven. The more earthly, human angels depicted in the Early Church were being replaced by images of self-consciously celestial creatures, as befitted those without bodies but who, Aquinas taught, were made up of nothing but condensed air. Gender dividing lines were becoming less important. Better, indeed, that the angels' innate otherworldliness was confirmed by them appearing to be neither man nor woman.

When the early thirteenth-century Cistercian Caesarius of Heisterbach was describing his visions of angels in *Dialogue of Miracles* (c.1223), he referred to them appearing 'under the form of the most beautiful maidens'.[12] (His words might today raise the question of whether the vision was less a statement about the sexlessness of angels, and more the revelation of an erotic dream.) Confining angels ever more to heaven 'brought about something of a sex change', Henry Mayr-Harting remarked, when drawing attention to this passage in his 1997 inaugural lecture as Regius Professor of Ecclesiastical History at Oxford University. 'One can see it clearly if one compares any Ottonian angel [from tenth- and early eleventh-century Germany] with the amiable hermaphrodites who smile out at us from thirteenth-century French Gothic portals.'[13]

In the company of angels

As Caesarius reveals, some individuals in the medieval Church didn't just gaze upon paintings or carvings of angels. They reported meeting them face to face. Hildegard of Bingen was one such. In this twelfth-century German Benedictine abbess the various threads weaving angels into the everyday life of medieval Europe came together in an extraordinary whole. Though women's voices were rarely heard in the theological debates of the day, Hildegard won so many admirers for her writings among the male clerical elite that she corresponded with popes, emperors, bishops and academics, sharing her own insights in her prayers and reflections on the scriptures from within the walls of her enclosed convent on the banks of the Rhine in the Palatinate.[14] She was also an accomplished scientist, exploring the medicinal uses of plants, as well as a musician whose compositions continue to be played 700 years later.

In every part of her life, this polymath introduced angels, nowhere more so than in her best-known prose work, *Scivias* (from the Latin *Sci vias Domini* – 'Know the Ways of God'), which details twenty-six visions she had during the course of her long life. They started, she reports, when she was three, and happened not in dreams – as was the case with her contemporary, fellow Benedictine and fellow mystic Elisabeth of Schönau – or after a prolonged period of fasting (which accompanied the visions of Catherine of Siena in the fourteenth century), but in the course of everyday life. 'I never suffer in them any unconsciousness induced by ecstasy,' Hildegard reported, 'but I see them when I am awake, day and night.' In the 'extremely strong, sparkling, fiery light, coming from the open heavens' that she experienced each time, she was given, she said, an insight into the Old and New Testaments that went beyond 'the meaning of the sentence structure and the hyphenation'.[15]

Her most detailed vision of angels takes the familiar notion of hierarchical ranks, but adds an extra dimension.

Then I saw in the secret places in the heights of heaven two armies of heavenly spirits who shone with great brightness. Those in one of the armies had on their breasts wings, with forms like human forms in front of them, on which human features showed as if in clear water. Those in the second army also had wings on their breasts, which displayed forms like human forms, in which the image of the Son of Man shone as if in a mirror. And I could see no other form either in these or in the others. These armies were arrayed in the shape of a crown around five other armies. Those in the first of these five armies seemed as if they had human forms that shone with great splendour from the shoulders down. Those in the second shone with such great brightness that I could not look at them. Those in the third had the appearance of white marble and heads like human heads, over which torches were burning, and from the shoulders down they were surrounded by an iron-grey cloud. Those in the fourth had forms like human forms and feet like human feet, and wore helmets on their heads, and marble tunics. And those in the fifth had nothing human in their appearance, and shone red like the dawn. And I saw no other form in them.

But these armies were also arrayed like a crown around two others. Those in the first of these other armies seemed to be full of eyes and wings, and in each eye appeared a mirror and in each mirror a human form, and they raised their wings to a celestial height. And those in the second burned like fire, and had many wings, in which they showed as if in a mirror all the Church ranks arrayed in order. And I saw no other shape either in these or in the others. And all these armies were singing with marvellous voices all kinds of music about the wonders that God works in blessed souls, and by this God was magnificently glorified.[16]

Hildegard is subtly shifting the usual focus for the organisation of angels from the neat, almost bureaucratic tiers set out by Pseudo-Dionysius, towards something more intuitive and mystical, as was demonstrated in the extraordinary illustrations (or illuminations, as they would have been known) that accompanied *Scivias* in the Rupertsberg edition, production of which she supervised at the abbey she had founded in the years leading up to her death in 1179.[17] In them, the angels are arranged not in ranks, but in concentric circles, interdependent and moving around a blank centre that is the unfathomable mystery of God. In place of the usual Christian emphasis on angels gazing into the face of God, Hildegard suggests that even their eyes cannot penetrate so profound a mystery.

This is a familiar sentiment among mystics. The celebrated sixteenth-century Spanish Carmelite John of the Cross wrote:

it is nothing wonderful that God should be strange to men who have never seen him, seeing that he is also strange to the holy angels and the souls who see him; for they neither can nor shall ever see him perfectly . . . Thus God is the strange islands not to men only, but to the angels also; only to himself is he neither strange nor new.[18]

In the illustrations to accompany her writings about angels, the twelfth-century German abbess Hildegard of Bingen arranged them into concentric circles around the unfathomable mystery of God.

Other details in Hildegard's illustrations of angels are worthy of note. Some of them are winged, some not. Some have clear but androgynous, almost feminine, faces; others do not. Theirs is, the arrangement seems to say, a collective effort, not a series of rungs on a ladder, which may just reflect Hildegard's view of the organisation of the Church that marginalised from any say in its affairs women in particular, and those of lowly birth in general.

'God keeps a watchful eye over every person,' she begins in one passage in *Scivias*, dispensing with the need for guardian angels representing a distant God, 'so that a lower order will not gain ascendancy over a higher one . . . for God establishes ranks on earth, just as in heaven with angels, archangels, thrones, dominions, cherubim and seraphim. And they are all loved by God, although they are not equal in rank.'[19]

If a point was being made about the need to reform the Church's structures, Hildegard was not doing it forcefully, though it is worth reflecting that among the best-known medieval mystics – who also include Mother Julian of Norwich, Gertrude of Helfta and Margery Kempe – there was a disproportionate number of women. 'In medieval life,' writes Hildegard's biographer, Fiona Maddocks, 'spiritual authority was the one real avenue for women to obtain leadership, just as the religious life was the only chance for them to enjoy a degree of privacy and the opportunity to educate themselves offered by access to the monastic library.'[20]

And Hildegard could not complain, herself, of lack of influence. *Scivias* was widely circulated. It was reading it that caused popes to write to her, and other leading figures to seek her counsel. She also produced in *Ordo Virtutum* (Play of Virtues) what some now refer to as the first musical play in Europe, initially performed by Hildegard and her fellow nuns at the formal blessing of the Rupertsberg abbey in 1152. Again it uses a different format beyond straight prose reporting to explore and convey her visions, and her own distinctive angelology. It is a morality play, with the addition of music, in which the Virtues, one of Pseudo-Dionysius' middle-ranking categories of angels, combine to bring a kind of order to the universe and to save souls from the devil's clutches.

Perhaps, though, Hildegard's most tangible influence on the story of angels in the Church was through her music. Every one of her visions, she said, was accompanied by a soundtrack of angelic song of such beauty and glory that it set a standard to which human voices could only aspire. But aspire she did, giving voice quite literally to that long-standing concept that the singing of choirs in churches should join with that of the heavenly host in praise of God. The results, she accepted, by her own yardstick, would always be imperfect next to the celestial chorus, since they were human, but music, she firmly believed, was one way in which angels dwelt within each and every one of us. Among the most enduringly popular of the hymns she composed was 'O Living Light, O Angels Glorious!', where angels 'below divinity / upon the eyes divine you gaze / within the darkness mystical / of all creation'.

That mystical tradition to which she is referring, and within which angels play such a prominent part, has often been regarded by official Christianity as, at best, a left-field endeavour, hard to control within its hierarchical structures and therefore a threat to their authority. Hildegard (despite her friendships with popes) and the medieval mystics more generally are better seen as free-thinkers within the institutional Church, pursuing an individual and direct knowledge of God through revelation. They share a view of the cosmos that favoured senses over intellect, dreams over dogma, revelation over rules.

As Christianity was exploring its relationship with angels over its first five centuries, Judaism had been gradually rowing back from its own obsessive preoccupation with them as seen in the various Enoch texts and apocalyptic literature. One reason for the shift was disappointment. For all the talk of angels heralding the arrival of God's kingdom on earth among his chosen people, the reality had been first the destruction of the Second Temple in Jerusalem by the Romans as they put down a Jewish uprising between 66 and 70 CE, and then the failure of the Bar Kokhba Revolt (132–5 CE) to prevent the establishment of a new Roman colony of Aelia in Judea, with laws that included a prohibition on male circumcision and the establishment of a shrine to Roman gods erected on the ruins of the Temple. Once the uprising had been ruthlessly crushed by imperial forces under Julius Severus, Jews were forbidden even to enter Jerusalem.

As a reaction, Judaism turned increasingly inwards, and over those centuries a thousand scholars of Jewish law were working, first in Palestine and later in the academies of learning, or *yeshivas*, in Sura and Pumbedita (part of a well-established diaspora community in Babylon) to develop the Talmud. When completed in the middle of the fifth century, it was second in importance only to the Hebrew Scriptures, and set out Jewish laws and beliefs, ethical guidelines and how Jews should conduct their lives. It included angels, since they were there in the Hebrew Scriptures, but, in the words of the distinguished twentieth-century American scholar Rabbi Morris Margolies, 'cut them down to size'.[21] The rabbis of the Talmud laid special emphasis in particular on an instruction given to Moses on Mount Sinai by Yahweh: 'You shall not make gods of silver, or gods of gold, to stand beside me.'[22] This meant, they said, that images of angels were banned, as was any attempt to give angels any kind of quasi-divine status.

That guidance found expression in the Talmud's downplaying of angels in the Seder service to mark the Passover, which recalled the Jews' liberation from slavery in ancient Egypt. 'The Lord brought us out from Egypt,' it stated, 'not by an angel, not by a seraph, and not by a messenger, but [by] the Holy One, praised be He, Himself.'[23]

Limiting angels' scope became the norm thereafter in Judaism. There was no longer any question of them power-sharing with God. Yet the appetite for these more forceful angels of the period between 300 BCE and 200 CE was not quite exhausted. So when Maimonides and others (as described in the previous chapter) worked to apply reason and logic to their faith, including on the celestial hierarchy, they faced a backlash that became a form of Jewish mysticism known as Kabbalah ('received tradition'). Its principal text was the *Zohar* (*Book of Splendour*), thought to have been composed or assembled during the thirteenth century by a Spanish rabbi, Moses de Leon.[24]

Outpourings of mystical thought from visionaries and poets have often come in both Christianity and Judaism at times of crisis. It had been a sense of abandonment by Yahweh, following their exile in Babylon and then subjugation by the Romans, that had first turned Jews to speculation about angels. And now, as Christianity was spreading across Europe, becoming ever more intolerant of dissenting or even different voices, Jews were facing prejudice and pressure to convert, with harsh persecution if they didn't. When in 1095 Pope Urban II summoned a crusade to liberate Jerusalem on behalf of Christianity from its Muslim rulers, the army that gathered across Europe to answer his appeal first tested its mettle by attacking Jewish communities in cities such as Cologne, Speyer, Worms and Mainz, offering their victims a choice of baptism or the sword.

Meanwhile, an expanding Islam, which hitherto had shown a greater willingness than Christianity to co-exist with Judaism, took a fanatical turn in the middle years of the twelfth century in the shape of the Almohad Caliphate, which seized control of Muslim Morocco and extended its rule across North Africa and into Al-Andalus, Muslim Spain, where it forced Jews to convert, and closed their centres of learning.

As a result, with Judaism once more feeling itself besieged on several fronts, that sense of being left to their own devices tempted Jews once more to look to angels to invoke God's protection. It is no accident that Moses de Leon tried to pass off the *Zohar* as a rediscovered second-century text by Rabbi Simon bar Yohai, dating back to the golden age of the angelic avalanche. The text of the *Zohar* is a part visionary and often opaque commentary on the Torah, the first five books of the Hebrew Scriptures. Mixed in are esoteric reflections on the nature of God and mystical cosmology, all written in Aramaic, the language of first- and second-century Israel. It contains a multitude of angel names, including that of the Archangel Uriel, restored to his equal position alongside Gabriel, Michael and Raphael around God's throne, surrounded by the cherubim who 'beat their wings above and spread them out' creating a daily chorus of praise.[25]

Angels in the *Zohar* are both male and female, composed of fire and water, occasionally with earth and air added in. They live in seven heavenly halls (as seen in Enoch's visions) and could, it suggests, be summoned by using intricate numerical combinations, deduced by those in the know from the various names for God. Part of the *Zohar*'s heady cocktail, too, was the return of Metatron, last seen in Enoch as the greatest of all angels, here elevated to a status halfway between the rest of the heavenly host and God, a 'lesser Yahweh'.

The *Zohar* wastes no time striving for consistency, or clarity, or even order, but instead concentrates on closing the gap between an unknowable and transcendent God and the material cosmos he created. It does this by exploring the hidden meanings (a particular theme of Kabbalah) of scriptural passages, especially the celestial visions of the prophet Ezekiel. It also features an army of fallen angels, who are products of a divine, creative 'presence' (or '*shekhinah*') that is characterised as fire. They pose an imminent threat, 'dazzling, demonic guardians, standing poised to emerge and rule the world'.[26] Like the Gnostics before them, the Kabbalists had strong dualist tendencies, seeing the world in their visions as split between good and evil.

In medieval Europe, Kabbalah remained popular among Jews as long as they were being persecuted. When in 1482, in a Spain now wholly under the control of Catholic monarchs, the Inquisition turned its intolerance onto the Jews, many began to leave the country to escape the resulting persecution. A decade later, the 150,000 that remained from a community that had been established in Spain for a thousand years were summarily expelled by royal decree. It was a tragedy, some Jewish historians have said, to rival the destruction of the Second Temple.

Some of the exiles headed for the Holy Land and washed up in the town of Safed in northern Palestine, which became, under first Moses Cordovero (1522–70) and then Isaac Luria (1534–72), the new centre for Kabbalah. Cordovero wrote an influential commentary on the *Zohar* and its angels, but it was the teachings of Luria (he wrote little save a few poems, his words being recorded by his disciples) that had the greatest influence in reshaping and reinvigorating this branch of Jewish mysticism as a response to the blow that had been dealt to the Jewish people. He described the angelic host in dualist terms as split between the *sitra di yemina* (those on the right side of divine emanations) and the *sitra ahura* (those on the left, or fallen, side).

One of the most intriguing adherents of Lurianic Kabbalah was Joseph Karo (1488–1575). Exiled from Spain as a four-year-old, he became a distinguished scholar of Jewish law, his *Shulkhan Arukh* remaining a definitive text to this day. Yet he combined such precise scholarship with a vivid mystical side that brought him to Safed and made his name known among Jews all across Europe and beyond. In his *Maggid Meisharim* (*Preacher of Righteousness*) he kept a diary of his visionary relationship with his *Maggid*, or celestial teacher, whom he referred to as his 'Answering Angel'.

This was traditional guardianship taken up and embellished to the nth degree by mysticism. It was, therefore, the 'Answering Angel' who dictated the diary to Karo in the Aramaic of the *Zohar*, who showed Karo multiple visions of the future (something Aquinas had specifically ruled out for angels), and who told him that he would die a martyr. Such eye-catching revelations attracted a steady stream of Kabbalah pilgrims to Safed. Karo lived to the grand age of eighty-seven, eventually dying not as a result of martyrdom, but undramatically as a result of natural causes.

This final detail was much remarked upon by subsequent generations of scholars, who suggested that his angel was one of his own making, that it was one side of his split personality (the other being the careful legal scholar).[27] In other words, angels are humans in disguise.

Dante's Divine Comedy

In the three-part *Divine Comedy*, an early fourteenth-century account of a journey around heaven, hell and purgatory that is variously referred to as the outstanding poem of the Middle Ages and the greatest ever literary work in Italian, Dante Alighieri (1265–1321) gathered together many of the aspects of medieval angelology. His depiction of a layered hell (or *Inferno*) inside the core of the earth, and then an arrangement of planets that led up to heaven, echoed the cosmic speculations of Thomas Aquinas and the Scholastics. Another label sometimes attached to the *Divine Comedy* – which is not funny in the sense that the word comedy is now used, but rather, its author explained, was a *comus oda*, or rustic song – is the *Summa Theologica* in verse. Both tag lines greatly underestimate Dante's ambition.

There is a strongly mystical feel in his *Paradiso* (the last of the three parts, written shortly before Dante's own death in 1321), especially in his descriptions of the *Primum Mobile*, the 'crystal-line heaven', the ninth sphere and place of angels just below the Empyrean, or highest part of heaven where God presides. Here, at the very heart of heaven, Dante describes not light, or circling angels, but something beyond words, like the blank space in the centre of Hildegard's depiction of the angelic ranks in *Scivias*. When the fifteenth-century master Sandro Botticelli came to illustrate the *Divine Comedy* in a series of ninety-two drawings, his final one, for the thirty-third and last canto (verse) of *Paradiso*, was a blank sheet.[28] To add to the complexities, some scholars have also suggested that Dante's descriptions may have been influenced by the *Book of Zohar* and the Kabbalah, and include encoded references to them.[29]

That case has not been proved. The debt owed by Dante to medieval angelology is clearer but his writings also exhibit many of the qualities of Renaissance thinking, the artistic, philosophical and cultural movement originating above all in Florence, Dante's home city, that gathered momentum throughout the fourteenth century. In the broadest of terms, it brought with it a new optimism about humanity's capacity, alone and collectively, to be and do good, in stark contrast to the often doom-laden and fearful obsession with sin and damnation that was so strong in the medieval Church and, by association, medieval Europe. And so, in Dante's *Inferno*, it is humans – albeit dead ones – who inhabit the nine concentric rings (to match those in heaven, with that typical Scholastic love of order and calibration) rather than the fallen angels. Even the devil, who resides in the lowest ring, is encased in ice, weeping and all but impotent. Punishment, Dante suggests, is not caused by winged demons/angels who have fallen out of favour with God and are seeking revenge, but rather by people who have brought sorrow on themselves by their abuse of the free will that gave them the potential to do good.[30]

Up in *Paradiso*, too, unlike the more standard medieval geography, angels are largely absent as Dante climbs up through the light-suffused stepping stones of the planets. His guide is not, as in the great Old Testament visions, an angel, but rather one of the dead, Beatrice Portinari, the woman whom he had met and fallen in love with when both were still children, but who had died young in 1290.

So the thousand *splendori*, or 'shining spirits' who welcome them on Mercury are specifically not angels, however tempting it is to think of them in that way. Instead they are, explains their spokesman – the sixth-century Roman emperor Justinian, who resides there in death – those who were so absorbed with fame and honour in life that they neglected their devotion and service to God. His presence suggests that this – in Dante's eyes – was Justinian's weakness.

This heaven is humanised, and therefore without angels, even if some of its inhabitants take on traditional angelic features. Saint Benedict, for example, is portrayed as a blazing light without a face. And when, on Saturn, Dante spots Jacob's ladder, it is the dead not angels who are ascending and descending it. Human virtue can put heaven within its grasp, Dante was emphasising. You don't have to be angelic.

Only very near the top, in the Primum Mobile – 'marvellous and angelic temple / which is bounded only by love and light'[31] – does he finally reach the habitat of angels who swirl around him and Beatrice 'in bodily rings'. Up to this point, Dante has been clear that afterlife in *Paradiso* dispenses with bodies – in line with Aquinas, Augustine, Paul and Plato – but here his words are sufficiently ambiguous for Botticelli in his celebrated illustrations to equip the angels with sweet faces, rounded limbs and softly billowing draperies to accompany their harp-shaped wings.[32] They are like a hurricane of movement, spiralling round the centre where, calmly, stand the visitors. Similarly calm alongside them are the first among the nine ranks of angels that Dante has prescribed, faithfully following Pseudo-Dionysius' formula. Those nearest to them, Beatrice explains, are the seraphim and cherubim, who possess an all-embracing power and intelligence that makes them content to stay still and sing the *Regina Caeli*, the hymn to the Virgin Mary.

> There was such sparkling
> From the circles, as is seen in the sparks
> Which are thrown off by iron when it boils.
>
> Every spark followed the fire it belonged to;
> There were so many that the number of them
> Was greater than all the combinations at chess.
>
> I heard Hosanna sound from choir to choir
> To the fixed point which holds them to the where,
> And will do always, in which they have always been.
>
> And she who saw the uncertain thoughts
> Within my mind, said to me: 'In the first circles
> You may have been shown the Seraphim and Cherubim.
>
> So swiftly they follow as they are bound,
> To be as like the point as they may be;
> And they may so far as their vision is exalted.'[33]

Rather than tilt down, like the levels of choir stalls, Dante's angels reach upwards to the highest level of all, the Empyrean.

> All these orders keep their gaze upwards,
> And downwards exert force, so that all are drawn
> Towards God and all draw others there.[34]

Here, Dante demonstrates again his engagement with the Scholastic discourse of Aquinas and others. He refers to those angels at the very top, closest to the Empyrean, as 'the highest point / Of the universe; in them was pure act'. It is an odd use of the word to modern ears, but 'act' in Scholastic discourse meant constant and eternal spiritual activity, unimpeded by matter. If angels are 'pure act', Beatrice explains to Dante, earth is 'pure potential', with the fusion of both, the cosmos, between them.

Angels are there too in the Empyrean, in the very centre of this heaven of pure light. To enter into it, Dante has to bathe his eyes with the waters of a glorious spring and then is greeted by a scene where the sparks he saw previously become angels:

> with their wings outstretched,
> I saw more than a thousand angels celebrating,
> Each one different in brilliance and in manner.

> I saw smiling on their games and songs
> A beauty which was all happiness
> In the eyes of all the other saints there.[35]

S

S is for **Shalgiel**, the angel 'appointed over the snow' in the fifth-century-CE rabbinical text the Hebrew Book of Enoch, also known as 3 Enoch. In the burgeoning angelology of this vivid text, all the natural elements are given an angelic controller – Ra'amiel for thunder, Ruchiel for wind, and Matariel for rain. In her 2011 novel *The Dovekeeper*, the Jewish American purveyor of magic realism Alice Hoffman writes of a rare covering of snow in Jerusalem, 'dusting the hills, sent by Shalgiel, the angel of snow. Some children had mistaken it for manna [from heaven] and eaten handfuls of it, freezing their lips.'

T

T is for **Tawsi Melek** – in English, the 'Peacock Angel' of the Yazidi people of northern Iraq. In their creation myth, the Supreme Being delegated to Seven Great Angels the task of creating the earth. Of them, Tawsi Melek was the greatest. In some accounts, he is briefly tempted away from the way of righteousness, but then weeps for seven thousand years as he repents, filling seven huge jars with his tears, which are then used to extinguish the fires of hell. As the lynchpin of creation, Tawsi Melek refuses, in Yazidi tradition, to bow to Adam, God's creation in Judaism, Christianity and Islam. Because in the Qur'an the devil-like Iblis also refuses to bow to Adam (Surah 17:61), some extremist Muslims have down the centuries accused their neighbours, the Yazidi, of being devil-worshippers, and persecuted them. Yazidis regard their twelfth-century-CE founder, Sheikh Adi Ibn Musafir, as an incarnation of the Peacock Angel.

IO

The Renaissance Angels

'O welcome pure-eyed Faith, white handed Hope, Thou hovering
angel girt with golden wings.'

John Milton, *Comus* (1634)

The medieval angelologists had presented angels ever more insistently as pure spirit. They were without emotion, Thomas Aquinas
had concluded in his *Summa Theologica*, and stood, therefore, in
stark contrast to humanity. The artists of the Renaissance, though,
equally insistently claimed them back, as our close, attentive,
lookalike companions who, as the modern expression goes, feel our
pain. This dramatic re-imagining took place from the fourteenth
century onwards, with even the upper echelons of the angelic hierarchy transported from their celestial perch in the inner circle of
heaven and instead installed in abundance not only on the walls
and ceilings, façades and roofs, of churches and monasteries, but
also in palaces, courts and – most significantly – in private homes.

Angels were being domesticated and placed in the midst of
earthly life. As a consequence, artists gave them back the bodies
that theologians had taken away. And not just any old bodies, but
three-dimensional physiques and faces that epitomised and
mirrored the best of human strength, vitality, vibrancy and – *pace*
Aquinas – feelings.

The word Renaissance – 'rebirth' in French – is believed to have
been first used only in the mid-nineteenth century by the anti-
clerical historian Jules Michelet to describe the period stretching

from the fourteenth to the seventeenth centuries when, first in Italy and then across Europe, the dominant mindset of the Middle Ages was overturned. Out went pessimism and obsession with the sinful, fallen nature of humankind, beholden to an unknowable God. No longer was it a question of simply enduring the trials of this world by lifting our eyes to heaven in the hope of salvation and a happy life after death. The Renaissance gaze focused on the here and now, and on the God-given potential of each individual for pleasure and achievement.

This was not an explicitly anti-Church development. Many of the Renaissance's greatest treasures were commissioned by clerics from artists whose number included faithful priests and monks. It did, though, push for greater freedom of thought and expression than hitherto allowed for by the Church's carefully calibrated and restrictive rulebook. And so, while the leading lights of the Renaissance continued to explore the familiar biblical scenes, and hence the familiar sightings of angels, they were now doing so from a new perspective that celebrated the human heart, brain and spirit as gifts from God.

The Renaissance only indirectly challenged the Scholastic method of questions and answers that Thomas Aquinas and his colleagues had developed to provide what, for them, was a fool-proof scientific and philosophical proof of God's existence, and an explanation of his operating methods across the universe. That remained the orthodoxy taught in the universities and seminaries, and preached from the pulpits, until a growing tide of discontent boiled over in October 1517, when an obscure German friar, Martin Luther (who had no time at all for Renaissance finery), issued his Ninety-Five Theses – or debating points – and so precipitated the Reformation that broke Catholicism's stranglehold over Europe.

What the Renaissance brings to our story, then, is a plentiful, nigh on ubiquitous, vision of a new sort of angel who existed side by side with human beings in natural, everyday landscapes (rather than dream-like, celestial realms). Aside from their wings and – in the early Renaissance – their haloes, they looked just like us, and our interactions with them were characterised not by flashes of lightning and almighty visions, but rather by an often cosy, stay-at-home intimacy.

Medieval artists, in both the Western and Eastern branches of Christianity, had long favoured a flattened, perspective-free, icon-like emphasis on symbol over working from life. The first significant break with this approach came in the early Renaissance years in the work of Giotto di Bondone (*c.*1267–1337) – usually referred to, as was the way then, simply by his first name. A Florentine painter and architect, his origins are obscure but his genius in pushing established boundaries ushered in a more naturalist style.

In his masterpiece, the thirty-seven scenes from the life of Jesus and his mother commissioned for the Scrovegni Chapel in Padua in northern Italy at the start of the fourteenth century, Giotto's angels share the faces and gestures of those with whom they connect. The chapel was dedicated, among other things, to the Annunciation – which, as the cult of the Virgin continued to thrive, became the indispensable Renaissance subject – and is reported to have been where an annual procession took place with local boys donning wings to play the Angel Gabriel, come to tell Mary the news of her pregnancy. And so, in focal positions above the chapel's chancel arch, Giotto has the two figures of Christ's mother and her messenger facing each other, side-on, similar in size, position and shape, matching the intensity of each other's stare in a meeting that captures the charge of that moment.

Elsewhere in the chapel, Giotto shows smaller, airborne angels, tearing at their breasts in sorrow as they observe powerlessly Jesus' crucifixion and its aftermath. In *Lamentation* – one of the most reproduced of this remarkable cycle – Mary, along with her son's apostles and followers, is tenderly cradling his battered and rigid corpse after he has been cut down from the cross, the anguish etched on all their faces. Above them, in this moving study in sorrow, their distress is echoed in the gaze of ten golden angels. These are not the contour-less, ethereal creatures of medieval art. They have personalities and are so engaged in the heartbreak that their misery is there for all to see.[1]

In Giotto's 1303–5 study in sorrow, Lamentation, *in the Scrovegni Chapel in Padua, ten golden angels mirror the anguish of Mary and the apostles as they cradle the dead body of Jesus.*

In general terms, Renaissance artists offer two sizes of angel. Those on terra firma tend to match the dimensions of the humans with whom they share an encounter. Those in the skies, looking down, are usually smaller, though still with well-defined bodies and faces that tell us what is going on inside their heads and hearts. Giotto provides both in the Arena Chapel. So, too, in his commissions did the Florentine sculptor Donato di Niccolò di Betto Bardi, known as Donatello (1386–1466). His *Annunciation* tabernacle is one of the highlights of Florence's Basilica of Santa Croce. The gilded limestone figures of a startled Mary, still clutching the book she has been reading, and of Gabriel, kneeling before her, are presented as equal partners in a gripping but private drama. Yet Donatello is celebrated, too, for his 'child angels'. Indeed, some art historians credit him with reviving interest in such figures by returning to the classical canon and turning them into one of the motifs of the Renaissance.

The treasury of the classical world was among the most significant of Renaissance enthusiasms, not only (as with the medieval angelologists) for its philosophy and learning, but also for its culture and artistic forms of expression. With his child angels, Donatello was drawing again on the winged *putti*, *spiritelli* and cupids of ancient Greece and Rome, once an inspiration for the early Christians. Two works of his in particular stand out. Originally in the Duomo, Florence's cathedral, his *Cantoria* (Singing Gallery) – one of two white marble and mosaic decorations on the choir balconies that were suspended on either side of the main altar – features a tangle of dancing, singing, vivacious, almost frenzied boy-*putti*, half naked but wingless in classical garb. It was completed in the early 1430s, soon after Donatello had been in Rome, where he had studied the decorations on sarcophagi that featured similar figures.

And then in the Basilica of Sant'Antonio in Padua in 1450, he took on a commission to decorate the whole high altar with scenes of the miracles attributed to the saint to whom the church was dedicated, mixed together with others from the life of Christ.

*Two of the 'musical angels' in Donatello's 1450 decorations at the
Basilica of Sant'Antonio in Padua. His child angels are based on
the* putti, spiritelli *and cupids of classical Rome and Greece.*

One notable feature is his bronze bas reliefs of twelve 'musical angels', again inspired by the *putti*, and this time including wings, with all of them blowing trumpets, or lyres, or singing with mischievous, joyful, child-like faces.

Quite when the Renaissance conflated these 'child angels' with the biblical cherubim – second only to seraphim in Pseudo-Dionysius' hierarchy, rather than over-excited, not-entirely-innocent youngsters – is a matter of debate. One of the clearest linking references comes in the writings of Teresa of Avila (1515–82), the Spanish nun, mystic and reformer of her own Carmelite order, who reported seeing repeated visions of an angel, as well as levitating, during spiritual raptures. 'He was not large, but small of stature, and most beautiful,' she wrote in her 1565 autobiography, 'his face burning, as if he were one of the highest angels, who seem to be all of fire: they must be those whom we call cherubim. Their names they never tell me; but I see very well that there is in heaven so great a difference between one angel and another, and between these and the others, that I cannot explain it.'[2]

The angels created by Renaissance artists for public, private and religious settings both contributed to and reflected the widespread conviction that a host of very human angels were close at hand. And it inevitably also fuelled wider speculation about them that went beyond the definitions agreed by the academic angelologists. Sandro Botticelli (1445–1510), another Florentine, is a case in point. He created many celebrated works featuring typically Renaissance angels, but in a small number of works went further. In his 1485 *Birth of Venus*, now found in the city's Uffizi Gallery, he eschewed the usual, standard and all-pervasive religious themes and instead tackled head-on something from classical mythology, an unusual choice for the times. The Roman goddess of love, Venus, arrives naked on the seashore in a giant scallop shell. To her right a female figure – often described as a minor goddess – hands Venus a cloak to protect her modesty, while to her left the airborne winged god of the wind, Zephyrus, carrying what some have identified as the flower nymph, Chloris, is blowing Venus onto land, all the while looking almost indistinguishable from an angel.

If one of Botticelli's intentions in *Birth of Venus* was to highlight the classical lineage, rather than the celestial origin, of Christian angels, then in *Mars and Venus*, a near contemporary work in the same vein, he surrounds the smitten god and goddess in their forest glade with horned infant satyrs, in Greek mythology drunken, lustful woodland gods, but to fifteenth-century Christian eyes resonant of the *putti* angels with whom they had become so familiar, albeit with more than a hint of fallen angels mixed in. And then in arguably Botticelli's most complex mythological work, *Primavera* (or *Spring*) from the late 1470s, he has a gathering in an orange grove of figures from the classical pantheon, including once again Zephyrus, Chloris and Venus. Hovering over them, just where the *putti* angel would be if this were a standard religious subject, he places a naked, winged cupid with an arrow. The connections between past and present, especially when it comes to angels, he is suggesting, are rather more complicated than any official church account, a thought reinforced by the striking resemblance between Venus's hand gesture and that widely given to Mary in the many Renaissance versions of the Annunciation.

The Renaissance was questioning the role allotted to angels, and in some cases subverting it as part of a new spirit of enquiry about religious faith. In his personal notebooks, the polymath Leonardo da Vinci (1452–1519) reveals himself as privately not as devout as some of his artist contemporaries. Yet, like them, he knew that the only way to earn his living as an artist in those times was by taking on religious commissions, such as his version of the Annunciation, now also in the Uffizi Gallery. In it, Gabriel's wings have attracted comment as oddly disconnected in their precision from the archangel's more naturalistic body. One explanation is that this is the product of what Leonardo's notebooks show to be a genuine obsession for him – how to build a flying machine. He was a keen observer of how birds managed flight and in his rendering of angels – especially Gabriel in the *Annunciation* – it has been suggested that he was taking the opportunity to produce a blueprint of the sort of wings that he believed might be capable of lifting a human being (as well as an angel) off the ground.[3]

And Leonardo's curiosity didn't stop there. If the Renaissance tended to make its angels increasingly androgynous, often quietly feminine and sometimes, in their semi-nudity, sensuous, it carefully steered clear of sexualising them. That would have put it directly at odds with the Church, which would have been a step too far in the climate of the time. The angelologists' line that angels were without gender, without sexual desire, and therefore without sexual organs, was publicly accepted and, in representations, they were draped in perfectly weighted layers of cloth to make such questions irrelevant. But in private the freethinking Leonardo pushed at this boundary, at least to judge by one of his sketches that was in the private collection of the British royal family in the late nineteenth century. Among some preparatory drawings for his now-lost 1505 work, *The Battle of Anghiari*, was found a depiction, known as the 'Angelo Incarnato' ('Angel Incarnate'), of a naked angel-like figure (though without wings), with both prominent female nipples and, beneath a thin piece of gauze, a large and unmistakable erection (though efforts had been made at some stage to rub it out). No one quite knows the whys and wherefores of this curious piece of work, and some dispute it is actually by Leonardo at all, suggesting it may instead be something mischievous by one of his assistants.[4]

Such breaking of taboos is a world away from two other Renaissance figures, both named after angels – Guido di Pietro (c.1395–1455), the Dominican artist from Fiesole, outside Florence, known as Fra Angelico, or 'the angelic friar', and Raffaello Sanzio da Urbino (1483–1520), more commonly referred to as Raphael. Opinion is divided on how Fra Angelico got his nickname – whether it was because he just painted so many beautiful and memorable angels, or because he was angel-like in his humility and modesty, or because in his frescoes in Florence and later Rome his paintbrush seemed to be touched by the divine. He refused ever to revise his works, saying that God had guided his hand and so he couldn't err. He saw painting scenes from the Bible as his own form of prayer and religious devotion.

In the history of angels, Fra Angelico is the last significant Renaissance artist to give his angels haloes, as had been the unwavering practice in medieval art. In his *Virgin of the Annunciation* (c.1450) for the Chapter House of the Convent of San Marco in Florence, Gabriel is seen meeting Mary on an outdoor, vaulted loggia. He is framed by two of its slender classical arches, she by the next two along. There is an austere elegance to the scene, with its extraordinary light, the artist's clever use of space and perspective, and the delicate fragility he gives to Mary. Both figures have their arms folded across their chests, as if hugging themselves as they lean forward to face each other with matching gestures, but Fra Angelico also gave the pair matching golden haloes.[5] His contemporaries may have argued that such adornments, and the symbolism they conveyed, got in the way of the naturalism of the scene, but Fra Angelico stuck in this regard to the traditional way. So much so that his haloes have become one of his hallmarks. When he was beatified by Pope John Paul II in 1984 – becoming Blessed Angelico – he was hailed by the *New York Times* as 'Master of the Golden Halo'.[6]

Raphael shared his name with an archangel.[7] His two impish, rascally cherubs at the bottom of his painted altarpiece of the *Madonna and Child*, commissioned by Pope Julius II in 1512 for the Church of San Sisto in Piacenza in central Italy, make up one of the most reproduced images of angels in circulation. The back-drop he gives to the Virgin Mary is the clouds of heaven, through which can only dimly be discerned the outline of the faces of dozen upon dozen of cherubim. At the foot of the painting, though, two of the *putti* have emerged from the mist into plain sight, complete with their wings. They are resting their elbows on what was to become, when the painting was complete and put in place, the top of the altar itself.

Raphael's rascally cherubs, from the bottom of his 1512 altarpiece in the Church of San Sisto in Piacenza, are among the most reproduced images of angels in circulation today.

It is a clever optical trick, and the faces of the two are not easily forgotten, today gracing many a poster, postcard, book jacket and any number of bits of angel memorabilia. One legend has it that Raphael copied their expressions from the two young sons of the woman who modelled for him for the Madonna. They were bored sitting waiting for her to finish her work with the artist. Another prefers the version that has Raphael going into a bakery and spotting two urchins looking in longingly at the bread and cakes they couldn't afford to buy, and then reproducing them.

Reformation and Counter-Reformation

Martin Luther made his one and only visit to Rome in 1511, when still a naïve Augustinian friar and devout Catholic, as yet unknown to anyone outside his cloister in Saxony. He had been sent the 900 miles on foot by his provincial so that he could act as his representative in a minor dispute within the Europe-wide religious order. As he approached the headquarters of Catholicism after forty days of walking, Luther threw himself to the ground and cried out in awe 'salve, santa Roma' ('hail, holy Rome'). But that pious enthusiasm quickly evaporated when he witnessed at first hand the papacy's profligacy in spending money raised from humble believers back in Germany (notably by the sale of indulgences, or free passes into heaven when they died, for them and their relatives) to fund a Renaissance building boom that included commissioning the leading artists of the Renaissance to create a new, sumptuously decorated Saint Peter's Basilica. 'I had not been in Rome very long before I had seen much that made me shudder,' Luther later recalled disapprovingly of the extravagance he had witnessed.[8]

Given his horror at the cost – and, he would say, the utter corruption and lack of theological rigour involved in raising money in this way to fund the Church's patronage of the arts – it seems logical to assume that, once Luther had made his final break from Rome in 1521 and established his own reformed Evangelical Church (he disliked the words Lutheran and Protestant), he would insist on plain white-walled churches with no room for images of angels. That expectation is further reinforced by Luther's own central and animating belief that the individual believer's relationship was always first and foremost with

God, as revealed in the scriptures, and not with messengers, whether they be the institutional Church with its man-made rules, rituals, practices and cults, or intermediary angels.

Yet Luther was a complex figure and his behaviour was rarely logical or consistent. Though he broke with the Catholic Church – or, more precisely, it broke with him when he refused to back down on his demands and was excommunicated – the Catholic element in his make-up remained strong. Right up to his death, a part of him continued to hope that Rome would radically reform itself to accommodate his agenda. This may explain his somewhat ambiguous attitude to angels.

During his Christmas Day discussions round his dining table in Wittenberg in 1538, Luther made a point of singling out angels for particular praise for the part they play in the Nativity story, and used them – as countless generations of Catholic clerics before him had used them – to berate the faithful for their lack of conviction.

> To think that we are so cold and unresponsive to this great joy given to us, which actually happened for us; this great benefaction, which is far, far superior to all other works of creation, and is nevertheless met with such weak faith, which was preached to us and sung for us by angels, who are heavenly theologians and who were so joyful on our behalf! Their song was by far the most beautiful possible, and included the entire Christian belief. For the 'Glory to God in the Highest' is the most supreme worship. That is what they wished for and brought us in Christ.[9]

Among Luther's guiding principles was the importance of listening to the voice of God in the scriptures – '*sola scriptura*' ('scripture alone') – rather than waiting for it to be filtered through the authority structures and politics of the Church of Rome. And there throughout the scriptures are hosts of angels (though he did exclude from the Lutheran canon the Book of Revelation, and therefore pruned their numbers). So it would have been impossible for Luther to reject angels outright, though he did cut them down to size by being selective about what aspects of their cult he was prepared to endorse.

He mentioned in that Christmas Day 'table talk' the song of the angels, and he certainly cherished the long-standing belief that the voice of the congregation raised in song in the liturgy joined seamlessly with that of the heavenly choirs of angels. Yet the type of song he preferred, and indeed pioneered in the hymns that he composed, was more earthily robust than the ethereal choral music heard in Catholic churches. It used the vernacular, spoken every day by congregations, rather than Latin, and you will search in vain among his best-known hymns, including 1529's 'A Mighty Fortress', for any references, however oblique, to the intercession by angels.

Likewise, if Luther didn't, in reality, sweep all ornament out of churches as an unnecessary, expensive and distracting obstacle to developing a relationship with God, neither did he encourage them to be adorned with angels, as was the way in Renaissance Italy. In the Stadkirche in Wittenberg, where Luther preached more sermons than anywhere else, the pulpit becoming his second home, there is certainly lavish and monumental decoration, including the vast altar triptych by his follower, Lucas Cranach. Nowhere, though, is there so much as a loose feather from an angel's wing, even when Cranach expands on scripture to add Luther to the participants at the Last Supper.

Beyond questions of style and taste, the central doctrinal thrust of Luther's revolution was, moreover, to challenge the still prevailing Scholastic orthodoxy in Catholicism, which believed that by faith and reason, debate and disputation, hard and fast rules could be produced about God, his creation and angels. Nonsense, retorted Luther. God was essentially a mystery to humankind, and any suggestion that angels could somehow explain him was pure heresy. Scholasticism, he charged in his 1518 *Sermon on Indulgence and Grace*, had allowed Thomas Aquinas to advance arguments 'scarcely or not at all to be found in Holy Scripture'.[10]

Luther had no patience, either, with those in Catholic ranks who claimed mystical insights and visions of angels. 'We weak and ignorant creatures want to probe and understand the incomprehensible majesty of the unfathomable light of the wonder of God,' he reported back after being directed to read some of the mystics. 'We approach; we prepare ourselves to approach. What wonder then that his majesty overpowers us and shatters!'[11]

If Luther was moved to laud angels on the odd occasion, and certainly did not specifically exclude them, overall he had little use for them compared with Catholicism. They were clinging to the margins of the new Lutheran Church that stood on its own feet following his death in 1546. His Reformation precipitated a whole series of other reformations. By breaking Rome's hold, and insisting on the paramount importance of the word of God, he had opened the door for others to pass through who interpreted that word in ways different from him. And among these Reformers who came in his wake, angels excited even less enthusiasm. John Calvin, for example, poured cold water on the hitherto cherished concept of each individual having a guardian angel. 'Whether each of the faithful has a particular angel assigned him for his defence, I cannot venture certainly to affirm,' this French Protestant wrote in 1536 in his *Institutes of the Christian Religion*, the founding theological text for what became known as Calvinism and had a much greater day-to-day influence on the development of the Reformed Churches than even Lutheranism. 'Not one angel only has the care of every one of us, but that all the angels together with one consent watch over our salvation.'[12]

Calvin harboured a particular dislike for the Catholic cult of the Virgin Mary, regarding it as idolatry. Since the rise of angels in the

Renaissance had been tied with the tide of enthusiasm for Mary –
as evidenced by the many versions of the Annunciation being
commissioned – that charge of idolatry was also made in Protestant
ranks against the Catholic fascination with angels. There followed,
in many Protestant lands, a stripping out of angels from churches,
as for example in 1643, by order of the British parliament, at
Peterhouse, Cambridge. 'We pulled down two mighty angels',
wrote the Puritan overseer, William Dowsing, in his diary, 'with
wings, and divers other angels . . . and about a thousand chirubims
[*sic*] and angels and divers superstitious letters in gold.'[13]

A word of caution, though. Angels had and have a strong
enough hold on the popular imagination for them to be overly
vulnerable to church pronouncements on their fate. And so, in the
Reformation years, grassroots practice didn't always conform to
the role officially allocated – or not – to angels in Protestantism.
At the same time as Dowsing was visiting some hundred parish
churches in Cambridgeshire, and about a hundred and fifty in
Suffolk, smashing stained glass and other 'superstitious' imagery,
in the neighbouring county of Norfolk, angels on the ceilings,
walls and windows of its medieval churches went undisturbed. In
the prosperous port of King's Lynn on the Wash, for example, the
flock of carved angels playing instruments on the spectacular late
fourteenth-century oak ceiling of Saint Nicholas Chapel
remained, and remain, including one who holds a bishop's staff,
sign of his episcopal authority, a suggestion that bishops might
also be angels, or vice versa.

This survival was no accident. 'It is not surprising,' writes
Professor Keith Thomas in his *Religion and the Decline of Magic*
on the subject of popular belief during the sixteenth- and seven-
teenth-century English Reformation,

that many old Catholic formulae retained their value in times of
emergency for Protestants . . . At first sight the Reformation

appeared to have dispensed with [the] whole apparatus of supernatural assistance . . . and referred the believer back to the unpredictable mercies of God . . . Yet the problems for which the magical remedies of the past had provided some sort of solution were
still there – the fluctuations of nature, the hazards of fire, the
threat of plague and disease . . . and all the uncertainties of daily
life.[14]

His remark captures a particular period, but it can also be applied
more widely to the history of angels. In the eyes of institutional
religion, and in cultural and artistic circles, angels' popularity
and appeal may wax and wane, but their attraction as a way into
some sort of supernatural force for salvation for those in need or
crisis remained largely undiminished, whatever the pronouncements of clerics, scientists and artists.

Even within the academic circles of official Protestantism, what
looks very like medieval angelology continued to feature in public
disputations at some of the Lutheran universities of Germany.
Meanwhile, in the neighbouring Netherlands, at the influential
Academy at Leiden, a popular compendium of Calvinist theology, published in 1625 by four leading professors, concerned itself
with rehearsing one more time the arguments about whether
angels had bodies, their exact place in the creation story, and how
to avoid idolatry when dealing with them.

In Jaköb Böhme (1575–1624), German Lutheranism even had
its own mystic, seeing visions of angels and demons locked in that
seemingly eternal fall-back of a cosmic battle between good and
evil. Böhme's angels, although shaped like humans but without
wings,[15] were, he explained in *Mysterium Magnum* (*The Great
Mystery*), published the year before his death, better regarded as
God's thoughts. They were his 'instruments in governing the
world'. To 'continue in God', he suggested – that is, to have
complete faith – had the power to make humankind 'higher

dignified than the angels'.[16] He was shuffling the celestial hierarchy again.

However familiar Böhme's visions, and however influential they were to be later in the Romantic movement of the eighteenth and nineteenth centuries, the net effect of the Reformation was still to downgrade angels in that part of the Christian world that embraced Protestantism in its many manifestations. And, as a consequence, to shift Catholicism's position on them. There, the result was neither promotion nor demotion. Angels instead became even more prominent in Catholic churches, but also more banal.

The Renaissance's willingness to project its own passions and concerns onto angels was, the Counter-Reformation Catholic Church decreed, henceforth to be avoided at all costs lest it further cause scandal to the faithful, and push them into the arms of Protestantism. Anything to do with angels had to be strictly controlled if it wasn't to cause dissent. Yet when Catholic leaders initially gathered at the Council of Trent in 1545 to plan their fight back, angels were not top of anyone's agenda. During the eighteen years the Council took to complete its business – between its twenty-five sessions there were gaps of months and even years – a realisation slowly dawned that, with Protestantism apparently set on offering an austere, simple and God-directed form of faith, ritual and worship, a real opportunity had opened up to counter its appeal by continuing to offer a channel, including through the cult of angels, to access the sort of supernatural assistance for which, as Keith Thomas argues above, appetites remained strong.

And so, in the twenty-fifth and final decree of the Council of Trent, the gathered ecclesiastical princes offered their directions on the future place and conduct of sacred art. As a discipline, they acknowledged, it had a major role to play in teaching and supporting the largely illiterate faithful, but only if it always

educated those in the pews in the correct (i.e. the Church's official) interpretation of scripture. Such interpretation, the Council
of Trent insisted, remained the prerogative of the Church, and
not of individual consciences as Luther had advocated. Neither
was it, the Council Fathers ruled, to be down to individual artists
to use church-funded or church-directed commissions to paint
religious subjects in a way that went beyond the strict limits of
Catholic orthodoxy, including on the subject of angels. Henceforth
all art was to be produced in such a way that 'no images [sugges-
tive] of false doctrine, and furnishing occasion of dangerous error
to the uneducated, be set up'.[17]

The implication is clear. The Council Fathers had decided that
the freedom and licence given to Renaissance artists had so
clouded the waters of doctrine and belief that it had contributed
to the build-up of discontent that became the Reformation. In
future the Church, as patron of the arts, was going to be more
vigilant, insisting on purer standards – there was also a reference
to banishing 'pagan' influences, which might be taken to include
classical allusions – and doctrinal orthodoxy.

If the general intention was plain, quite how, in practice, it was
to be achieved and enforced was not. Application was therefore
somewhat haphazard. By 1608, when Pope Paul V trumpeted the
still central but strictly controlled role of angels in the lives of
Catholic believers by proclaiming an annual feast day for the Holy
Guardian Angels on 2 October, an artistic style had already
started to emerge in Baroque that managed to convey the intellectual and spiritual vigour of Catholicism without causing
church-goers to ask awkward or dissenting questions.

Baroque combined a doctrinal rigour with drama, and propaganda with an extravagance that tipped into over-the-top, especially when, in the eighteenth century, it spawned the even more
exuberant Rococo. The stock in trade of the Baroque was a plentiful sprinkling of always showy, often gilded but essentially

hollow angels, as seen, for example, in the Flemish artist Peter Paul Rubens' 1625 *The Triumph of the Church over Fury, Discord and Hatred*, now hanging in Madrid's Prado Museum. The Protestant heresy is trampled and crushed by the hooves of the horses that pull the papal carriage, while winged angels, suitably demurely clothed as Trent had demanded, dance attendance like an approving chorus. There are both full-size angels – one holds a parasol decorated with the keys of Saint Peter, symbol of the papacy's authority – and cherubim, some of them peeping round the painted folds of material that surround the scene. The child-like innocence of their bodies indicates the purity of their witness, while their adult faces betray some knowledge of the trials of this world.

The thought-provoking, domesticated angels of the Renaissance were being discarded in favour of something altogether less challenging. On the great Baroque façade of the Basilica of Sant'Andrea della Valle next to Rome's Campo de Fiori flower market, a giant angel in white limestone perches to one side, its mighty wing raised high and touching the upper storey as if holding it up. By association, suggests this detail that was personally approved by Pope Alexander VII in the mid-seventeenth century, angels were there purely and simply to support the structures of the Church.[18] Even when an angel did move centre stage – as in Pietro da Cortona's *The Guardian Angel*, commissioned by the same pope in 1656,[19] where a mighty but androgynous angel, all benign smiles and billowy neck-to-ankle robes, leads a small child towards the bright lights of heaven – the effect is largely sugary.

Not all artists of the Baroque, however, could be relied upon to fall into line. A few used angels as what we might today call disrupters. Principal among the rebels was Gian Lorenzo Bernini (1598–1680), whose main patron was the cultured Pope Urban VIII (1623–44). Bernini's towering black marble *baldacchino* – or canopy – over the main altar of the new Saint Peter's Basilica in Rome is the size of a four-storey building. Atop each of its four giant gilt-bronze pillars stands an outsized angel. So far, nothing to which theological purists could object. At the bottom of the four pillars, though, are plinths, each decorated on the sides that face outwards with a series of eight white marble motifs. They all feature a papal crown, and below it the crest of the Barbarini popes, stretched over what appears to be a swollen stomach. Finally, beneath it all, on seven of the eight, is a woman's face going through various contortions, while on the last, in the same place, is the face of a cherub.

Quite what Bernini was getting at in this clearly strategic deployment of an angel is disputed. Some see it as a subversive reference to papal mistresses having their officially celibate lover's children. Others, though, ascribe it to the medieval legend of Pope Joan, the German woman of English descent who is said to have tricked her way into the papacy in the ninth century disguised as a man. She was only discovered when she gave birth in the street while on a papal procession.[20]

What is not disputed is that, as the master of Baroque, Bernini did not feel so constrained by church stipulations that he couldn't make mischief with his angels. And more than mischief. In his celebrated sculpture *The Ecstasy of Saint Teresa*, in the Cornaro Chapel in Santa Maria della Victoria in Rome, ten minutes' walk from Saint Peter's, Bernini was arguably being both provocative and thoughtful. He based the work, he said, on the Carmelite nun's account (already mentioned) of the cherub who visited her in her dreams, but this angel is no *putti*-like knowing child. It is a magnificent man as befits the second ranking in the angelic hierarchy.

'I saw in his hand', Teresa had written in her autobiography,

a long spear of gold, and at the iron tip, there seemed to be a little fire. He appeared to me to be thrusting it at times into my heart, and to pierce my very entrails: when he drew it out, he seemed to draw them out also, and to leave me all on fire with a great love of God. The pain was so great that it made me moan; and yet so surpassing was the sweetness of this excessive pain, that I could not wish to be rid of it.[21]

Some of Teresa's biographers insist that this passage is about a spiritual desire for God, which is awakened by the angel's visit, and that any erotic/sexual connotations are all to do with Bernini himself.[22] Everything is pure to the pure at heart, as the traditional church maxim goes. And it is true that, while he was a daily attender of vespers at the nearby Church of the Gesú, and a regular at confession, the sculptor was notoriously promiscuous, with an often health-threatening appetite for women. There is, though, an unmissable sensual charge to Bernini's creation that borders on the sexual as his white marble angel, his face androgynous, but his shoulder and muscle-bound arm unmistakeably masculine, causes the flailing Teresa's face to swoon.

Talking to angels

Where Bernini's angels were challenging their relegation to mere ornament by the Counter-Reformation, some notable figures on the other side of the denominational divide among the reformed Protestants were also falling under the angelic spell, albeit for what appear at first glance more bizarre reasons. The eminent Elizabethan and English polymath John Dee (1527–1609) spent much of the last three decades of his life trying to communicate with angels by learning their language – the same tongue spoken in the Garden of Eden, he suggested, before the fall of Adam and Eve.

To a twenty-first-century audience that makes Dee sound like a crank, and even in his own age there were those who labelled him an occultist and therefore dangerous. Yet this was also a man of considerable achievement. In the academic field, he was a child prodigy who was offered chairs at Oxford and Paris, but who turned them down to become a scientific adviser to, and favourite courtier of, Queen Elizabeth I, encouraging her in the quest for colonies (he is credited as being the first person to use the phrase 'the British Empire'). His learning was the stuff of legend. In his home in Mortlake, south-west of London, he assembled at ruinous cost a library of 4,000 books, larger than that of either Oxford or Cambridge universities, along with a collection of the latest mathematical and astronomical instruments.[23]

Dee's quest for knowledge was unceasing, and his goal – like that of Thomas Aquinas before him – was to find the key that unlocked a complete and comprehensive understanding of the visible and invisible world. One possibility he explored was mathematics. Drawing on Plato, Pythagoras and other Greek philosophers, he attempted to show that numbers could explain the workings of the universe. When that failed to convince, he switched his attention to angels. If he could somehow tap their knowledge of creation, this devout church-goer believed, he would finally get answers to the questions that interested him.

In the early 1580s, with his stock at the royal court falling, he embarked on a partnership with Edward Kelley, a 'scryer' or medium through whom Dee believed himself able to participate in 'spiritual conferences' with angels. As he learnt to decipher their language, he recorded what they said in his diaries. Among their instructions to him was one from the Archangel Uriel, who in 1587 told him that humans should share their goods with each other, up to and including their wives. With a certain reluctance Dee did as he was told. Kelley was, by all accounts, rather keener on the angelic message he had conveyed, and his liaison with Jane Dee drove a wedge between the two men, exacerbated when the following year Jane gave birth to a son, who many believe was Kelley's.

It is easy to dismiss Dee's efforts to talk to angels as a hoax – in part against him (Kelley was already a convicted fraudster when the two met) – but there is no doubting his sincerity. What is remarkable about his story, though, is that it illustrates the power that even a distinguished man of science in the late sixteenth century was willing to ascribe to angels to quench his thirst for knowledge about nature. Subsequent biographers have tried to suggest that Dee's angelic language may have been a smokescreen for a secret code (he did devise several of these during his lifetime) that allowed him to act as a spy during his travels in Europe, passing information back to the English royal court. Yet in his surviving records of his exchanges with angels, a different and more profound agenda is apparent.

Dee believed that angels had two sides, one active, visible and earthly, the other just as real but invisible and part of their place in the cosmos. It meant that angels – these 'pure verities',[24] as he described them – could be both material and corporeal, part of this world in their communications with humans, as well as spiritual and immortal in another. But it could also make their means of communicating complicated since, he recorded, they 'have no organs or instruments apt for voice: but are mere spirituall and nothing corporall: but [they] have power and property from god [sic] to insinuate [their] message or meaning to eare or eye'.[25]

It sounds remarkably like previously advanced theories about how Gabriel conveyed to the Virgin Mary the message of her impending pregnancy, but Dee went on to define it as a practical distillation of the sort of mystical vision experienced by the likes of Teresa of Avila. The angels who conveyed their messages to him by passing them through his imagination were, he wrote, able to imitate divine thought processes. Dee clearly felt himself getting close to the mind of God. And because the angels were far above the limitations of even the greatest of human intellects, they could convey a knowledge of the workings of the natural world – 'of things intangible and immaterial'[26] – that was otherwise beyond the grasp of any other.

This fusion of natural philosophy and revealed theology saw Dee walking in the footsteps of others before him in invoking angels as the means to bring together science and religion. Those of his possessions that have survived – the crystal ball used in his 'spiritual conferences' now in the British Museum, or the piece of crystal that he said was given to him by the Archangel Uriel, which resides in London's Science Museum – fail to convey to sceptical modern eyes the essential seriousness of his purpose. It reads now, almost laughably, as fake science, though in its day it would have appeared much more, if not entirely, respectable.

And, indeed, there were those, nearer in time to Dee, who annexed him and his memory to their own cause – the fantasy world of the occult, with its belief in communicating with the dead. Yet in his lifetime there were also others who better esteemed the complexities that Dee embodied. Many Shakespeare scholars, for instance, would point to him as the model for the magician Prospero in *The Tempest*, first performed shortly after Dee's death.

Milton's angels

At the heart of John Dee's fascination with angels was not magic, of course, but rather his sincere belief that they could somehow help him unlock the meaning of the universe that God had created. And it was that similar thirst for all-encompassing understanding, similarly unorthodox in its expression, that inspired the Puritan poet John Milton (1608–74), born in the same year Dee died, to surround himself with angels. His epic *Paradise Lost* is a rival in the detail it provides to anything Aquinas produced in the field of angelology.

Indeed, its appearance in 1663 and subsequent influence highlights a shift in the study of angels. It may have been ever more marginalised in the seventeenth century as new ideas of science and reason challenged the whole God-dominated mindset of Europe, but it continued to inspire individuals who were drawn to the place where theology interacted with nature, politics and culture. Angels remained, as Professor Joad Raymond has written of the period, 'part of the intellectual furniture, and they were a particularly creative part'.[27]

Among those most drawn to them were poets. Some of the reasons are obvious. Angels continued to be a concept that most people understood, even if they didn't accept the claims made for them. As spiritual vocabulary, they were familiar and therefore made for easily grasped metaphors. Yet for those who made them the central figures in their poetic epics the pull was more profound.[28] Angels had captured their imaginations, as surely as they had previous generations of Catholics, Muslims and Jews, not only as characters and plot devices in their literary works, but as a way of understanding.

In *Paradise Lost* Milton allows his angels to edge up closer to humanity than anything that had gone before. They eat freely, and actually do digest. They 'quaff immortality and joy'.[29] They fight and get wounded, and are unashamedly sexual beings, both male and female, who make love to each other, as the Archangel Raphael explains when Adam questions him about angels' intimacies in the Garden of Eden, the setting for much of the work.

> To whom the Angel with a smile that glow'd
> Celestial rosy red, Love's proper hue,
> Answer'd, 'Let it suffice thee that thou know'st
> Us happie, and without Love no happiness.
> Whatever pure thou in the body enjoy'st

(And pure thou wert created) we enjoy
In eminence, and obstacle find none
Of membrane, joint, or limb, exclusive bars:
Easier than Air with Air, if Spirits embrace,
Total they mix, Union of Pure with Pure
Desiring; nor restrain'd conveyance need
As Flesh to mix with Flesh, or Soul with Soul.'[30]

You want Raphael to expand more, to be clearer about precisely what he means. Aquinas would certainly have tried to pin it down further by debate and disputation so as to arrive at a copper-bottomed definition. But that is not what this late flourishing of angelology meant for Milton, so he cuts the exchange short as the sun starts to set over Eden. More intuitive, psychologically astute and imaginative than anyone writing about angels before, Milton believed that human ideals of romantic love were something we share with angels[31] – though he excluded the 'casual fruition' of promiscuity from his definition.

He was – as a Puritan – making a moral point. Romantic love was good. Promiscuity bad. Therefore angels were, he argued, in sex as in other things, an example to us all. This set limits to their kinship with humanity, notably in the detail he offers that when angels make love they do not create children. But, in general, Milton's angels were to a greater extent than ever before mirrors into which the faithful could peer to see themselves, even if it was not an exact likeness that stared back out at them.

Milton was – like Dee – another child prodigy, and had travelled Europe in his youth, meeting leading Renaissance figures. For Milton, the Church of Rome was irredeemably heretical, which all stemmed from its failure to follow scripture. With the victory of the Parliamentarians over the Royalists in the English Civil War, he became a propagandist for the new republic until the death of its Lord Protector, his fellow Puritan, Oliver Cromwell in 1568 precipitated its collapse. The restoration of the monarchy in 1660 landed Milton in prison.

Released through the good offices of friends, and believing the work of the Reformation incomplete, he spent his later years, as he progressively lost his eyesight, writing *Paradise Lost* and the much shorter *Paradise Regained*, published in 1671, three years before his death. In the texts, his ambition is boundless. His epic starts before creation, attempts to describe the history of the universe, and concludes with the end of time.

Aquinas would have approved of the scope, if not the content. Milton, for example, tells of angels as simultaneously creatures of God and characters in a narrative. Prominent among them is Satan, 'Arch Angel ruin'd and th'excess / Of glory obscured'[32] who was 'glorious once . . . till pride and worse Ambition threw me down / Warring in Heav'n with Heav'n's matchless King.'[33] Here is one who was so close to God but still fell. It was ultimately God-given free will that caused Satan's fall, just as it is free will that causes humanity to spurn the promise of salvation. In the fallen angel and his companions, our human faults are reflected but magnified.

At the start of *Paradise Lost*, Milton states his intention as to 'assert Eternal Providence / And justify the ways of God to men'.[34] By his own words, he is another trying through angels to make sense of the universe. How does evil fit into God's creation? Why do we reject God's offer? And how does he then remain so detached as we suffer the consequences of our misuse of free will, seemingly unknowable even to his angels?

All of these Milton explores through the prism of good angels – Raphael has a leading role, Uriel too, though neither part they play is in any way justified by reference to scripture, which Milton claimed as his bedrock. Yet Milton also probes the natural world through the role of the bad angels. Indeed, the note of tragedy in *Paradise Lost* is struck by these fallen creatures, for their tragedy, Milton believes, is humanity's tragedy.

One part of the angels' fall, he argues, is their jealousy at the attention God lavishes on the first man and woman, Adam and Eve. The angels feel displaced. As a result of their break with God, they become no longer our protectors and messengers, the bridge to the divine. Instead, Milton's rogue angels are, in some ways, humankind's rivals – the antithesis of those benign Baroque angels prescribed by Counter-Reformation Catholicism. That is why in Genesis they come to earth and seduce the daughters of men and so lead them away from God. That is their victory over us.

And Satan, the chief fallen angel, is not an object of pity. He is the most beguiling among the cast of *Paradise Lost*, if ultimately fatally flawed.

> So spake the false dissembler unperceiv'd;
> For neither Man nor Angel can discern
> Hypocrisy, the only evil that walks
> Invisible, except to God alone,
> By his permissive will, through Heav'n and Earth.[35]

Angels, good and bad, canonical and not, still had their champions who were asking the difficult questions about them, but these investigators were fewer in number, and their impact on the society around them was diminishing. As the Scientific Revolution of the seventeenth century gave way to the age of Enlightenment in the eighteenth, that process was accelerating.

U

U is for the Archangel **Uriel,** who is to Michael, Gabriel and Raphael what 'the fifth Beatle' (variously Stuart Sutcliffe or Pete Best) is to John, Paul, George and Ringo. Though often to be found listed alongside the other three in various Christian texts that have subsequently been excluded from the canon – notably the Second Book of Esdras/Ezra, where he is sent from heaven to the prophet Ezra – Uriel enjoys none of their renown, save when traditional Christian formulations (for example, of the Four Cardinal Points or the Four Winds) require one more name for a quorum. In some traditions in Christianity, though, Uriel is credited with rescuing the infant John the Baptist and his mother Elizabeth from the slaughter of all small children ordered by King Herod, and with then carrying the mother and child to safety in Egypt to reunite them with Mary, Joseph and the baby Jesus, a moment captured by Leonardo da Vinci in his *Virgin of the Rocks*.

V

V is for **Victor**, guardian angel to Saint Patrick, who brought Christianity to the Irish in the fifth century. It was not a name that Patrick gave the figure 'composed of air' who appeared to him regularly throughout his life (including to dry his tears on Croagh Patrick, the mountain where the saint was tempted by the devil), but one announced by Victor himself as the two 'conversed familiarly, even as with a friend', as Patrick's twelfth-century biographer, the Cistercian monk Jocelyn, puts it. When Victor comes to the rescue on Croagh Patrick, he is accompanied by 'snow-white birds'.

The Enlightenment – Moving to the Margins

'Cherish pity, lest you drive an angel from your door.'
William Blake, 'Holy Thursday' (1789)[1]

In November 1619, the young René Descartes – later to be hailed as 'the father of modern Western philosophy', and a key figure in the Scientific Revolution of the seventeenth century – encountered 'the Angel of Truth'. It was evening, in an overheated room in Neuburg, a town on the River Danube in Bavaria, where he was working as a mercenary. The large stove, relentlessly pushing up the thermometer, is important to the story, whoever is telling it, because its warmth lulls twenty-three-year-old Descartes to sleep.

He has three dramatic dreams. In the first he is spun around by a whirlwind and surrounded by ghosts, all the time terrified by the sensation of falling. In the second, it is all thunderclaps and sparks flying round the room. In the third, the most contemplative of this particular trinity, is an out-of-body experience where he watches himself as he is moved to open at random a collection of poetry wherein his eyes fell upon the line, 'what path in life shall I take?' At that point, a stranger – the Angel of Truth – appears and promises to show him the answer, but then promptly disappears.

No mention of wings, or any of the other typical distinguishing features, but angel is the word that Descartes used of this figure, according to his first biographer Adrien Ballet, writing forty years after the philosopher's death.[2] Straight afterwards Descartes began to pray and set about planning a sackcloth-and-ashes pilgrimage in order to find the purpose in his life. Before these preparations came to fruition, however, he decided that the angel's real intention was to guide him towards the development of a whole new philosophy – what ultimately became known as a 'Cartesian' way in pursuit of wisdom and truth in science, where the wheat is separated from the chaff, and the speculative realms of astrology, necromancy and alchemy from the properly scientifically based disciplines of astrology, chemistry and physics. By these latter, Descartes believed, like many before him, the mind of God might ultimately be known.

There was nothing so very unusual about this angelic visitation by the standards of the times. Others had set themselves the same goal of harnessing together religion and science when inspired by angels. And what we know of Descartes' family background suggests he would have known of this tradition. He came from a piously Catholic French family, was educated – including in the sciences – by Jesuits, to whom he remained devoted all through his life,[3] and went to his death as a believer. Why wouldn't he make mention of an angel?

Yet the very suggestion sits uncomfortably with his subsequent reputation, not least among the *philosophes* of the eighteenth-century Enlightenment. They warmly embraced the Scientific Revolution and its leading lights, including Descartes, as they ratcheted up the debate to the point where science and religion found themselves at loggerheads. Many of Descartes' later admirers have preferred to dismiss accounts of his angel, pointing out that the Adrien Ballet who penned the 1691 biography was *Father* Adrien Ballet, a priest who also wrote lives of saints, and was therefore an unreliable witness. Others prefer to treat the angel as either a momentary aberration or a metaphor for something more palatable to the age of science. 'Descartes' overheated mind caught fire [in the stuffy room in Neuburg] and provided answers to tremendous problems that had been taxing him for weeks,' wrote Philip Davis and Reuben Hirsh in 2005 in *Descartes' Dream: The World According to Mathematics*.[4] 'He was possessed by a Genius, and the answers were revealed in a dazzling, unendurable light.'

Curiously, though, the language of angelic visitation is still employed here. Others have gone further, posthumously diagnosing the whole 'angel episode' as a case of Episodic Cranial Sensory Shock, also known as Exploding Head Syndrome. This occurs when someone, on the cusp of waking and sleeping, experiences loud, jarring and often frightening sounds that are not real.[5]

What is not disputed, however, is that this vision/aberration/ metaphorical jolt caused Descartes to abandon soldiering in favour of the scholarly study of mathematics, philosophy and science, where his aim became to 'lay the foundations of a new method of understanding and a new and marvellous science'.[6] He set to work on a treatise that he called 'Rules for the Direction of the Mind', which though later abandoned went on to become his four 'rules of thought' in his celebrated 1643 *Discours de la Methode*. The first – and most influential – of these rules was 'never to accept anything for true which I did not clearly know to be such . . . to comprise nothing more in my judgment than what was presented to my mind so clearly and distinctly as to exclude all ground of doubt'.

Here is one of the starting points for that now all-consuming demand for 'proof' as the prerequisite of anything being taken seriously in our modern world. The best-known line from the *Discours* – '*cognito ergo sum*' ('I think therefore I am') – continues to be quoted to defend the proof-based approach to metaphysical questions to this day. There is, then, a certain irony in one of the sparks for the contemporary marginalisation of religion having been an angel, even if, admittedly, one that was more blinding flash of light than the bewinged, benign Gabriel who came to talk to Mary at the dawn of Christianity, or later (as

Jibr'il) squeezed the breath out of Muhammad in a cave near the summit of Mount Hira on the 'Night of Destiny', the birth of Islam. While Christians and Muslims went on to make these initiating angels central to the practice of their beliefs, Descartes and those who followed his scientific lead largely marginalised any further examination of the Angel of Truth from the faith they came to profess in science. And, indeed, every other angel, too. When it came to categorisation, angels were judged to belong with astrology, necromancy and alchemy rather than with astronomy, chemistry and physics – though Descartes himself, in highlighting the divide between the material from the spiritual, saw value in both sides of that particular coin.[7]

In his lifetime, he found that others were reluctant to embrace the broad vision he promoted that potentially combined (good) science and (good) religion. If the scientific community wrote off angels, the Inquisition, brutal enforcers of orthodoxy within Catholicism at the time, were intolerant of those seeking any sort of accommodation. In 1633 they condemned Descartes' contemporary, Galileo Galilei, for reporting his astronomical observations that the earth revolved around the sun, and not vice versa, as it was immoveable Catholic doctrine. To escape a similar fate in his own faithful pursuit of truth, Descartes lived for many years in the Protestant Netherlands, and then later under the patronage of Lutheran Sweden's Queen Cristina (though, after his death in 1650, she abdicated her throne and became a Catholic).

The chasm between religion and science was now impossible to ignore, though Descartes and others were still trying to bridge it. His near contemporary, fellow Frenchman, mathematician, true believer in the 'scientific method' as well as questioning Catholic, Blaise Pascal (1623–62), bemoaned in his *Pensées* 'the eternal silence' that had fallen in 'these infinite spaces' of the universe, and which filled him with 'dread'.[8] Among those who had gone quiet, and those whom he missed, were the angels.

A *new kind of light*

The word enlightenment denotes a letting in of light, and for many – as the seventeenth century's exploration of the new world of science segued into the eighteenth-century Enlightenment – that light was directed onto the darkness and superstition of religion so as to reveal its flaws. The leading luminaries, the French *philosophes*, championed Enlightenment values in their writings and public pronouncements, disdaining the churches as imposing a mental strait-jacket on human potential. Faith, they claimed, was no match for reason, which was for them the primary source of authority. Connected with this primacy of reason were notions of liberty, of the individual, of tolerance and of the separation of Church and State. It wasn't a wholesale rejection of religious ideas – though in practice that is often what it ended up amounting to – but rather a demand that they be put under the same spotlight as everything else and tested by Enlightenment methods. And so, the historical accuracy of the scriptures was challenged, and the scientific logic (or lack of logic) in talking of miracles and the resurrection of Jesus examined.

In the process, even those writers who had lately taken angels seriously were dismissed. *Paradise Lost* was a 'disgusting fantasy', wrote the leading *philosophe*, Voltaire (1694–1778), in his *Essay on the Manners and Spirit of Nations* of 1756, as he applied the new thinking to take a fresh look at European history and culture. While Jesuit-educated Voltaire was prepared to countenance a creator God who had set everything in motion, thereafter he dismissed Aquinas's notion of a chain that linked heaven and earth, angels with humans, arguing that what came next was all down to humankind, for better or for worse. He left no room for intervening angels.

The Catholic Church, inevitably, vigorously condemned any such suggestion, but the methods it adopted to repel the attack demonstrated that, for all the vim it had shown in the

Counter-Reformation fight back, it had learnt little. Simply outlawing the great Enlightenment texts – including the most influential, the thirty-five-volume *Encyclopedie* compiled on the basis of reason and logic by chief editor Denis Diderot (1713–84) and others – did not stop the ideas they contained being circulated. Quite the opposite. It enhanced their influence.

On his deathbed, Diderot – raised Catholic and at one time even considering becoming a priest before he embraced atheism – is said to have bequeathed his Enlightenment confrères a new rallying cry as they took forward their challenge to the Church–State established order of Europe: 'the first step toward philosophy is incredulity'. It became a potent slogan for those who wished to dispel the superstition (in their terms) of religion, and who were fundamentally suspicious of any instruments of control other than reason. Yet enduringly popular and influential though Enlightenment beliefs did indeed become, especially in the age of the French Revolution of 1789, with its demands of 'liberty, equality and fraternity' and its attempted abolition of Catholicism, an older God-centred way of understanding the world was not so easily wiped away.

In an age of still-widespread illiteracy, the full power of the *Encyclopedie* was going to take at least a few generations to filter down. In the meantime, appeals to the god of reason went largely unheard by those who continued to be more drawn to God's angels – as a prop in bringing sustenance to lives of hard toil, order to the fragile, war-torn, topsy-turvy revolutionary world in which they lived, and a sense of belonging to something larger than themselves in an age of turmoil, challenge and fragmentation. Among those churchmen who believed that the best way to challenge the new spirit abroad of rational enquiry was to speak with greater fervour and plain language about the scriptures, angels remained a favourite subject.

It was, granted, an uphill fight, with the world made more hostile still by some of the fruits of Enlightenment values – for example, the rise of a free press that took an anti-church stance, or the promotion of open debate in increasingly state-controlled (rather than church-operated) schools and universities. Yet it was also one that many articulate, charismatic and driven believers took up, and with significant success. For as well as Voltaire, Diderot and their admirers, this was also the age of the Wesley brothers – John and Charles – and of their Methodism, which attracted large numbers of converts from other parts of Christianity, notably among the working classes in both urban and rural areas, with its scripture-based preaching coupled with a robust anti-Establishment, anti-clerical bias, plus an ethos of hard work, clean living and rousing hymns, many penned by Charles. These included 'Hark! The Herald Angels Sing' and 'Come, O Thou Traveller Unknown', an account of Jacob and the angel at the River Jabbok that is often referred to by chapel-goers as 'Wrestling Jacob'.

His brother, John, published three significant sermons on the subject of angels – the first, early in his career, on guardian angels, delivered on the Feast of Saint Michael and All Angels in September 1726, and then a pair, in 1783, on angels and demons and their role in the lives of believers. The good angels, Wesley suggested to his followers, taking an already tried and trusted line, were role models. 'We may imitate them in all holiness; suiting our lives to the prayer our Lord himself has taught us; labouring to do his will on earth, as angels do it in heaven.'[9]

The eighteenth and nineteenth centuries witnessed, too, the rise of a wider Non-Conformism that again saw powerful preachers draw congregations, especially from among those who felt most downtrodden in a world that was fast becoming unrecognisable thanks to industrialisation and urbanisation. Among Non-Conformity's earliest advocates was Isaac Watts (1674–1748), who encouraged his listeners to place their trust not in reason, logic, science or talk of human progress, but instead in the age-old promise of heaven, where the angels waited to welcome the faithful into eternal life with God. In his 1722 sermon 'Death and Heaven; or the Last Enemy Conquered and Separate Spirits Made Perfect' – which went into sixteen printed editions – Watts painted paradise as where 'angels are so variously and delightfully employed in the service of God, in his several known and unknown worlds'.[10]

There was a shift of emphasis in such preaching about angels. It was no longer a question of them descending to earth to act as guardians or assist the God-fearing in the emotional traumas of life, as had been the Renaissance way. Now angels were glimpsed on the high ground of heaven and became a focus for the aspiration to celestial afterlife that would reward those who had suffered hardships in this world. Angels were no longer sustaining the oppressed in their lives, but rather encouraging them to be content with their lot here on earth by redirecting their hopes for justice to the next life.

Swedenborg's angels

Few had more to say on the subject of heaven than Emanuel Swedenborg (1668–1772), one of only a handful of post-Reformation thinkers to develop the sort of big, elaborate and all-encompassing worldview of angels that had once been so commonplace. Swedenborg was travelling in the opposite direction from Descartes, whom he greatly admired,[11] the first half of his life having been dedicated to science, engineering and his family mining business, where he achieved great distinction, and then the second almost exclusively to spiritual and mystical matters, where he attracted a large and loyal following.

Swedenborg came from a wealthy background, with royal connections. The son of a Swedish Lutheran bishop, as a young man he had been caught up by the Scientific Revolution and its possibilities, designing canal locks and his country's first salt works. Intriguingly, among other projects he worked on in this period was a flying machine, a preface in his case (as with Leonardo da Vinci[12]) to taking a special interest in the flight of angels. It was only when his attention shifted on to the science of biology that Swedenborg's life fundamentally changed. What started with a search to understand the body's workings drew him into philosophical reflections about the nature of the soul. As he read and reread the scriptures, he resolved to dedicate himself, with a scientist's precision, to understanding the physical reality of what the sacred texts promised in eternity.

This quest, however, was taken up with much more than reading about heaven. Swedenborg the rational scientist started to experience angel-strewn visions of paradise, which he recorded in his eight-volume *Arcana Caelestia* ('Heavenly Mysteries'), published in Latin between 1749 and 1756 throughout northern Europe, and then in his *Heaven and Hell* of 1758. His writings remain robustly popular to this day, with the London-based Swedenborg Society, an educational charity boasting a worldwide membership.

In his visions, Swedenborg conversed with heaven's angelic inhabitants, but in August of 1744, he reported seeing Jesus, who gave him instructions on the urgent need to reform Christianity, and a personal mandate to lead that reform. Among the tools provided from on high to carry out this daunting task, Swedenborg claimed to have the ability to use Jacob's ladder and to pass, angel-like, between heaven and earth.

If that wasn't startling enough, he made an even more earth-shattering revelation on the basis of his conversations with those in heaven. The Day of Judgement, he said, the Second Coming of Jesus long promised and long awaited by Christianity, had already happened. It had taken place, he said, in 1747, at a point halfway between heaven and earth. The promised New Jerusalem – also the title of the book in which he revealed this – was to be a rolling programme of spiritual renewal rather than the material return of God's son to earth promised in Jewish literature and the apocalyptic Book of Revelation. That version had had to be abandoned, he explained, because Christianity had strayed so far from what God the Father had intended for it.

The picture Swedenborg painted of heaven was more human than anything yet proposed. It was essentially a cleaned-up earth, where all that was virtuous in this life carried on into the next, but all that blunted that virtue was discarded. He was the first to state quite so plainly that, in death, humans who have been virtuous and God-fearing would become angels. Previous accounts had imagined the souls of the faithful departed existing in heaven side by side with angels. Now the two were as one.

And it was not a question of 'becoming' an angel once elevated in death to heaven, but rather of those who made it there returning to their essential angelic state, Swedenborg suggested. Life on earth was, he said, but a short chapter in an angel's existence. 'If a person is regenerated [listens to the word of God], he is as regards his internal man [his spirit] in heaven, and therefore is an angel among angels, and after death [of his physical body] he comes to join them.'[13]

In heaven, therefore, the internal and the external combine, so the dead, as angels, continue to think, to move, to eat and to sleep – even though their earthly bodies have been left behind. Those who have been happily married in life, Swedenborg wrote in 1768 in *Conjugal Love*, will be reunited in death, while those who have endured loveless or faithless pairings will be allocated a new partner. His angels live not on clouds, as had previously been imagined by artists, but in houses:

> precisely like abodes on earth, but more beautiful. In them are chambers, parlours and bedrooms in great number; there are also courts and there are gardens and flowerbeds and lawns around about. Where they live together, their houses are near each other, arranged one next to the other in the form of a city, with avenues, streets and public squares, exactly like cities on earth.[14]

Swedenborg's heaven was an extension of human desires. In the simplest of terms, he was telling those attracted by angels that their guardian was not something outside of them, but part of their very being, so much so that when they returned to heaven, they would also return to the angelic state. All accounts testify that Swedenborg was a sincere man, and believed passionately in the truth of what he had seen in his visions, but still he was telling those who heard him what they wanted to hear about the afterlife, namely that it was eternal reunion with loved ones, in a familiar but benign setting.

There was little to dislike, but Swedenborg himself highlighted some of the challenges. Principal among them was adaptation – how to let go of human vanities and 'self-love' when becoming an angel again. Martin Luther, he reported back from a heavenly brush with the great reformer, was finding life in heaven as an angel tough going because he was so puffed up with pride and self-regard.[15] And, of course, the *real* obstacle remained gaining re-entry to heaven. For Swedenborg was clear that it was by no means guaranteed. First, there was judgement based on the life you had lived on earth, and some would be condemned to hell, a place which Swedenborg also described in spine-chilling detail.

But it is Swedenborg's vision of heaven that dominates his writing. If the initial stages of paradise are a better version of earth, then the higher he climbs, the more vague and light-infused his descriptions become. In those early 'spiritual' levels, there are even churches in heaven to attend, as if God himself remains far away. Once the dead/spirits/angels have ascended further upwards towards 'celestial' heaven, however, all material matters give way and Swedenborg's vision switches to something more mystical as it charts a return to a state of eternal innocence and purity that is increasingly (as in Dante's *Paradiso*) beyond Swedenborg's powers to describe.

The influence of his writings in his lifetime was widespread, though he established nothing so institutional as a church. Instead

– largely in Sweden, the Netherlands and Britain – reading groups assembled to study his books, reflect on his visions, and consider the ideas that lay behind them of the connections (or 'correspondences') between the physical world and the spiritual world.

One of Swedenborg's major contributions to the story of angels arguably lies in how many of his ideas inspired those who came after him. Those who acknowledged a debt include August Strindberg, Charles Baudelaire, Honoré de Balzac and Jorge Luis Borges. Swedenborg kept a careful diary of his dreams, where his extensive analysis of their symbolism predates the work of Sigmund Freud and Carl Jung by over a century, including his identification of a 'half-dream' world.

Into that equation of influences, too, should be added those on whom his works had a more indirect effect, such as popular nineteenth-century writers like Elizabeth Stuart Phelps, an American Calvinist minister's daughter whose *The Gates Ajar*, published in 1868, described a reassuring heaven of home-cooking, reunion with relatives, singing around a piano and gingham tablecloths. It was one of the bestselling books of its era, notching up 180,000 copies on both sides of the Atlantic.[16]

To some, though, Swedenborg's change of direction from science to religion halfway through his life negated any legacy. The anti-clerical Victor Hugo, in his 1862 novel *Les Miserables*, dismisses him as a 'very great man' who 'slipped into insanity'. Others felt his angels – in their very evident humanity – to be too literal, and therefore insufficiently transcendent.[17] And when psychics took up Swedenborg and claimed him as a fellow clairvoyant, able to communicate with 'the other side', it distorted his wider message about death, judgement and the afterlife.

When challenged directly to prove he had been to heaven and back, Swedenborg was often asked why he didn't just stay there given how wonderful he made it sound. His usual response was to offer a detailed prediction of the circumstances of his own death, when he would finally return to the angelic state. He even laid down the date – 29 March 1772. On the appointed day, just as he had said, a stroke felled him. It was one way, some have argued, to demonstrate that he had indeed come to know the mind of God.

Blake's vision of eternity

Another of those significantly influenced by Swedenborg was William Blake (1757–1827[18]). It used to be said that this artist, poet, engraver and visionary had been brought up by Swedenborgian parents. This has more recently been shown to be a myth; his background was solidly Non-Conformist and so he grew up knowing his Bible intimately. Blake did, though, possess three books by Swedenborg, all complete with notes and comments in the margins. In 1789, moreover, Blake and his wife Catherine attended a Swedenborgian gathering in London, though later he was to turn against Swedenborg, even to the point of sending up some of his claims in *The Marriage of Heaven and Hell* (1793).[19] It was something of an on–off relationship. As he grew old, Blake changed his mind once again, now showing renewed sympathy for the man he once so admired. In his epic illustrated poem *Milton*, completed in 1810, Blake includes on the lips of one of his characters the line: 'O Swedenborg! strongest of men, the Samson shorn by the churches!'[20]

Trying to identify all the influences that came together to create Blake's angels, which are everywhere in his life, his poetry and his art, is reductive. Yes, there are elements in his celestial visions of Swedenborg, an echo too of Milton's prophetic voice, not to mention a strong resonance of Michelangelo in the powerful physique of his *Angel of the Revelation* (1803–5), a colossus clothed in cloud, his face radiating sunlight and his feet and ankles pillars of fire. But Blake's free-ranging imagination, and the techniques he employed to give expression to it, were all his own. If some of his angels were taken from the scriptures, or mythology, others were uniquely his own complex creatures, as far removed from humankind as Swedenborg's were close and cosy. They are as impossible to grasp fully, as are the ever-expanding worlds Blake created in verse and imagery from the mystical ideas that germinated inside his own head, the one place where he truly lived.

Though his background was Christian, the extraordinary Blake fashioned his own church, his own Jesus as the embodiment of humanity, and his own God, whom he named Urizen: both the traditional bearded old, white man and a malign, unlovely and vengeful creature, sometimes depicted with nets with which he ensnared believers' lives – a reference to the rules and regulations of institutional religion. Blake was as hostile to institutional religion as were the French *philosophes* and the English-born, American-raised radical Tom Paine (1737–1809), whose *Rights of Man* (1791) Blake admired, and with whom he had a friendship.

He did not, though, dismiss religion entirely. Instead he sought alone to discover its true potential and power to change the world; for example, to banish the destitution, prostitution and child labour he saw on the streets of London where he himself lived, mostly in poverty.[21] Blake was, moreover, appalled by the damage being done to ordinary lives by the Industrial Revolution – the 'dark Satanic mills' he refers to in his preface to *Milton*, later set to music in 'Jerusalem'. His response was, via his angels, to reintroduce the texture of the spiritual within what he saw as the increasingly tattered fabric of material reality. In his first, illustrated poetic work, 1794's *Songs of Innocence and of Experience*, he describes the life of pain and peril of a young chimney sweep, who is then liberated by an angel.

> And by came an Angel who had a bright key,
> And he opened the coffins & set them all free;
> Then down a green plain, leaping, laughing they run,
> And wash in a river and shine in the Sun.

Then naked & white, all their bags left behind,
They rise upon clouds, and sport in the wind.
And the Angel told Tom, if he'd be a good boy,
He'd have God for his father & never want joy.

And so Tom awoke; and we rose in the dark
And got with our bags & our brushes to work.
Though the morning was cold, Tom was happy & warm;
So if all do their duty, they need not fear harm.[22]

The angel – like much in Blake – defies easy interpretation. He is not only liberator of the afflicted, but also can be read as encouraging those who suffer exploitation to accept their lot and pin their hopes on heaven. What is indisputable, though, is that – like Milton, Descartes and Swedenborg before him – Blake was transporting angels outside the realm of organised religion. And simultaneously being transported by them. 'I am under the direction', he wrote on 10 January 1803, 'of Messengers from Heaven, daily and nightly. But the nature of such things is not, as some suppose, without trouble or care. [That could have been a dig at Swedenborg.] Temptations are on the right hand and on the left. Behind the sea of time and space roars and follows swiftly . . . he who keeps not right onwards is lost.'[23]

Blake was not a conformist in any sense. What he created did not fit easily into any artistic school or movement. Largely, he shunned collaborators and chose to live his life in his own way, turning his back on the artistic establishment as much as it turned its back on him and his work, which it found hard to understand. In his wider social activism, too, he was once charged with sedition but then acquitted. He was, in short, a rebel, and so was naturally attracted to the story of the rebel angels, depicting them giving as good as they got in their battle with the good angels. He endowed Satan (in his illustrations for Milton's *Paradise Lost*) with a striking majesty and heroism.

Angels, though, were not just for Blake a means of providing the world around him with an alternative imagined narrative. They had also been his companions from earliest days. Even before he could have articulated the idea, he saw no absolute physical barrier between the realm of the living and the realm of the dead.

He had started seeing angels when he was eight. He was walking on Peckham Rye, a common in south London, near his family home, when he spotted 'a tree filled with angels, bright angelic wings bespangling every bough like stars'. When he got home, he told his parents what he had seen, and only escaped his hosier father's belt for telling lies through his mother's intervention. On another occasion, when still a child, watching haymakers at work, he saw angels walking among them.[24] And when, for three short years from 1800 onwards, he and his wife moved out of London (for the only time in his life) to the village of Felpham in the Sussex countryside, he reported that there were angels everywhere. 'Heaven opens here on all sides her golden Gates; her windows are not obstructed by vapours; voices of Celestial inhabitants are more distinctly heard, & their forms more distinctly seen.'[25]

Again, the challenge is to interpret what he meant. Was his talk of angels a metaphor for his intuition that the countryside was spared the sufferings of the city; that it was somehow blessed? Or did he believe himself to see in nature the signs of God's presence? Or both? Certainly what was invisible to others in the world around them was often all too visible to Blake. 'Like some other great poets,' writes Harold Bloom, '[Blake] has the power to awaken his readers to an implicit answering power, to a previously unfelt sense of possibilities for the self.'[26] Blake himself provided one answer to the questions raised by his invocation of angels when he defined his 'great task' in his 1834 *Jerusalem: The Emanation of the Giant Albion*, the last and longest of his prophetic books. It was 'to open the Eternal Worlds, to open the immortal Eyes / Of Man inwards into the Worlds of Thought: into Eternity'.[27]

To add to the list of challenges that Blake offered to the world around him, he was also fierce in rejecting the increasingly popular scientific orthodoxy that discarded anything that could not be proved to be real – including, of course, angels. In surviving notes to accompany a now-lost 1808 artwork, *A Vision of Last Judgement*, he wrote:

> when the sun rises, do you not see a round disc of fire somewhat like a guinea! Oh! no, no! I see an innumerable company of the heavenly host crying 'Holy, holy, holy is the Lord God Almighty!' I question not my corporeal eye any more than I would question a window concerning a sight. I look through it, and not with it.[28]

Newman's blessed servants of God

If William Blake began the 1800s with a boundless, intense and innovative vision of angels, their treatment in the remaining decades of the nineteenth century was, for the most part, much more traditional, bordering at times on the sentimental. Not, it should be noted, that many in that century would necessarily have been aware of William Blake's legacy. An isolated figure in life, in death he became a neglected one. In his 1863 biography, Alexander Gilchrist reflected that Blake 'neither wrote nor drew for the many, hardly for work'y-day men at all, rather for children and angels; himself "a divine child", whose playthings were sun, moon, and stars, the heavens and the earth'.[29] Wider appreciation of his genius, and of the challenge to think afresh intrinsic to his work, only came in the twentieth century. It took until 1925 for a complete illustrated collection of his work to be made widely available.

Meanwhile, among those 'work'y-day men' – and women – perceptions of angels changed little throughout the nineteenth century. If they were devout church-goers, as many remained, in both the Catholic and Reformed traditions, then angels continued to be a familiar presence in rituals, figures in the stories they heard from the pulpit, and therefore one means by which they might conceive of God's presence in their world, most likely as guardians sent down from heaven to protect them in times of crisis.

In Catholicism, there was in the mid-1800s another great surge of enthusiasm for the Virgin Mary. In 1858, a sickly fourteen-year-old peasant girl, Bernadette Soubirous, reported seeing seventeen apparitions of Christ's mother near the rural French town of Lourdes, in the foothills of the Pyrenees. At first, the church authorities treated her claims with scepticism, but pilgrims flocked to the spot and, eventually, it was granted official status as a Marian shrine. As before, the increased focus on Mary necessarily also directed the spotlight back onto the Archangel Gabriel, who brought her the first news of the Christ child she was expecting, and more generally onto her role as 'Queen of Angels'. In Mary Walsh's 1871 Marian hymn 'Bring Flowers to the Rarest', in its day immensely popular, not least in convent schools, but now heard less often, the chorus hammers home over and again that celestial connection: 'O Mary! We crown thee with blossoms today / Queen of the Angels, Queen of the May.'

Among Anglicans, the Oxford Movement brought renewed interest in the Catholic way of doing things that had been lost since the Reformation. It gave rise in England's Reformed state Church to a sizeable Anglo-Catholic wing, often known as High Church. It mirrored many Roman habits, including an enthusiasm for Mary and for angels. John Henry Newman (1801–90), poet, theologian and orator, was one of the Oxford Movement's leading lights in the 1830s, but went one step further than most of his colleagues in 1845 when he converted to Rome, later being named by the pope as a cardinal.

In one of his most reproduced sermons, 'The Powers of Nature', delivered on the Feast of Saint Michael and All Angels,

29 September 1831, Newman looked to the past to argue that the medieval Catholic focus on angels, gradually eclipsed thereafter, could still have relevance in the daily lives of his congregation. These 'Blessed Servants of God', he began, 'who have never tasted of sin; [and] who are among us, though unseen, ever serving God joyfully on earth as well as in heaven', may in the past have been paid 'excessive honour' in a Church that 'honoured them so perversely as to forget the supreme worship due to Almighty God'. Such idolatry, Newman contended, was 'the sin of a dark age'. Yet, he continued, 'the sin of what is called our educated age . . . is just the reverse . . . to ascribe all we see around us, not to their [angelic] agency, but to certain assumed laws of nature. This, I say, is likely to be our sin . . . of resting in things seen, and forgetting unseen things, and our ignorance about them.'[30]

In his spiritual biography *Apologia Pro Vita Sua*, published in 1864 once he was within Catholic ranks, Newman returned once more to that 1831 sermon on angels, delivered while he was still an Anglican. He quoted in particular the section where – like the medieval angelologists before him – he ascribes to the heavenly host the role of being the invisible hand behind the universe.

> Every breath of air and ray of light and heat, every beautiful prospect, is, as it were, the skirts of their garments, the waving of the robes of those whose faces see God in heaven. And I put it to any one, whether it is not as philosophical, and as full of intellectual enjoyment, to refer the movements of the natural world to them, as to attempt to explain them by certain theories of science; useful as these theories certainly are for particular purposes, and capable (in subordination to that higher view) of a religious application.[31]

It is more poetry than anything the nineteenth century would recognise as science, but the timing of Newman's reiteration of this passage in *Apologia Pro Vita Sua*, championing a spiritual dimension to the natural world, is significant. Five years earlier, Charles Darwin had published his landmark *On the Origin of Species*, with its game-changing advocacy of natural selection and the survival of the fittest. It caused great controversy in the churches, where it was feared that evolutionary biology left little enough room for a creator God, and none at all for angels to control rivers, winds and the movement of the planets.

Newman's own angelology, by contrast, belonged to an earlier age. Its significance lies more in his resonant manner of expressing what he saw as eternal truths – even in the face of growing scepticism and the advance of god-free science – than in the novelty of the ideas that his well-chosen words conveyed. *The Dream of Gerontius*, his popular 1865 poem about a dying Everyman, explores the unseen world of afterlife. Before he can take his place in heaven, Gerontius is guided by a guardian angel to be cleansed in purgatory. It was a narrative that had a particular resonance in the Victorian age, with its unusually strong focus on death and the etiquette of mourning.

Later set to music in seven parts in 1900 by Edward Elgar, *The Dream of Gerontius* captures too the undiminished appeal of the guardian angel – a male in Newman's text, but a part given to a woman to sing by Elgar. As Gerontius approaches death, he is united with the angel who, unseen, has been watching over him all his life, but who now can finally reveal itself and take Gerontius home to his creator.

> My Father gave in charge to me
> This child of earth
> E'en from its birth,
> To serve and save,
> Alleluia,
> And saved is he.[32]

Pre-Raphaelite escapism

Newman's championing of traditional angels was shared by his contemporaries the Pre-Raphaelite Brotherhood, a group of English painters, poets and critics founded in 1848 by Dante Gabriel Rossetti, William Holman Hunt and John Everett Millais, and later, in its various branches, to include the critic John Ruskin and Edward Burne-Jones (1833–98). The latter is of particular significance, since it is his angels, floating ethereally in the stained-glass windows of many an English church of the period (commissions often undertaken with William Morris, the textile designer, poet and socialist), that continue to feature prominently on our Christmas cards.

The Pre-Raphaelites wanted, as the name suggests, to return to the artistic values of the period before Raphael; that is, to late medieval and early Renaissance ideals. Among their agreed beliefs – at least initially, before they splintered – was a passion for the study of nature, and a fascination with the combination of creative and spiritual inspiration. It was an agenda that led them inexorably to the subject of angels.

An idealisation and dream-like quality characterise many Pre-Raphaelite works, so the Pre-Raphaelite angel is usually to be seen playing a musical instrument, eyes gazing into the far distance. In John Melhuish Strudwick's 1895 portrait of *Saint Cecilia*, she is at the piano as an enraptured angel looks on. Both figures are given haloes, the symbolism lost since the days of Fra Angelico now restored.

The painting hangs in Sudley House, the perfectly preserved home of a wealthy Victorian merchant in Liverpool. It is a city that boomed in the Victorian era as the self-styled 'Port of Empire', the thriving commercial hub of the extensive and far-flung British colonies. The fortunes that paid for such Pre-Raphaelite works of purity and perfection were amassed on the backs of the abject poverty and misery that existed a stone's throw away from Sudley House in Liverpool's docklands. There was, then, a note of domestic escapism to be found in such works of heavenly perfection, collected avidly by wealthy patrons whose fortunes had been made out of the human suffering outside their front doors.

The Victorian Pre-Raphaelites' ethereal angels broke with tradition by being female – as in Edward Burne-Jones's Angel Playing a Flageolet *of 1878.*

Burne-Jones's *Angel Playing a Flageolet* from 1878 is also on display in Sudley House, the rich golds and reds of drapery behind the female figure with elaborate wings who plays this French flute suggesting the extreme sumptuousness of the welcome that awaits the God-fearing in heaven. But it is Evelyn de Morgan, a rare sister among the Pre-Raphaelite Brotherhood, who conveys the movement's all-consuming fascination with angels in her *c.*1887 *Aurora Triumphans*. The subject is the Roman goddess of the dawn, waking from her reveries, but – draped in roses – she is relegated to one small corner of the painting. The rest of it is taken up with three huge angels in gold tunics, with even bigger red wings, who summon Aurora by the blasts they give from their trumpets.

Evelyn de Morgan was a rare sister in the Pre-Raphaelite Brotherhood, but she shared the group's fascination with angels in her c.1887 Aurora Triumphans.

All three works are typical of the Pre-Raphaelite penchant for a backward-looking notion of angels, something recovered from the medieval period to stand for a spirituality rooted in nature that had been lost in the brutal Victorian commercial world. Yet that is not the whole story of the Pre-Raphaelite angels. In some regards, they also carry the story of angels forward. One tradition they did not honour was that angels should be male or androgynous. Pre-Raphaelite angels were, for the most part, unmistakably female and, to boot, rejected the conventions of the past whereby angels, as creatures of light and goodness, were blond, pale or golden. Many of Burne-Jones's stained-glass angels have abundant long dark hair, well-formed lips and a lightly worn sensuality.

The dominant note, though, in Pre-Raphaelite angels is one of sentimentality. It fits neatly with another staple of the Victorian age – its penchant for child angels. Chubby cherubim, with children's bodies but adult faces, had become popular in Renaissance, Baroque and Rococo art, drawing on the *putti* and *spiritelli* of classical Rome and Greece. So the connection between children's innocence and cherubim was therefore long established, but the Victorians made a cult of it. Just as the Romans had mourned their dead children by adorning their stone coffins with *putti*, the Victorians would weep over theirs in the new model graveyards they developed from the 1830s onwards at graves that were decorated with cherubic angels.

And it wasn't only *dead* children who became angels. The pioneering British photographer Julia Margaret Cameron made her reputation in the 1860s and 1870s in part by taking bored, restless, fidgety children of prosperous Victorian parents and turning them – by use of soft lighting, faraway looks, untied hair and loose white gowns – into angelic creatures.[33] There was, again, that element of escapism. While mothers and fathers sought Cameron's services to capture perfect images of their offspring, they and others tolerated and indeed profited by the labour of other people's children. And for every Charles Dickens, highlighting the pain of blighted young lives by recounting the misery of David Copperfield or Oliver Twist, there was a Favell Lee Mortimer.

Her 1833 *The Peep of Day* sold over half a million copies, was translated into thirty-seven languages and was part of a new industry of children's books and associated imagery, strongly tinged with religious and moral messages. In its pages, she tackled for her young readers – and for their parents – the reality of child mortality, but smoothed the rough edges with talk of angels.

> When a little child, who loves God, falls sick, and is going to die, God says to the angels, 'Go and fetch that little child's soul up to heaven.' Then the angels fly down, the little darling shuts its eye, it lays its head on its mother's bosom, its breath stops. The child is dead. Where is its soul? The angels are carrying it up to heaven. How happy the child is now! Its pain is over; it is grown quite good; it is bright like an angel. It holds a harp in its hand, and begins to sing a sweet song of praise to God. Its little body is put into a grave, and turns into dust. One day God will make its body alive again.[34]

There was, doubtless, comfort in such saccharine sentiments. Giving succour to individuals in need has always been part of the brief of angels. In the second decade of the twentieth century, popular demand for the protection and guardianship of angels was to be seen on an unprecedented scale.

W

W is for **Wormwood**, the junior demon, or fallen angel, in C.S. Lewis's 1942 novel *The Screwtape Letters*. He receives letters from his uncle, a more senior demon in the hierarchy of hell, instructing him on how to be more successful in wooing humans into the path of evil. The novel's theme is temptation and how to avoid it. Lewis took Wormwood from the Book of Revelation (8:10), where what some biblical scholars describe as a star, others as an angel, of that name tumbles to earth during a cosmic battle between the forces of good and evil, and pollutes the water system with his bitterness.

X

X is for the **X-Men Angel**, first seen in the popular X-Men comic strip created by Stan Lee in 1963, and then later in big-screen adaptations of the X-Men superhero franchise. Angel (sometimes Archangel) is a core character. In daily life a wealthy playboy, Warren Worthington III discovers that he comes from a sub-species of humans known as mutants, who have super-human abilities that can be used for good or bad. In his case, he has wings, originally depicted as made of feathers, though later of metal, and he flies in and rescues those in danger.

12

Angels on the Modern Shelf

'Whoever it was that used to heed us and care for us, who had concern for our fate and the world's, has been replaced by another who glories in our servitude to matter, and to the basest part of our own nature.'

Lawrence Durrell, in *Monsieur or The Prince of Darkness* (1974)

On 22 and 23 August 1914, at Mons in Belgium, in one of the early major engagements of the First World War, the British Expeditionary Force confronted the fast-advancing German First Army. Though outnumbered three to one, the BEF acquitted itself well, holding the line for forty-eight hours, inflicting a disproportionately high number of casualties on the other side, and delaying the Germans' rapid push towards Paris. Though it ended with the British retreating, back home in wartime propaganda about Mons, the battle was presented as a triumph. Part of that spin was the creation of the legend of the Angels of Mons.

It began in the *London Evening News*, where Arthur Machen published an article contributing to the range of morale-raising explanations as to how this 'victory' had come about. His account told of how soldiers in the battle had spoken of ghostly 'bowmen' coming to their aid, and drew a parallel with similar supernatural figures said to have played their part in the famous British defeat of the French at the Battle of Agincourt in 1415. Only this time, the supernatural help had come in the form of what Machen referred to as 'heaven's knights' – who quickly became angels in the minds of his readers. 'And as the soldier heard these voices he saw before him, beyond the trench, a long line of shapes, with a shining about them. They were like men who drew the bow, and with another shout their cloud of arrows flew singing and tingling through the air towards the German hosts.'[1]

The story of the 'Angels of Mons' took hold, despite Machen's best efforts later to retreat from such an interpretation of his 'knights'. He was, he pointed out, a writer of 'mystical' tales and what we would now call horror stories, and had intended his article in the *Evening News* to be clearly marked as fiction. His audience insisted, though, on taking it as fact, a sign of divine messengers intervening on the British side as they had in the Old Testament on behalf of the Israelites. Soon, accounts of the Angels of Mons were appearing everywhere, in national newspapers, magazines, parish journals and even popular songs. 'It seemed my light fiction had been accepted . . . as the solidest of facts,' Machen later ruminated.[2]

It wasn't only the British who, in their hour of need, rushed to embrace talk of a helping hand from above on the battlefield. Accounts of other supernatural visitations surfaced during the First World War. Joan of Arc, dead for almost six hundred years, was reported to have been seen guarding the French trenches, while German soldiers described ghostly white horses that had charged their positions. In the context of the sheer, unfathomable scale of death in the Great War, angels found themselves once more in the front line.

There are, of course, many more straightforward theories regarding the spread of this legend about Mons. Some historians point to British military sources making up and disseminating the story as a way of deflecting attention from otherwise gloomy headlines – the sinking by German U-boats of the ocean liner the

Lusitania, Zeppelin attacks on London, and stalemate on the Western front.[3]

Yet, it is unavoidable to conclude that, as at other points in history, the Angels of Mons, whether actual, imagined or manufactured, spoke of, and to, something all too real in the human experience. Belief in them wasn't primarily about facts, but rather about seeking a comforting balm in a wretched situation. The Anglican theologian Jane Williams has written of this reflex: 'In what we think about angels, it is as though we allow ourselves access to needs that normally we would deny or suppress. Angels give us a way of expressing our longing for beings who are more powerful than ourselves, and who care for us.'[4]

The rise of science, logic and scepticism may have caused some to predict the death of religion – the 'melancholy, long, withdrawing roar' of 'the Sea of Faith' as described by Matthew Arnold in his 1867 poem 'Dover Beach' – yet here, at this particular point in the midst of a conflict that resulted in anywhere between 17 and 37 million casualties,[5] angels continued to answer a need. People returned in adversity to the traditional rituals and sense of belonging that religion offers, in the same way that, in more everyday moments of crisis, many can still think of nothing else to do other than say a prayer, however firmly in the rest of their lives they have rejected belief in God.

In the context of the 'war to end all wars', the Angels of Mons were just one manifestation of this phenomenon. *The Story of a Soul*, a simple, pious spiritual autobiography about her childhood and vocation by Marie Françoise-Thérèse Martin, better known as Saint Thérèse of Lisieux, a nun who had died young in Normandy in 1897 of intestinal tuberculosis, became hugely popular during the war years with its core message of relying on God in the 'little way of trust and love'.[6] It was said to have been found in the knapsack of countless French soldiers in the trenches – and in those of Germans too.

They would also carry photographs of her into battle, or wear medals, stamped with her face, that could, they claimed, stop bullets that would otherwise have killed them.

How, then, did the churches respond? In the twentieth century, and on into the twenty-first, there has been a widespread loss of belief in God, especially in Western societies, and a corresponding rapid decline in the influence of institutional religion and the practice of church-going. Talking up angels would, at first glance, seem like a good way to reverse the tide by highlighting the essential difference in approach between religious institutions and secular ones to the challenges of modern life. If angels offer hope in hopeless times, so too can the Church.

Yet, generally, that has only happened quietly and sporadically. The mainstream churches have largely all but given up on angels as anything more than ornament. Reference to them may, on occasion, be sprinkled like a cake decoration into sermons and public pronouncements, but any sort of detailed study and reflection, theological and spiritual, that takes angels as the starting point and the key to a thorough-going understanding of the world, nature, the universe and the mind of God, is now vanishingly rare. Indeed, the legacy of Aquinas and the angelologists is often laughed off, and at, by senior clerics, keen to sound in step with our rational times, as just the sort of medieval superstition that gives their institutions a bad name. They are tacitly, at least in the case of angels, accepting the scientific orthodoxy that anything physically invisible has no value.

Others, though, have realised the danger posed by going along with the spirit of the times. In his August 1950 encyclical, *Humani Generis*, Pope Pius XII – whose record during the Second World War has subsequently been such a focus of discussion and dispute between Catholic and Jewish scholars[7] – confronted what he described as 'some false opinions threatening to undermine the foundations of Catholic doctrine'. Among these threats he listed those – within and without his Church – who doubted angels and thereby 'destroy the gratuity of the supernatural order'.[8]

Pius, though, represented for many Catholics an outdated approach. The winds of change were blowing and, less than a decade later, his successor, John XXIII, summoned the Second Vatican Council, a meeting of all the world's bishops. It convened in Rome in regular sessions between 1962 and 1965, and ushered in wholescale change and modernisation. Its pronouncements remain at the core of today's Catholicism, but they pay no heed at all to the place of angels, any references in the texts being fleeting and incidental.

Subsequent popes have, though, spoken of angels with a tiny bit more engagement. In one of his weekly general audiences in 1986, John Paul II chose to give a succinct summary – and hence endorsement – of the views of Aquinas on angels being spirit rather than body, and above the 'laws of corruptibility, which are common to the material world'. Such definitions, he conceded, 'may seem far away or less vital to the modern mentality', but he acknowledged that something was being lost. 'It is precisely the religious encounter with the world of the purely spiritual beings that becomes valuable as a revelation of [each individual's] own being, not only as body but also as spirit, and of his belonging to a design of salvation.'[9]

Fine words, and a stout defence by a religious leader of the metaphysical as it is eclipsed by the physical, but never developed or further explored by a pope who was prolific in producing teaching letters and encyclicals. His successor in 2005, Benedict XVI, was equally sparing, his only notable contribution to the modern angelology coming in November 2012, shortly before his resignation, when he published the latest of 'The Infancy Narratives', his scholarly accounts of Jesus' life. In it, he picked over the details of the stable in Bethlehem and, based on the exact wording of the Gospels, suggested – running against a belief that dated back to the earliest centuries of the Judeo-Christian tradition – that the angels who attended the birth did not sing but rather spoke their words of acclaim.[10] It was another demotion of angels by the modern Church, this time of the long-cherished notion of heavenly choirs – though in staging their annual Nativity plays around the world, there is little evidence that Catholic schools and parishes have taken the pope's remarks as gospel and changed their scripts.

Benedict's successor, the Argentinian Pope Francis, has a surer feel for what goes on at the grassroots of the Church and a corresponding affection for popular piety. He has gone some small way to rehabilitating angels. 'The doctrine on angels is not fantasist,' he insisted in October 2014 while celebrating mass on the Feast of the Guardian Angels in the small chapel in the pilgrims' hostel where he lives in the Vatican. 'No, it's reality ... According to church tradition we all have an angel with us, who protects us and helps us understand things.'

This restatement of the role of guardian angels, consistent with 2,000 years of Catholic practice, was said with enthusiasm, but again it has not at the time of writing been a theme to which Francis has returned. If angels today remain part of the official church furniture, they have rarely been given a polish in the twentieth and twenty-first centuries.

A notable exception, in the Reformed tradition, is the highly esteemed and much studied Swiss theologian Karl Barth (1886–1968). In his *Church Dogmatics*, a thirteen-volume study that he began in 1932 and continued up to his death, Barth dwelt at length on angels – or rather 'the limits of angelology' – and argued against those popular notions of angels that exist inside and increasingly outside the churches. He dismisses the tried and trusted guardian angel concept. To treat angels as individuals with links to specific human beings, he argues, is to make them too like us, tailored to our needs rather than to their real function, which is serving God. 'They do not ... act independently or autonomously,' he asserts, but are instead part of a 'force' around God that gives out energy. If they have been perceived, or even seen, as individual figures, it is the result, according to Barth, of them having been 'specifically summoned and separated from the rest [of the force] with a specific commission', but as soon as that commission is completed they dissolve back into the mass.[11]

More so than many twentieth-century theologians, Barth's impact spread beyond church and academic circles. In 1962, he even featured on the cover of *Time* magazine.[12] Some of his maxims have become well known and are often repeated, notably the line that angels are 'not a proper subject' for theologians. It sounds as if he was off-loading angels because they presented an obstacle to the churches' embracing the modern world. His remark, however, had been uttered in a particular context. Angels were not a proper subject, he wrote, because the only proper subject was God. What he was really saying, then, goes all the way back to the old argument about idolatry. If you have a specific angelology, Barth suggested, it gets in the way of doing the only thing that matters: trying to understand God.[13] Inside that framework, though, Barth does concede that angels still have a purpose – even if the exact explanation he offers is short on the practical details that fire our imaginations and sweeps away some of the best-loved traditional roles of angels as guardians, musicians and tireless workers for the good.

The very thing which they lack in comparison with us includes within itself their infinite advantage over us. In face of God they have no cause of their own in the espousing of which they have to submit to His will. They do not exist in any reciprocal relationships. These must be confined to the divine model. They do not sing any hymn of praise, which well or badly they have to strike up. They are themselves an eternal hymn of praise. And their existence is not tedious, as tedious theologians usually imagine, because as the entourage accompanying God they have their hands full with what He wills and does and therefore with us. Their liturgy is their service to Him and therefore to us.[14]

Barth was going all the way back, via Pseudo-Dionysius, to the Jewish teachers of the intertestamental period. Angels are part of heaven, he was saying, much more than they are part of earth.

The Mormon angel Moroni

If contemporary mainstream churches are, at best, restrained in their enthusiasm for angels, the Church of Jesus Christ of Latter-day Saints, better known as the Mormons and 15 million strong around the world, has no similar reservations. Joseph Smith, the scarcely educated fifth of eleven children born to poor, ethnically Irish parents in 1805, later the inaugural Mormon prophet and seer, was visited three times on 21 September 1823, in his home town of Palmyra in New York State, by an angel. In Smith's later accounts,[15] the angel identified himself by the previously unheard name Moroni, and recounted to Smith how he was part of an ancient Judeo-Christian civilisation that had died out after defeats in battle many centuries previously on the American continent. Moroni was a human prophet (like Elijah and Enoch) who had become an angel. Indeed, he claimed to be the last prophet of his particular civilisation to contribute to a record, 'written upon gold plates, giving an account of the former inhabitants of this continent, and the sources from which they sprang'. The book was named after Moroni's father, Mormon, and had been buried in a stone box in a hillside near Smith's home.

In his definitive 1838 account of Moroni's visitation, Smith describes him in conventional terms as an 'angel of light' who 'had on a loose robe of most exquisite whiteness. It was a whiteness beyond anything earthly I had ever seen . . . His hands were naked and his arms also a little above the wrists . . . Not only was his robe exceedingly white but his whole person was glorious beyond description.'[16]

Following those initial appearances, though, Moroni took four long years before finally providing Smith with the ability to translate the lost language of the hidden text, even as he continued to appear not just to Smith but to three of his close companions, known to Mormons as the Three Witnesses.[17] However, once Smith could decode the text on the golden plates, he published its content as the Book of Mormon in 1830, with a full explanation of its origins and how it had come into his hands. It is now the founding document of the Church Smith established in the same year. The original golden plates, he said, he returned to Moroni for safe-keeping.

Mormonism, then, is another religious tradition that started with an angel, and there are parallels between Smith's account of his interaction with Moroni and Muhammad's with Jibr'il. The Mormons position themselves within the bigger Christian tradition, placing the Bible alongside the Book of Mormon (though insisting that the latter contains none of the errors to be found in the former). They point to the promise in the Book of Revelation that a trumpet-blowing angel will roam the earth, proclaiming the gospel until the Second Coming, as a prophecy of Moroni.[18] The golden statues of Moroni that sit on top of Mormon temples everywhere, usually in restrained and uniform neoclassical style, feature that angelic trumpet prominently.

However, Smith's development of his religious movement was anything but traditionally Christian. His endorsement of polygamy, and what seemed to some around him as his toying with a pantheon of gods, did not endear him to many of those who had initially followed him with great enthusiasm. He was to die at the hands of a mob, at the age of thirty-eight, in 1844, at Nauvoo in

Illinois, one of a series of ever more remote places to which Smith and his followers retreated in face of sustained criticism and persecution by mainstream Christian churches that included thirty spells in prison and one occasion of being tarred and feathered.

In his theology Smith came up with another of those formulations that seek neatly to categorise angels and harness them to both church doctrine and human yearnings. He identified three distinct groups of angels. The first are spirits, he said, sent to earth to deliver messages to believers. These spirits will themselves one day be born as humans. There is an echo of Swedenborg in there. The second are righteous human beings who have died, been perfected in heaven and are now coming back to earth with messages and a mission that they know better how to deliver or carry out – having once been human – than the first category of angels. This category is roughly akin to ghosts, unable to leave earth behind, though Mormonism teaches that the tasks they undertake can only be things that humans cannot do for themselves (there is a strong self-improvement imperative that prevents angels being seen as an emotional crutch).

These righteous angels contain both those yet to be resurrected, and those – like Moroni – who have been through that process and therefore have an immortal body, which is made up of flesh and bones, but no blood (blood being the preserve of mortals). And then there is the third category – the fallen angels, led by Lucifer.

Here again Smith's angelology shows all sorts of influences, but notable is the heavy presence of the Book of Enoch. Smith is said also to have studied the Kabbalah. The combination – plus a degree of arrogance that is perhaps part and parcel of being a prophet – led him to the conclusion that when he assumed his immortal body, he would follow in the footsteps of Enoch, who became the supreme angel, Metatron, also known as the 'lesser Yahweh'.

What the three-level structure Smith proposed shows most clearly, however, is a desire to create a tangible, comprehensible and convincing – for believers – link between angels, humans and eternal life. It has to be remembered that he first started seeing visions while part of a religious revivalist community. Those who embraced his accounts in nineteenth-century America came from similar upbringings, predominantly belonging to rural or less affluent groups, usually living far away from the expanding cities. They reacted favourably, in what they heard Smith preach, to the flavour of straightforward, Non-Conformist views of an earlier age that defined and separated out good from bad, with not much space in the middle, but which were now under threat. Central to Smith's appeal, too, was a new and unabashed angelology that provided his followers with comfortingly black and white answers about their own salvation, and promised life after death as angels. You might now call it a magical worldview, though those who followed and follow Smith's literalism certainly wouldn't recognise or accept the description.

'Angel of History'

As theologians, mostly, ceased to work with angels to shape bigger visions, believing them to have become irrelevant to the modern world, there were those in other fields who continued to be drawn to them to provide narratives about human existence and suffering. Among the most notable during the twentieth century was the Swiss-German Modernist artist Paul Klee, especially in his wraith-like, unsettling *Angelus Novus*, from 1920. Its cylindrical face, framed by jug ears and a curious unruly curly mop, and distinguished only by its protruding teeth and slack jaw, sits on top of a feeble, fragile body, completed by chicken feet and spindly legs. Even its wings, grand in proportion, are tangled and somehow inadequate.

Paul Klee's Angelus Novus *of 1920 saw the German Modernist trying to make sense of the world he lived in between the First World War and the start of the Second.*

One response might be to deduce that Klee (1879–1940) was signalling the irrelevance of angels to the modern age, but nothing could be further from the truth. This angel was, his most fervent admirers believe, his way of making sense of the world. It is a work that followed on from one world war – where Klee served behind the lines in the German army, but saw colleagues and friends killed – and anticipated another. Klee was to suffer under the Nazis, who labelled him a 'degenerate' artist, closed the Bauhaus School in Weimar in the early 1930s where he taught, and persecuted him until he left the country in 1933, returning to his native Switzerland (which refused him citizenship right up to his death in 1940). Did Klee wish to convey in his distressingly un-angelic angel the trampling and corruption in the opening decades of the twentieth century of everything that had been held dear throughout history?

That is certainly what Klee's patron and champion Walter Benjamin believed. He bought the painting in 1920 and counted it as his most treasured possession. A well-known German Jewish philosopher, critic and essayist, Benjamin committed suicide in 1940 to avoid capture by the Nazis. Just before his death he wrote a reflection on the *Angelus Novus*, recasting it as the 'Angel of History'. It showed, he argued,

> an angel looking as though he is about to move away from something he is fixedly contemplating. His face is turned toward the past. Where we perceive a chain of events, he sees one catastrophe, which keeps piling wreckage upon wreckage, hurling it before his feet . . . A storm is blowing from Paradise; it has got caught in his wings with such violence the angel can no longer close them. This storm irresistibly propels him into the future to which his back is turned, while the pile of debris before him grows skyward.[19]

Klee's angel, in such an analysis, was a statement about the fate of the world, political in intent. More private and personal are the angels he produced once exiled by the Nazis. He was in poor health and his mind turned increasingly to angels as he approached death. His technique is as powerful as it is simple, eschewing the naturalistic in a series of line-drawings, without colour or definition and not obviously beautiful. His angels were not even trying to be beautiful in the way of past generations of angels in frescoes, paintings, sculptures and illustrations. Klee gives them casual titles such as 'forgetful' or 'still ugly', as if searching in the everyday for that hard to capture, almost invisible, only ever briefly glimpsed mystical and spiritual dimension that had long intrigued him, even though he was not formally religious.[20] As symbols for the angels that exert a more powerful pull on the human imagination today than God (according to opinion polls), these works remain strikingly modern and relevant.

Others in the twentieth century took more direct inspiration from the Hebrew Scriptures to depict angels, notably Klee's fellow Modernist Marc Chagall (1887–1985), whose 'religious' works (including a series of illustrations he completed from 1931 to 1934, and commissions in stained glass for churches and cathedrals) extensively explore the Book of Genesis. Chagall celebrated in particular in his work his own Jewishness and the customs and traditions he had grown up with in Russia, but – again like Klee – he approached angels as an essentially human, domestic story. 'His figures of angels are rhymed or combined with human ones,' writes his biographer Jackie Wullschlager, noting that in his exploration of Abraham and his three mystery visitors at Mamre, the four of them end up sitting around over a glass or two 'as if they have just dropped by for dinner'.[21]

Klee and Chagall encourage us to embrace angels so as to understand ourselves. The German lyric poet Rainer Maria Rilke

(1875–1926), though, found that encountering an angel could be a terrifying experience. He was staying, in January 1912, as a guest at Duino Castle on the Adriatic. Walking along a cliff-top path, deep in thought, struggling to compose a letter, he suddenly heard a voice. 'Who, if I cried out,' it asked, 'would hear me among the angelic orders?' According to an account written at the time by his hostess, Princess Marie von Thurn und Taxis, Rilke hurried back to his desk, wrote down the line in his note-book, and proceeded to create the first of his *Duino Elegies*, published fourteen years later.

Whether the voice was muse or angel, or both, is not clear, but in the *Elegies* – written in bursts over a period when Rilke served on the front line in the First World War and suffered repeated episodes of depression – angels become, as the poet himself once put it, symbols of the 'higher level of reality in the invisible'. Rilke understands the appeal of angels, of their role in a visible world, but he also appreciates how unlikely they are to get a response. Angels, he believes, are creatures of such great beauty that – far from being the benign guardians imagined by countless genera-tions of Christians – they are all but unreachable. And if they can be approached, they are representatives of such perfection as to be terrifying, pointing as they do towards the metaphorical, meta-physical and mystical that is beyond imperfect and finite human imaginations:

> Every Angel is terror.
> And so I hold myself back and swallow the cry
> of a darkened sobbing. Ah, who then can
> we make use of? Not Angels: not men,
> and the resourceful creatures see clearly
> that we are not really at home
> in the interpreted world. Perhaps there remains
> some tree on a slope, that we can see

again each day: there remains to us yesterday's street,
and the thinned-out loyalty of a habit
that liked us, and so stayed, and never departed.[22]

There is, in Rilke's awe-inspiring, unattainable angels, something that goes all the way back to the eighth century BCE and
those mighty six-winged seraphim in the Book of Isaiah at the
start of this story. But the poet pointed to a different inspiration. He is reputed to have told his translator, shortly before his
death, that his angels should not be thought of as part of the
Judeo-Christian tradition, but rather as Islamic – he was an
avid reader of the Qur'an – since they contained a divine fire
and therefore could burn those who dared touch them. In a
century that was to make angels ever more cosy, Rilke understood the appeal of having angels close at hand, but judged it
impossible.

His vision of distant and distanced angels is both bleak and
distinctive, qualities that inspired the German film-maker Wim
Wenders. His 1987 *Wings of Desire* stands apart in the minor
genre of twentieth-century films about guardian angels that
includes other more heart-warming examples such as *Here
Comes Mr Jordan* (1941) and *It's a Wonderful Life* (1946). It
features two trenchcoat-wearing guardian angels, Cassiel and
Damiel, who have been in Berlin since time immemorial, are
invisible to those they try to assist, and do not intervene directly
in human affairs (Cassiel cannot prevent a suicide, for example,
unlike the angel who saves James Stewart's character in *It's a
Wonderful Life*).

Berlin was still divided by a wall between East and West when
the film was made, adding to the sense of melancholy and existential alienation. Wenders captures the gap that Rilke highlighted
between angels and humans by filming sequences with Cassiel
and Damiel in a sepia-infused black and white. Of the two, Cassiel

is, broadly, content with his lot (though there is the sense that as a 'worker' angel, he resents being far down the celestial ladder from God). Damiel, though, tries to bridge the great gulf between the two worlds when he falls for a lonely circus trapeze artist, Marion (who performs wearing angel wings).

His decision to exchange the spiritual realm for the material – to fall as the fallen angels of Genesis fell – so as to be able to talk to Marion, eat food, drink coffee, feel the touch of another being, is juxtaposed in Wenders' script with the story of a visiting American, played by Peter Falk (best known as the TV detective *Columbo*), who it turns out is also a former angel who gave up his wings, but regrets his choice.

Wings of Desire is as much about the unhappiness of humans as it is about that of angels, serving and decommissioned. Like Rilke, the film understands our attachment to guardian angels, but imagines, too, how tough it can be as one of those guardian angels.

A *new age of angels?*

You might just find a DVD of Wim Wenders' *Wings of Desire* in the 'Angel' sections that have appeared in recent years in bookshops and among online retailers. Other staples include writings by Lorna Byrne, who has followed *Angels in My Hair* with six more books, all of them bestsellers and translated into thirty languages worldwide. Equally popular is the American author Doreen Virtue, who describes herself as a clairvoyant and 'fourth-generation metaphysician who works with the . . . ascended-master realms'. She offers what she calls 'angel therapy' – 'a non-denominational spiritual healing method . . . to heal and harmonise every aspect of life'.

Others, in the same genre, co-opt angels to connect with 'past lives', reviving the late Victorian enthusiasm for spiritualism (which peaked around the First World War with the involvement of Sherlock Holmes's creator, Arthur Conan Doyle). And there are plenty of websites where you can buy your own 'authentic' set of wings, date a fellow angelologist, or book an 'angel retreat'.

While the churches, traditional custodians of angels in the West, have gone into retreat on the subject, others have stepped in to satisfy what appears to be a robust and continuing demand. Several specific factors have driven this development, first seen in the United States in the late 1980s, and then in Europe from the 1990s, notably the popularity of a 'New Age' approach to religion that reflects both a widespread loss of trust in religious institutions and a pre-millennial enthusiasm for trying alternative approaches to what is loosely defined as spirituality. The huge growth of the internet has also helped and emboldened those who might once have felt isolated and reluctant to talk publicly in their community about their interest in angels to connect with like-minded individuals.

Dispassionate research about those who today claim to have seen angels is in short supply. Angelology is no longer regarded as a respectable academic discipline. In 2001, however, the British academic Emma Heathcote-James published a collection of 350 accounts of celestial visitations. All had been shared with her by members of the British public, in response to appeals she had placed in local and church newspapers and radio stations.[23] While the respondents were self-selecting – over 50 per cent described themselves as varieties of Christian – Heathcote-James herself came to the subject with no denominational or religious baggage. She was, she writes, simply curious.

The details shared with her fall into several broad categories. Some 31 per cent of her respondents saw what might be termed a traditional angel – wings, white gown, often a halo – little changed from the image used by the painter of the fifth-century frescoes in

Rome's Santa Maria Maggiore Basilica. Science might ascribe this to neuro-plasticity, the flexible way we now know that the human brain works, where the images and shapes we see around us every day are, sometimes subconsciously, sometimes by design, projected onto our beliefs, hopes and deepest yearnings. These witnesses are seeing the most familiar angel image in Christian-inspired Western civilisation.

A further 17 per cent saw an angel in everyday garb, indistinguishable from any other human being. Identifying them as angels in such circumstances is therefore very much their individual choice but, if conditioning or the collective subconscious does play a part in what we believe we see, then a debate that has been going on throughout Christian history as to whether angels are heavenly creatures or take on earthly form seems to have left its mark.

Of the other respondents, 12 per cent described what they experienced as an infusion of light, 9 per cent a special smell, another 9 per cent 'felt a presence', and just 5 per cent heard the angel, often singing as if in a heavenly choir. Other images familiar from the story of angels occur in these individual accounts Heathcote-James gathered: of angels disappearing up a Jacob's ladder-like flight of stairs; of them appearing in a dream; and of angelic messengers coming back from beyond the grave to reassure grieving relatives, especially those who had lost children, that their loved one was safe. This last manifestation is connected to the Near Death Experience movement, which in the later decades of the twentieth century sought to provide 'proof' of heaven by sharing the visions of white tunnels and blinding lights seen by those who have stopped breathing for periods of several minutes before being rescued by the skill of doctors, and the genius of modern technology.

Perhaps the most intriguing among Heathcote-James's interviewees, though, were those who were blind, but still saw angels.

As one of her correspondents put it, she was able 'to see angels as [the sighted] see people'. Here, science does have something concrete to say, pointing to Charles Bonnet syndrome and Anton–Babinski syndrome. In the former condition, more common, with around a hundred thousand people being affected each year in the UK, those who have lost all or most of their sight, often through macular degeneration, experience visual hallucinations that cause them to claim they are still able to see things, even when they can't. And in the much rarer Anton–Babinski syndrome, those who have suffered damage to the occipital lobe, one of four main lobes in the cerebral cortex, insist in the face of all evidence to the contrary that they, too, are able to see.

What should not be overlooked, though, is what Heathcote-James's respondents said they sought and/or gained from their reported encounters with angels. Over a quarter referred to a resulting feeling of 'general comfort/reassurance'. Some 18 per cent received a message that 'helped' them, and another 17 per cent connected their experience with troubling times they had been through in facing terminal illness or the death of someone close to them. A similar percentage placed the appearance in the context of someone unidentified stepping in to save their life, or prevent them from having what could be a nasty accident, and then afterwards disappearing without trace.

Again, rational explanations exist, even if rejected by those involved. There is no way of reconciling the different accounts, but what intrigues is that so many people believe they have experienced angels, and moreover experienced them in a manner that resonates with history. Every one of the narratives that Heathcote-James has collected would once have fitted easily with the beliefs and frameworks of organised religion. And while Judaism, Christianity and Islam continue to have a place for angels, and even refer to them occasionally, their lack of any real engagement with the subject – despite angels being everywhere in their holy books – has resulted in angels now largely operating as freelancers outside the mainstream of faith.

Y

Y is for **Yeyalel**, the fifty-eighth out of seventy-two angels in a list found in the Kabbalah, the Jewish mystical tradition that traces its origins back to the *Book of Zohar* in the thirteenth century, and beyond. This visionary text is a commentary on the Torah, the first five books of the Hebrew Scriptures, but casts its net much wider to include a host of angel names not there in the original. Among them is Yeyalel, which in Hebrew means 'God who is sung above', appropriately enough since this angel is one of those in the celestial choirs whose music stretches from heaven to earth.

Z

Z is for **Zebuleon**, one of nine angels who will be in charge 'at the end of the world' according to the second-century-CE *Apocalypse of Ezra*, a vision of end-times when the kingdom of God would be established on earth. It is a Christian text (which survives in a Greek version) that was not included in the authorised version of the Bible. The list of the nine begins with familiar names such as Michael, Gabriel and Raphael, happily accepted by Christianity, continues with the more problematic Uriel, and then ends with the wild, wonderful and non-approved Gabuthelon, Aker, Arghugitonos, Beburos and Zebuleon. The latter is not to be confused with Zebulun, one of the biblical patriarch Jacob's twelve sons (who also include Joseph of *Amazing Technicolor Dreamcoat* fame), or Grandpa Zebulon Walton from the popular wholesome 1970s TV series played by Will Geer.

EPILOGUE

Dwellers All in Time and Space

'Angels, help us to adore Him
Ye behold Him face to face;
Sun and moon, bow down before Him,
Dwellers all in time and space.'
From the hymn 'Praise, My Soul,
the King of Heaven', by Henry
Francis Lyte (1834)

My local church, Saint Mary's in South Creake, is where I go
when I want to spend time with angels. It has stood since the
fifteenth century in that ancient, ecclesiastical part of north
Norfolk, England's fourth-largest county, that clusters around the
Marian shrine at Walsingham, destroyed in the Reformation but
revived on a modest scale in the twentieth century. The break with
Rome saw many churches stripped of their decorations, deemed
too Catholic as official tastes in matters of religion became more
Protestant, even Puritan. Yet places of worship such as Saint
Mary's were left largely untouched.

Smiling down from Saint Mary's 'angel roof', as they have been
for the last 500 years, are two rows of carvings of winged heavenly creatures, carrying musical instruments and reminders of
Jesus' crucifixion, as well as objects with more specific local references such as the triple crown of Saint Edmund of East Anglia.
Though it defies logic, they have come to feel to me like friends,
and not just because their benign gaze, gathering me in as it has

gathered others for half a millennium, represents a kind of continuity, an expression of that chain that links us as tiny, unimpor-
tant specks backwards and forwards in human history.

The church itself was built in the 1450s, funded by lavish
bequests from pious lords of the manor keen to curry divine
favour at a time the county was booming on the back of the wool
and cloth trade. That prosperity is long gone, and in today's secular world Saint Mary's is a giant out of all proportion with the
tiny village it now serves. Inside, though, it remains a place of
wonder and – despite its size – of intimacy thanks to the angels.

There is also a medieval wine-glass pulpit and a rood screen, as
well as an ancient seven-sided baptismal font. All three show definite
signs of having been defaced in the post-Reformation turmoil, but the
real draw, at least for me, is the angels, hovering high, high above, like
the skeins of geese who fly over north Norfolk's big blue skies, so vast
that when under them you can see that the world is round.

The angel roof is said to have been put in place, belatedly, to
mark Henry V's victory at the Battle of Agincourt in 1415, where
those 'heavenly knights' (later summoned up again by Arthur
Machen at Mons in the First World War) had played their part.
Along each side of the nave, the angels double as the hammers
that support the hammerbeam ceiling, their wings in red and
green (the colours slightly garish, the result of an over-eager
restoration in the 1950s). Their bodies, though, are the originals.
No compressed air here, as Thomas Aquinas had prescribed, but
solid oak. When the invisible was made visible, the angelologists'
theological precision didn't always translate.

There have been, it is recorded in the church's records, some zealous efforts to disfigure the angels, but not by disapproving Protestants.
Rather a group of local farmers in 1680 sprayed them with musket-
shot in their over-vigorous efforts to polish off an invasion of jack-
daws who were disturbing worshippers. Bits of ancient lead were
found lodged in the angel bodies during the 1950s' restoration.

Perhaps the angels' survival in the post-Reformation stripping of altars and cleansing of churches was down to the roof of Saint Mary's being so high up that even the most extreme hater of 'graven images' of 'anything in heaven' wasn't sufficiently confident of having God on his or her side that they would risk climbing a ladder to tear down the too 'popish' angels. Or, even if the flesh was willing, they were nevertheless practical enough to realise that if they did hack away at the hammers of the roof, it might come tumbling down on top of them. Smashing statues, breaking stained glass and destroying wall-paintings, by contrast, was a form of vandalism that didn't risk life or limb.

Or perhaps, I find myself thinking when I am sitting in Saint Mary's on a quiet weekday afternoon, never quite feeling alone in the silence of the empty church with these survivors of religious wars and enthusiasms hovering overhead, it may have been that the countless largely unlettered congregations who filled this place in centuries gone by wanted the angels to remain, always available for them. In that wish, they are rather like us today. And so they ignored whatever orders were sent down the line from the civil and church authorities to destroy them.

To generations of Creakers these angels were their very own gateway into the scriptures, as well as protectors and signs of hope in what were lives of hard toil and cruel fate. What strikes me most about them now is their democracy. They are there for everyone, regardless of creed, rank or belief, their amused, expectant beams never demanding anything in return. Many ancient churches, cathedrals, monasteries and convents were designed to reflect the man-made hierarchies – the clerical elite on the altar, elevated and separated off by rails; the choir up in the gallery, closer to God in his heaven than the rest of the congregation; the nuns, if nuns there were in the area, in their special enclosure, behind a grille, into which no ordinary mortal might trespass; and the preacher in his ornate pulpit, looking down on those he lectured. But the angels on the ceiling were just as available to the righteous and the self-important as to the sinners in the back rows. And today, dawn to dusk, they are just as much there for the trickle of visitors who wander in to inspect the church as they might a museum, as they are for the handful of remaining worshippers at the Sunday morning rituals.

For organised religion is in decline in the West, most obviously in dwindling church attendance figures that are but one measurement. The shift has been going on for a long time. One way the once all-powerful Christian Church responded to the challenge posed to its authority by first the Scientific Revolution and then the Enlightenment, with their mantras of proof and reason, was to insist ever more loudly that the details found in the scriptures, and especially in the Gospels, were literally true. That way, too, they could theoretically pass the 'proof' test. But, of course, they can't. That was never the point of these narratives, with the consequence today that those who have decided that those Gospel details aren't historically accurate have written them off as discredited, along with institutional religion.

Yet so much of the Judeo-Christian and Islamic holy books, and those of other faiths too, is about something other than the strictly historical. Instead they convey a poetic, emotional, timeless and very human truth in much the same ways as Greek myths do. In the latter case, we seem happy enough to accept them as such; but not the religious narratives. Because they have been presented as literal, and have then been exposed as nothing of the sort, they are sidelined. Five hundred years ago, when these angels were first carved in Saint Mary's, the much bigger congregations who once gathered understood more clearly than we do now, when listening to the scriptures read aloud, including accounts of angels, that there was a bigger human truth in them that was valuable and sustaining.

I have lost count while researching and writing this book of how many times I have been asked if I 'believe' in angels. Can you tell me, a distinguished oncologist I met at a party demanded when he had winkled out of me that I was writing about angels, that the Angel Gabriel was actually there at the Annunciation, telling Mary she was going to have God's child? Of course I couldn't – any more than I could produce a feather from an angel's wing, or a broken string from a celestial harp that one of them had left behind. I talked instead of my angel friends in Saint Mary's and he assumed a look of victory.

What I can prove, though, is that people have, in their own way, however inimical it might be to today's orthodoxy and tests of veracity, believed in angels for millennia. And continue to believe in them, for much the same reasons as they always have. Sales of angel cards, angel therapies and angel retreats are, in this context, nothing other than a continuation of the popular strain of religion that has down the ages insisted, whatever the outward physical absence, on having an angel close at hand, whether it be every day at the table, or in moments of strain and crisis, personal or collective. The only difference today is that this reliance on angels as dwellers in time and space is happening outside of organised religion.

There are many words, not all of them approving, that can be used to describe this hankering for the presence of angels: need; wish fulfilment; brain-washing by the churches; a child-like desire for an invisible best friend that we really ought to have grown out of; or, for those who haven't, the adult variation that likes the idea of a Superman of unknown origin but unimpeachable goodness who sweeps in and sorts out our messes and mixed-up emotions. How instantly comforting and calming that sounds.

Oscar-nominated British actress Carey Mulligan has spoken of how angels helped her get over the panic attacks she suffered when rehearsing for *Girls & Boys*, her one-woman play about male violence that was staged to rave reviews in London and New York in 2018. An artist friend decorated her dressing room with drawings of angels, including 'an incredible picture of a person on stage, who's meant to be me, then there's an angel leaning down pushing me on the shoulder, sort of pushing me forward'.[1] We can all, surely, recognise how good that must feel. Likewise the remark made by Hillary Clinton, former First Lady, Secretary of State and defeated US presidential candidate in 2016, when she confessed to wearing a brooch with angel wings, 'on the days when I need help'.[2]

All whimsy, and meaningless superstition? That is the modern consensus, but pause a moment before dismissing it so lightly. Throughout history, and in our continuing attachment to angels and their stories, especially that notion of them as our guardians, we are surely responding to an emotional need that is part and parcel of human existence, and which they can address. It is what we seek out too in poetry, something that touches on the elusive, the potentially transcendent, found, or not found in beauty, in life's ups and downs, the possibility that, somewhere out there, there is a type of 'unknown almost', just close enough for us instinctively to feel its presence, but also just far enough to be beyond our grasp. Like poetry, angels talk to spirit, not body; the within, not the without; the metaphysical, not the physical; the invisible, not the visible.

That has been their role through history. It used to be what religion did, too, but we are turning our backs on it. Angels once largely belonged in religious narratives and religious institutions, integrated (not always without a struggle) into the systems and structures of belief that once afforded believers a powerful sense of belonging. That is still their role in some areas of the world, though not so much now closer to home. And yet angels have somehow detached themselves from the declining institutions and are now thriving on their own.

They have achieved this because their appeal has always been more powerful and real to individuals than to hierarchies. That is still the case now. Remember those one-in-six atheists mentioned in the Prelude who believe in angels but not in gods. That one-to-one connection is flexible enough to stretch over the boundary between tangible and intangible. So much of what has been explored in this book is about individuals, visited in dreams, in visions, in ecstasies or in plain day by an angel. Religion may be in decline but it hasn't stopped us all having those moments of grief and loss, of inexplicable suffering and torment, of loneliness and isolation, of danger, terror, desperation or despair at existence itself. And when we do, angels continue to represent the aspiration that something inexplicable will guard us against our woes.

The exchange is as weightless as an angel's feather. Our would-be guardians come with no explanations, and they make no demands (like approving the sometimes dehumanising dogma that goes with signing up to membership of a religious tradition). They are just there. At their simplest, throughout this story of angels, what they have often been about is the power of love, whether you see it as the best of humanity or the best of divinity, or both, and how to reach for it at precisely those moments when we are confronted by the worst of life and each other. Their story, then, becomes part of ours. In its simplicity, it continues to resonate.

The medieval 'angel roof' of Saint Mary's Church at
South Creake in Norfolk offers visitors an open invitation
to contemplate being dwellers in time and space.

Acknowledgements

Angels are one of those subjects on which everyone has an opinion to offer, a pictorial or literary reference to quote, or a personal story to share. My thanks go to all who have over the past couple of years made time to talk to me about their angels. Without you the range of the examples given in the text would be narrower and poorer.

The final selection of writers, architects and artists mentioned, though, necessarily is my own. And that means I will inevitably have omitted many that others cherish and believe are unmissable, but – and I suppose it is one indicator of the popularity of angels – there were just too many to include in this book if it was going to be capable of being picked up and read without a crane.

For my Bible quotations, I have stuck as ever to my faithful 1974 *New Jerusalem Bible*, published by Darton, Longman & Todd. And for the Qur'an I have used the English translation by M.A.S. Abdel Haleem, published by Oxford University Press in 2004. Both combine accuracy with language that is readily accessible.

I owe the following a debt of gratitude for providing me with particular guidance: Michael Arditti, Simon Banner, the Revd Professor June Boyce-Tillman of the University of Winchester, Lorna Byrne, Jean Callanan, Christian Donlan, Sarah Dunant, Father Tom Goonan, Careen Hertzog, Liz Hunt, Teresa Hunt, Professor Henry Mayr-Harting, Melanie McDonagh, Wendy Pritchard, Anthony Quinn, Professor Bettina Schmidt (director of the Alister Hardy Religious Experience Research Centre at the University of Wales: Trinity Saint David's) and Sara Scott.

My grateful thanks go as always to my exceptional editor, Katherine Venn, and to her hard-working colleagues at Hodder – Rachael Duncan and Jessica Lacey – who all take such good care of me. Also to Nick Fawcett, who so carefully copyedited the manuscript. And to my agent Piers Blofeld who, professionally speaking, is something of a guardian angel to his authors.

If a book is going to turn into anything worthwhile, it has to get under your skin as you research and write it, but that process has come at a cost to my domestic life. My children Kit and Orla have, as always, been patient with my distraction, and with those infuriating occasions when I interrupt family trips to look in on churches and galleries in search of angels. And my wife Siobhan is the most patient, sustaining and encouraging of all.

Peter Stanford
September 2018

Notes

Prelude

1 Published in 1974 in the collection of the same name.
2 The quote from Billy Connolly appears in many places, most recently in the 2016 'Heavenly Creatures: Angels in Faith, History and Popular Culture' exhibition at Saint Mungo Museum of Religious Life and Art in Glasgow.
3 See Peter Stanford, *Bronwen Astor: Her Life and Times* (London: HarperCollins, 2000).
4 Ibid.
5 Peter Stanford, 'To Me, Seeing Angels Is Natural', *Daily Telegraph* (17 July 2008).
6 Ibid.
7 The episode was captured by Bernini in his celebrated *Ecstasy of Saint Teresa* sculpture in the church of Santa Maria della Vittoria in Rome, examined in more detail later in Chapter 9.
8 According to an ICM poll for the Bible Society, reported in 'A Third of Britons Believe They Have a Guardian Angel', *Daily Telegraph*, 28 December 2016.
9 Will Dahlgreen, 'British People More Likely to Believe in Ghosts Than a Creator', yougov.co.uk/news, 26 March 2016.
10 Nick Spencer and Holly Weldin, *Post-Religious Britain? The Faith of the Faithless* (London: Theos, 2012).
11 In a 2005 poll, 'Angels' was ranked the song that Britons would most like played at their funeral (BBC News, 10 March 2005).
12 It was on display at the British Museum in London in 2017 as part of its 'Living With the Gods' exhibition.
13 Harold Bloom, in *Omens of Millennium: The Gnosis of Angels, Dreams and Resurrection* (New York: Riverhead Books, 1996).
14 Iain McGilchrist, *The Master and His Emissary* (London: Yale University Press, 2009).
15 Jane Williams, *Angels* (Oxford: Lion, 2006).
16 Will Dahlgreen, 'You Are Not Alone: Most People Believe that Aliens Exist', yougov.co.uk/news, 24 September 2015.

17 Translated by Stephen Cohn, Rainer Maria Rilke's *Duino Elegies* (Manchester: Carcanet Press, 1989).

Chapter 1

1 From his collection, *Silex Scintillans*, which established his reputation as arguably the most biblical poet in the English language.

2 Isaiah 6:3–4.

3 Isaiah 6:2.

4 Isaiah 6:6–9.

5 Revelation 4:1–11.

6 Revelation 4:8.

7 See John Sawyer, *The Fifth Gospel: Isaiah in the History of Christianity* (Cambridge: Cambridge University Press, 1996).

8 In some medieval churches, the design specifically aimed to create a 'heavenly' echo so that the choir's singing appeared to the congregation to be coming from above.

9 Canto 28 of *Paradiso* 93–5: translated by C.H. Sisson, *Dante's The Divine Comedy* (Oxford: Oxford University Press, 1980).

10 1 Samuel 1:3.

11 Genesis 3:24.

12 Genesis 18:1–33.

13 Mentioned as someone's father in 1 Chronicles 5:15.

14 Book V 805: ed. John Leonard, John Milton, *Paradise Lost* (London: Penguin, 2003).

15 The Russian-American writer Isaac Asimov, best known for his science-fiction novels, speculated in his *Annotated Paradise Lost* (1974) that Abdiel was intended by Milton as a self-portrait.

16 See Valery Rees, *From Gabriel to Lucifer* (London: I.B.Tauris, 2013).

17 And some later Jewish theologians were to argue that both seraphim and cherubim should be seen as separate from angels.

18 Isaiah 30:6.

19 Numbers 21:6–9.

20 2 Kings 18:4.

21 Translated by M.L. West, *Hesiod's Theogony and Works and Days* (Oxford: Oxford University Press, 2008).

22 For example in sections 107–8 and 113 of *Phaedo* (edited by David Gallop) (Oxford: Oxford University Press, 2009).

23 An idea more recently explored by Philip Pullman in the *His Dark Materials* series of novels.

24 Translated by F.H. Colson and G.H. Whitaker, *Collected Writings of Philo* (Harvard: Harvard University Press, 1949).

25 Where many Jews and Christians came to believe the Garden of Eden had been located.

26 Pazuzu appears in William Peter Blatty's 1971 novel *The Exorcist*, and its celebrated big-screen adaptation.

27 See Karen Armstrong, *A History of God* (London: Heinemann, 1993).

28 Though this is predominantly the view of more recent scholars. Traditionally, he was dated more around 1000 BCE.

29 From the Jewish scholar or *amora*, Shimon ben Lakish (230–70 CE and usually called Reish Lakish).

30 See Peter Frankopan, *The Silk Roads* (London: Bloomsbury, 2015).

31 Originally by Karl Jespers in *The Origin and Goal of History* (translated by Michael Bullock) (London: Routledge, 1953).

32 For a fuller account, see Karen Armstrong's *The Great Transformation* (London: Atlantic, 2006).

33 1.139.11, translated by H.H. Wilson, *The Rig-Veda-Sanhita* (Michigan: Michigan University Library, 2005).

34 Joseph Campbell, *The Hero with a Thousand Faces: Collected Works* (California: New World Library, 2012).

35 Joseph Campbell, *The Power of Myth* (New York: Anchor Books, 1991).

Chapter 2

1 Late Victorian poet, mystic, laudanum addict, sometime rough sleeper on the streets of London – see *The Hound of Heaven and Other Poems* (Wellesley, MA: Branden Books, 2014).

2 The former Archbishop of Canterbury, Rowan Williams, published a collection of his writings in 2007 under the title *Wrestling with Angels*.

3 Including Rainer Maria Rilke's 'The Man Watching' and Emily Dickinson's 'A Little East of Jordan', which contains the lines: 'A Gymnast and an Angel / Did wrestle long and hard'.

4 Charles Wesley (1707–88), the founder of Methodism, explores the clash in 'Come, O Thou Traveller Unknown', often referred to by chapel-goers as 'Wrestling Jacob'.

5 Genesis 32:26–31.

6 Genesis 32:32, which adds that Jacob's injury is why Jews do not 'to this day' eat the sciatic nerve, which is in the socket of the hip.

7 'A Little East of Jordan', written in 1860, ed. R.W. Franklin, *The Poems of Emily Dickinson* (Harvard: Harvard University Press, 1999).

8 Genesis 28:11–14.

9 Genesis 31:11–13. Esau is the older of the two sons of Isaac, and he and Jacob fight bitterly, brutally and often dishonestly over who is their father's successor, with Jacob finally coming out on top.

10   From Margaret Joyce Field's 1971 book, quoted in *Perceptions of Angels in History* by Henry Mayr-Harting (Oxford: Clarendon Press, 1998).

11   This seems to be Jacob's own take on the incident. On his deathbed, he speaks of 'the angel who has been my saviour from all harm' (Genesis 48:16).

12   Though Epstein, in his carving, has Jacob's eyes closed.

13   Exodus 33:20.

14   Harold Bloom, *Omens of Millennium: The Gnosis of Angels, Dreams and Resurrection* (New York: Riverhead Books, 1996).

15   Hosea 12:4.

16   Stephen Orgel and Jonathan Goldberg (eds), John Milton, *Paradise Lost* (Book XI) (Oxford: Oxford University Press, 2004).

17   Genesis 18:1–15.

18   Ibid.

19   Ibid.

20   Ibid.

21   11:69–71 from M.A.S. Abdel Haleem's translation of *The Qur'an* (Oxford: Oxford University Press, 2004).

22   In the Babylonian Talmudic tractate (or treatise) (Bava Metzia: New York, Soncino Press).

23   Genesis 15:7.

24   Genesis 15:4–6.

25   Genesis 16:7.

26   Genesis 16:10–12. This story becomes an essential part of the founding story of Islam in the Qur'an, for later Yahweh tells Abraham that he will make Ishmael, his son with Hagar, 'into a nation' (Genesis 21:14).

27   Genesis 17:1–19.

28   Genesis 18:16–33.

29   Genesis 19:1.

30   Genesis 19:11.

31   Genesis 19:24.

32   Genesis 21:6.

33   Genesis 22:1–12.

34   Genesis 22:16–17.

35   Exodus 6:14–27.

36   Exodus 20:1–21. The other list, in Deuteronomy 5:1–22, is more familiar to church-goers.

37   Exodus 25:8–16.

38   Exodus 25:17–22.

39   A phrase with its origins in the English Bible translated by the Protestant Reformer William Tyndale, in the first half of the sixteenth century.

40 And continues to have – the curious phrase 'the mercy seat' has been revived for a new age by Australian rock star Nick Cave, well known for his interest in Old Testament imagery, in his 1988 song of that name, where he draws a parallel between it and the electric chair used to execute convicted prisoners in the United States.

41 Leviticus 10:1–3, the first of several occasions when those who dare to approach the Ark are smitten down (see 2 Samuel 6:6–7 and 1 Chronicles 13:7–11).

42 1 Kings 6:24.

43 See Professor David Albert Jones, *Angels* (Oxford: Oxford University Press, 2010).

44 2 Samuel 22:10–11.

45 See Jeremy Hugh Baron, *50 Synagogue Lectures* (New York: Hamilton Books, 2010).

46 Ibid.

47 Ibid.

48 Exodus 3:1–2.

49 Exodus 23:20–1.

50 Exodus 23:22–3.

51 Judges 6:11–24.

52 Joshua 5:13–14.

53 Joshua 5:15.

54 2 Kings 19:35.

55 2 Samuel 24:1.

56 2 Samuel 24:16–17.

57 Numbers 22:2–35.

58 Judges 13:3–4.

59 The angel also told her not to cut her son's hair, hence the familiar story of how Sampson's long locks were the source of his strength until Delilah, his lover, cut his hair while he was sleeping.

60 1 Kings 19:3–8.

61 Ezekiel 1:3.

62 Ezekiel 1:5–14.

63 Ezekiel 1:27.

64 Ezekiel 1:40–44.

65 Ezekiel 10:20.

66 Von Däniken claimed in his bestselling books, *Chariot of the Gods* (1968) and *Gods from Outer Space* (1972), that what Ezekiel saw were not angels but aliens. Inspired by his theory, NASA engineer Josef Blumrich in 1974 produced *The Spaceships of Ezekiel*, a book that purported to translate the wheels within wheels described by the prophet into a design for a spacecraft.

67 Ezekiel 1:24.

68 1 Kings 22:19.

69 Psalm 8:5 – though some translations refer not to angels but to 'a god'.

Chapter 3

1 Quoted in Ricky Riccardi, *What a Wonderful World: The Magic of Louis Armstrong's Later Years* (New York: Pantheon, 2011).

2 Including Philo of Alexandria in the first half of the first century CE.

3 'And they took all the holy vessels of the Lord, both great and small, with the vessels of the Ark of God, and the king's treasures, and carried them away into Babylon', it is written in the First Book of Esdras (1:54), a text that is not part of the biblical canon in Western Christianity, but is in some branches of Eastern Orthodoxy.

4 Zechariah 5:9 – see Professor Serinity Young's article 'With the Greatest of Ease: Airborne Female Saints' (*Church Times*, 24 August 2018).

5 Daniel 1:4.

6 Daniel 8:11.

7 In Daniel's specific references to the 'son of man' who will bring about this reversal of fortune, Christians were later to see a forerunner of Jesus, who used the same words of himself in the Gospel accounts.

8 Daniel 12:1.

9 Daniel 9:20–3.

10 Daniel 7:9.

11 Daniel 12:1–3.

12 2 Kings 2:11–12.

13 James Charlesworth (ed.), *The Old Testament Pseudepigraphia – Volume 1* (Peabody, Massachusetts: Henrickson, 2010).

14 Matthew 16:13–19.

15 Daniel 8:15–18.

16 The face of Satan in this work is said to be that of a cardinal from a rival family who had designs on the papacy.

17 And is all too familiar as the school song of my daughter's north London secondary school, Saint Michael's, where it was always belted out to a quasi-military beat.

18 See Frances Gies, *Joan of Arc: The Legend and The Reality* (New York: Harper & Row, 1981).

19 Ibid.

20 It was visited in the fifth century CE by the Eastern Christian writer Sozomen, who told of the many pilgrims there and of his own miracle cure thanks to Michael's intervention. The church became famous throughout Eastern

Christianity and was much copied, but by the fourteenth century had fallen into disrepair and was dismantled.

21 The fourteenth-century Chudov ('of the miracle') monastery in Moscow is named after this act of Michael.

22 Tobit 12:15 – and the words are later repeated in Revelation 8:2. Other translations of the Bible render the description more vividly, describing the angels as 'going in and out before the glory of the Holy One'.

23 In *Angels: A History* (Oxford: Oxford University Press, 2010).

24 Tobias and his dog, from the Book of Tobit, feature in German Baroque artist Johann Georg Schmidtner's *Mary, Untier of the Knots*, a painting said to have a special significance in the life of Pope Francis, who saw it while a troubled young priest in Germany – see Paul Vallely's *Pope Francis: Untying The Knots* (London: Bloomsbury, 2013).

25 Mary Smallwood (ed.), Josephus, *The Jewish War* (London: Penguin, 1981).

26 Tobit 1:3.

27 Tobit 3:7–8.

28 Tobit 5:5.

29 Tobit 5:12.

30 The vows they make to each other at their wedding, extolling the purity of marriage, are often read at ceremonies to this day.

31 Tobit 12:19–20.

32 Tobit 12:18–19.

33 In her Eric Symes Abbott Memorial Lecture, 'Faith & Imagination: How the Arts Speak to the Reality of the Unseen' (Westminster Abbey, 11 May 2017).

34 Ibid.

Chapter 4

1 Harold Bloom, *Omens of Millennium: The Gnosis of Angels, Dreams and Resurrection* (New York: Riverhead Books, 1996).

2 Speaking on BBC Radio 4's *Thought for the Day* on 10 November 2017.

3 Reported in *Antiquities of the Jews* 13:10:6 (translated by William Whiston), *New Complete Works of Josephus* (Michigan: Kregel Academic, 1999).

4 Though Saint Jerome, compiler of the first Latin Bible in the fourth century, regarded it as illegitimate and positively dangerous.

5 Wisdom 2:22–4.

6 Genesis 5:18–30.

7 2 Kings 2:1.

8 1 Enoch 1:1 from *The Book of Enoch* (translated by R.H. Charles) (London: SPCK, 1917).

9   1 Enoch 72.

10 See Peter Schafer, *Rivalitat zwischen Engeln und Menschen* ('Rivalry Between Angels and Humans') (Berlin: De Gruyter, 2014).

11 1 Enoch 20:1–8.

12 Ibid.

13 Zechariah 6:6.

14 Genesis 6:13 – though most translations refer to it being God, not an angel, who comes to Noah.

15 Book III, John Leonard (ed.), John Milton, *Paradise Lost* (London: Penguin, 2003).

16 1 Enoch 43:1–3.

17 2 Enoch 22:1–3, translated by W.R. Morfill, 1896.

18 1 Enoch 19:1–3.

19 Jude vv. 5–6.

20 Genesis 6:1–4.

21 1 Enoch 6:1–5.

22 Isaiah 14:12.

23 Luke 10:18.

24 Deuteronomy 13:13.

25 Leviticus 16:6–10.

26 1 Enoch 10:9.

27 1 Enoch 10:11–14.

28 Psalm 8:5.

29 James Charlesworth (ed.), *The Old Testament Pseudepigraphia – Volume 1* (Peabody, Massachusetts: Henrickson, 2010).

30 3 Enoch 9:2–4 (translated and edited by Hugo Odeberg), *The Hebrew Book of Enoch* (London: CreateSpace Independent Publishing, 2012).

31 From the Babylonian Talmud, Hagigah 15a, as reported in *The Journal of Post-Graduate Jewish Studies*, Volumes 34–5 (Oxford, 1983).

32 For example, 2 Kings 19:35.

33 Exodus 12:21–8.

34 Revelation 14:1–20.

Chapter 5

1   Luke 1:8–17.

2   Luke 1:18–21.

3   In the Second Vatican Council document, *Nostra Aetate*.

4   Their correct chronological order, with Matthew postdating Mark, though it appears first in the New Testament.

5   Traditionally said to be Luke, the companion of Paul named in Colossians 4:14, but modern biblical scholars question whether Paul is the real author

of Colossians, and therefore tend to see the Gospel of Luke as something created by an anonymous writer from a variety of existing sources, including eye-witness accounts of Jesus.

6 Zechariah 1:7–17.
7 Luke 1:29.
8 Luke 1:28–38.
9 Luke 2:9–10.
10 Luke 2:9–13.
11 The seven are Velon, Rakia, Shehakim, Zebul, Maon, Makon and Arabot.
12 See David Albert Jones, *Soul of the Embryo: Christianity and the Human Embryo* (London: A & C Black, 2004).
13 Eric Osborn, *Clement of Alexandria* (Cambridge: Cambridge University Press, 2008).
14 Matthew 1:18–25.
15 Matthew 1:22–3.
16 Isaiah 7:14.
17 Via the three kings who had visited the infant in the stable in Bethlehem – Matthew 2:1–5.
18 Matthew 2:1–23.
19 Luke 6:14–16.
20 Another named in Matthew 13:55.
21 Described in chapter 15 of the Acts of the Apostles.
22 Jude 1:5–10.
23 Mark 13:24–6.
24 Genesis 3:1–7.
25 Revelation 12:7–11.
26 See Valery Rees, *From Gabriel to Lucifer* (London: I.B.Tauris, 2013).
27 Book VI, 316–20, John Leonard (ed.), John Milton, *Paradise Lost* (London: Penguin, 2003).
28 Revelation 9:11.
29 See, for example, Job 26:8.
30 Revelation 9:7–9.
31 Revelation 8:2.
32 Revelation 8:2–4.
33 Revelation 8:6–8.
34 Revelation 11:14–19.
35 Revelation 5:12.
36 Revelation 7:1–2.
37 Revelation 21:10–12.
38 Acts 18:3.
39 Acts 9:1–19.
40 Acts 27:23–4.

41 Colossians 2:18–19.

42 Ephesians 3:1.

43 1 Corinthians 11:11. If this is not intuitive misogyny, Paul may be referring back here to Enoch and its account of the Watcher Angels being lured from heaven by lust for women.

44 Harold Bloom, *Omens of Millennium: The Gnosis of Angels, Dreams and Resurrection* (New York: Riverhead Books, 1996).

45 Ephesians 3:10–12.

46 Enoch 61:10ff.

47 Ephesians 3:10–12.

48 Ephesians 3:13.

49 Ephesians 9:11–12.

50 2 Corinthians 12:2.

51 Romans 8:38–9.

52 Colossians 1:13–16.

53 1 Peter 3:21–2.

54 Hebrews 2:5–18.

55 Hebrews 1:5–14.

56 Matthew 18:1–10.

57 Matthew 22:23–30.

58 Hebrews 1:14.

59 Mark 16:5.

60 Matthew 28:1–8.

61 John 5:1–9.

62 Luke 22:41–4.

63 Matthew 4:1–11.

64 John 1:1.

65 Isaiah 9:5–6.

66 See David Albert Jones, *Angels: A History* (Oxford: Oxford University Press, 2010).

67 Acts 1:10–11.

68 Acts 5:17–20.

69 Acts 12:1–8.

70 Acts 12:9–11.

Chapter 6

1 Karen Armstrong, *Islam: A Short History* (London: Weidenfeld & Nicolson, 2000).

2 Surah 96:1–2 from English translation by M.A.S. Abdel Haleem (Oxford: Oxford University Press, 2004).

Notes

3   Surah 2:97–8.
4   Surah 2:285.
5   Surah 3:65–8.
6   Genesis 16:16.
7   Genesis 21:8–14.
8   Genesis 21:17–19.
9   Surah 37:102.
10 Surah 53:5–11 – which describes the Night Journey (see later in chapter).
11 One of Muhammad's closest companions, and one of the first four caliphs (successors) who were leaders after Muhammad's death.
12 From a translation available online of Fath al-Bari, Ibn Hajar's fifteenth-century commentary on the Hadith.
13 See Maxime Rodinson, *Muhammad* (New York: Pantheon, 1971).
14 Surah 21:89–90.
15 Surah 19:7–20.
16 Surah 85:21.
17 Surah 56:80.
18 Surah 41:31.
19 Surah 15:7.
20 Surah 3:124–5.
21 Surah 40:7.
22 Surah 35:1.
23 Surah 37:1–3.
24 Surah 37:149–50.
25 Surah 40:7.
26 Surah 16:102.
27 Surah 13:11.
28 Surah 82:10–12.
29 Surah 50:16–19.
30 Babylonian Talmud, Shabbat 119b.
31 See Jean Danielou SJ, *The Angels and their Mission According to the Fathers of the Church*, translated by David Heimann (Notre Dame: Christian Classics, 1957).
32 From his lecture *Fihi Ma Fihi* ('In It What's In It'), edited by A.J. Arberry, *Discourses of Rumi* (New York: Samuel Weiser, 1972).
33 See Henry Corbin's *Spiritual Body and Celestial Earth: From Mazdean Iran to Shi'ite Iran*, translated by Nancy Pearson (New Jersey: Princeton University Press, 1977).
34 Surah 23:100.
35 Surah 23:104.
36 Surah 2:102.
37 Surah 15:26–7.

38   Surah 15:28–30.
39   Surah 15:31.
40   Surah 15:32–5.
41   Surah 15:37–44.
42   Surah 17:1.
43   This and what follows is based on the account in *The History of al-Tabari – Volume 6: Muhammad at Mecca*, based on the writings of a Persian historian working 300 years after Muhammad's death and translated by W. Montgomery Watt and M.V. McDonald (Albany: State University of New York Press, 1988).
44   Surah 39:68.
45   *The Complete Poems and Stories of Edgar Allan Poe* (New York: Knopf, 1946).

Chapter 7

1   Denys Turner, *Thomas Aquinas: A Portrait* (London: Yale University Press, 2013).
2   See Joad Raymond, *Milton's Angels: The Early-Modern Imagination* (Oxford: Oxford University Press, 2010).
3   Neil Gaiman and Terry Pratchett, *Good Omens* (London: Gollancz, 1990).
4   Matthew 28:19.
5   The last one based on Christians' claim that the bread and wine at the eucharist was the body and blood of Jesus.
6   Acts 12:5–17.
7   See *Ordained Women in the Early Church*, edited by Kevin Madigan and Carolyn Osiek (Baltimore: Johns Hopkins University Press, 2005).
8   A letter written by Saint Ignatius of Antioch (died 107) just before his death contains the phrase 'Catholic Church'.
9   David Rankin, *Athenagoras: Philosopher and Theologian* (London: Routledge, 2009).
10 Origen, *Against Celsus*, translated by Henry Chadwick (Cambridge: Cambridge University Press, 2008).
11 David Rankin, *Athenagoras: Philosopher and Theologian* (London: Routledge, 2009).
12 See Eric Osborn's *Clement of Alexandria* (Cambridge: Cambridge University Press, 2008).
13 See Stephen Hildebrand, *Saint Basil of Caesarea* (London: Routledge, 2018).
14 See *Butler's Lives of Patron Saints*, edited by Michael Walsh (London: HarperCollins, 1987).

15   Origen, *De Principiis* (London: CreateSpace Independent Publishing, 2016).

16   Matthew 18:10.

17   David Rankin, *Athenagoras: Philosopher and Theologian* (London: Routledge, 2009).

18   Surah 15:28–30.

19   William Barnstone and Marvin Meyer (eds), *The Gnostic Bible* (London: Shambhala, 2011).

20   Genesis 1:3.

21   Augustine, *The City of God*, edited by G.R. Evans and translated by Henry Bettenson (London: Penguin, 2003).

22   1 Corinthians 15:44.

23   Matthew 8:14–15 speaks of his mother-in-law, though the Catholic Church suggests that he was a widower.

24   See Elizabeth Abbott, *A History of Celibacy* (Cambridge: Lutterworth Press, 2001).

25   Chapter Seven of *The Rule of Saint Benedict*, edited by Carolinne White (London: Penguin, 2008).

26   Adomnán of Iona, *Life of Saint Columba*, translated by Richard Sharpe (London: Penguin, 1995).

27   In the writings of Prosper of Aquitaine (390–455), a disciple of Augustine.

28   Tertullian, *On Baptism* (London: CreateSpace Independent Publishing, 2015).

29   See Erik Peterson, *Theological Tractates*, edited by Michael J. Hollerich (Stanford: Stanford University Press, 2011).

30   Judith McClure and Roger Collins (eds), *Bede's Ecclesiastical History of the English People* (Oxford: Oxford University Press, 2008).

31   From *The Dialogues of Gregory the Great*, book 4, translated by Edmund Gardner and available online at the Tertullian Project (tertullian.org).

32   Luke 16:19–31.

33   From *The Dialogues of Gregory the Great*, book 4, translated by Edmund Gardner and available online at the Tertullian Project (tertullian.org).

34   See Arietta Papaconstantinou, *Le Culte des Saints en Egypte* (Paris: CNRS Editions, 2001).

35   Others, with similar legends attached, developed at Mont-Saint Michel in northern France and at Saint Michael's Mount in Cornwall in south-west England.

36   The other two named angels, Gabriel and Raphael, were also given feast days (24 March and 24 October respectively), but these were subsequently combined with that of Michael on 29 September and became popularly known as Michaelmas Day, also one of four 'quarter days' in the financial year. At Oxford University, the autumn term continues to be known as Michaelmas term, after the archangel.

37 Acts 17:34.

38 'Celestial Hierarchy', from an 1899 translation of *Works of Dionysius the Areopagite* (Tennessee: General Books LLC, 2010).

39 Ibid.

40 Gregory, *Moralia in Job*, (Minnesota: Liturgical Press, 2014).

41 Ibid.

42 In Sermon 9 in Volume 3 of Hughes Oliphant Old, *The Reading and Preaching of Scripture in the Worship of the Christian Church* (Michigan: Eerdmans, 1999).

43 In Tony Kushner's 1991 Pulizter Prize- and Tony Award-winning play *Angels in America*, the six angels who sit in a control room in heaven are called 'The Continental Principalities'.

44 The Italian scientist Roberto Volterri, a proponent of the idea that earlier ages were more aware than our own of the presence of extra-terrestrial beings, has suggested in his writings that the dome in Botticini's altarpiece is really a flying saucer and that the ranks of angels represent an army of aliens coming down to earth.

Chapter 8

1 Jean Danielou, *The Angels and Their Mission* (New York: The Newman Press, 1957).

2 1 Corinthians 6:9–11.

3 See Henry Mayr-Harting, *Perceptions of Angels in History* (Oxford: Clarendon Press, 1998).

4 Revelation 3:14.

5 From 'The Legend of the Three Companions' in *St Francis of Assisi: English Omnibus of the Sources for the Life of St Francis*, edited by Marion Habig (Illinois: Franciscan Press, 1991).

6 Catherine of Siena (1347–80), Jean Vianney, the French priest better known as the Cure d'Ars (1786–1859) and Padre Pio (1887–1968), all subsequently declared saints by Catholicism. In each case there was debate about whether the wounds had been self-inflicted, or in the case of Francis of Assisi made on his corpse soon after his death by his followers. The scepticism, in the case of Padre Pio, initially extended into the upper echelons of the Vatican.

7 Galatians 6:17.

8 *The Works of Bonaventure*, translated in five volumes by Jose de Vinck (New Jersey: St Anthony Guild Press, 1960–70).

9 Ibid.

10 Ibid.

11 From *Bonaventure: The Soul's Journey into God, the Tree of Life, the Life of Saint Francis*, translated by Ewert Cousins (New York: Paulist Press, 1978).

12 This was before it was accepted that the sun was at the centre of the solar system.

13 See Lenn E. Goodman, *Avicenna*, (London: Routledge, 1992).

14 Ibid.

15 From Immanuel M. O'Levy's translation of Book One of *Mishneh Torah*, available online at Jewish Virtual Library.

16 Moses Maimonides, *The Guide for the Perplexed*, translated by Michael Friedländer (New York: Dover Publications, 1956).

17 Ibid.

18 Maimonides liked to quote the example of a ship to show that religious language could be used negatively to produce a positive outcome. By asking a series of questions to which the answer was no, you found out what a ship wasn't, and from that deduction you could work out what it was.

19 Jean Danielou, *The Angels and Their Mission* (New York: The Newman Press, 1957).

20 The story is included in G.K. Chesterton's 1933 life of Thomas Aquinas (New York: Dover Books, 2008).

21 Tobit 12:19–21.

22 Thomas Aquinas, *Summa Theologiae* (London: Blackfriars, 1967).

23 Ibid.

24 It was also suggested by some Scholastics that the saints in heaven were in this same state.

Chapter 9

1 Exodus 20:4.

2 See Peter Stanford, *How to Read a Graveyard* (London: Bloomsbury, 2013).

3 John 19:25.

4 John 2:4.

5 John 2:1–12.

6 Attributed to Pope Gregory V (died 999).

7 Though she was only officially given the title Queen of Heaven by Pope Pius XII in 1954.

8 *The Works of Bonaventure*, translated in five volumes by Jose de Vinck (New Jersey: St Anthony Guild Press, 1960–70).

9 Luke 1:26–38.

10 Luke 1:28–9.

11 See Marina Warner, *Alone of All Her Sex: The Myth and Cult of the Virgin Mary* (London: Weidenfeld & Nicolson, 1976).

12 Caesarius of Heisterbach, *Dialogus miraculorum*, edited by J. Strange (Cologne, 1851).

13 Henry Mayr-Harting, *Perceptions of Angels in History* (Oxford: Clarendon Press, 1998).

14 It is in her writings, for instance, that some of the earliest known references are made to the concept of Purgatory, as an interim state between heaven and hell.

15 *Hildegardis Bingensis Liber Vitae Meritorum*, edited by Angela Carlevaris (Brepols: Turnhout, 1995).

16 *Scivias*, translated by Columba Hart and Jane Bishop (New York: Paulist Press, 1990).

17 The manuscript was lost during the Second World War, but a black-and-white photographic record of it survives, and it is on this record that contemporary versions of the illustrations are based.

18 From his 'Spiritual Canticle of the Soul', in *Collected Works of John of the Cross*, translated by Kevin Kavanagh and Otilio Rodriguez (Washington, DC: ICS, 1976).

19 *Scivias*, translated by Columba Hart and Jane Bishop (New York: Paulist Press, 1990).

20 Fiona Maddocks, *Hildegard of Bingen: The Woman of Her Age* (London: Headline, 2001).

21 Morris B. Margolies, *A Gathering of Angels: Angels in Jewish Life and Literature* (New York: Ballantine Books, 1994).

22 Exodus 20:23.

23 See Morris B. Margolies, *A Gathering of Angels: Angels in Jewish Life and Literature* (New York: Ballantine Books, 1994).

24 There is a debate around this. The *Zohar* was originally claimed as a rediscovered second-century-BCE text by Rabbi Simon bar Yohai, then as Moses de Leon's reworking of it, but there was always a question over its authenticity. The twentieth-century philosopher, historian and Kabbalah scholar Gershom Scholem settled the matter for many, pointing to de Leon as the author.

25 *The Zohar*, Pritzker Edition, Volume 1, translated by Daniel Matt (California: Stanford University Press, 2004).

26 Ibid.

27 See Harold Bloom, *Omens of Millennium: The Gnosis of Angels, Dreams and Resurrection* (New York: Riverhead Books, 1996).

28 *Sandro Botticelli: The Drawings for Dante's Divine Comedy* (London: Royal Academy of Arts, 2000).

29 See Jonathan Black, *The Sacred History: How Angels, Mystics and Higher Intelligence Made Our World* (London: Quercus, 2013).

30 See Peter Stanford, *The Devil: A Biography* (London: Heinemann, 1996).

31 'Paradiso' Canto 28:52, from *The Divine Comedy*, translated by C.H. Sisson (Oxford: Oxford University Press, 1980).

32 Closely resembling the angels in Botticelli's celebrated *Coronation of the Virgin* in his altarpiece for the Dominican monastery of San Marco in Florence, painted in 1491–3.

33 'Paradiso' Canto 28:88–105, from *The Divine Comedy*, translated by C.H. Sisson (Oxford: Oxford University Press, 1980).

34 'Paradiso' Canto 28:127–9, from *The Divine Comedy*, translated by C.H. Sisson (Oxford: Oxford University Press, 1980).

35 'Paradiso' Canto 31:127–35, from *The Divine Comedy*, translated by C.H. Sisson (Oxford: Oxford University Press, 1980).

Chapter 10

1 In his final, posthumously published collection, *Last Stories* (2018), the peerless William Trevor includes 'Giotto's Angels', the tale of an amnesiac picture-restorer, utterly enthralled by Giotto's frescoes as he tries to remember who he is.

2 *The Life of Teresa of Jesus*, translated by J.M. Cohen (London: Penguin, 1957).

3 A theory advanced by the British art critic Jonathan Jones, who included it in his *Guardian* column, 'How Leonardo da Vinci's angels pointed the way to the future', 25 December 2012.

4 Images of angels with genitals retain their capacity to shock. Celebrated Australian sculptor Ron Mueck's 1997 *Angel*, one of his trademark, outsized, hyper-real figures that focus on their innermost, unspoken thoughts, caused controversy when first shown. It features a small naked man on a too-big stool, with large wings and his legs open to reveal his penis.

5 Among those it has particularly inspired was the twentieth-century American abstract painter Mark Rothko, often lauded for the spiritual intensity of his work.

6 Michael Kimmelman, 'Fra Angelico: Master of the Golden Halo', *New York Times*, 11 September 2005.

7 Like his near contemporary Michelangelo Buonarroti (1475–1564).

8 See Peter Stanford, *Martin Luther: Catholic Dissident* (London: Hodder, 2017).

9 Table Talk 4201, from *Off the Record with Martin Luther*, translated and edited by Charles Daudert (Michigan: Hansa-Hewlett, 2009).

10 See Peter Stanford, *Martin Luther: Catholic Dissident* (London: Hodder, 2017).

11 Table Talk 6561, from *Off the Record with Martin Luther*, translated and edited by Charles Daudert (Michigan: Hansa-Hewlett, 2009).

12 John Calvin, *Institutes of the Christian Religion – Volume 1*, translated by John T. McNeill (London: John Knox Press, 1960).

13 *The Journal of William Dowsing: Iconoclasm in East Anglia during the English Civil War*, edited by Trevor Cooper (Woodbridge: Boydell Press, 2001).

14 Keith Thomas, *Religion and the Decline of Magic* (London: Penguin, 1973).

15 And without teeth, since angels had fed only on the fruit of the Garden of Eden.

16 Jaköb Böhme, *The Great Mystery* (New York: Hermetica Press, 2007).

17 From the decrees of the Council of Trent, on www.thecounciloftrent.com.

18 Alexander is said to have vetoed a matching angel on the other side of the façade, giving a lop-sided feel to the front of this basilica, one of three great Counter-Reformation churches built in the seventeenth century to provide a platform for a new generation of preachers whose oratory would turn the tide against Protestantism. The Gesù and the Chiesa Nuova are the other two.

19 Along with a medallion by the same artist of the Archangel Michael.

20 See Peter Stanford, *The She Pope: A Quest for the Truth Behind the Mystery of Pope Joan* (London: Heinemann, 1998).

21 *The Life of Teresa of Jesus*, translated by J.M. Cohen (London: Penguin, 1957).

22 See, particularly, Shirley du Boulay's trenchant *Teresa of Avila* (London: Hodder, 1991).

23 A plaque to him is on the wall of Mortlake's Church of Saint Mary the Virgin, and the local council has named a road there after him.

24 Deborah Harkness, *John Dee's Conversations with Angels* (Cambridge: Cambridge University Press, 1999).

25 Ibid.

26 Ibid.

27 Joad Raymond, *Milton's Angels: The Early-Modern Imagination* (Oxford: Oxford University Press, 2010).

28 Other texts to consider in this regard include Thomas Heywood's *Hierarchy of the Blessed Angels* (1635) and Samuel Portage's *Mundorum Explicatio* (1610).

29 John Milton, *Paradise Lost*, edited by John Leonard (London: Penguin, 2003), V:637.

30 Ibid., VIII:618–29.

31 And caused Milton's angels to inspire the Romantic poets of the eighteenth and nineteenth centuries.

32 John Milton, *Paradise Lost*, edited by John Leonard (London: Penguin, 2003), I:594.

33 Ibid., IV:37–41.
34 Ibid., I:25–6.
35 Ibid., III:681–5.

Chapter 11

1 From *Songs of Innocence and Experience* in *William Blake: The Complete Poems* (London: Penguin, 1977).

2 *La vie de Monsieur Descartes* (1691) (Paris: Éditions des Malassis, 2012).

3 In his 2005 biography, *Descartes: The Life and Times of a Genius* (London: Simon & Schuster), the militant atheist philosopher A.C. Grayling claims that his subject was in reality a Jesuit spy, operating against the backdrop of the Thirty Years War between Catholics and Protestants.

4 Philip Davis and Reuben Hirsh, *Descartes' Dream: The World According to Mathematics* (Chatham: Dover Books, 2005).

5 A.I. Otaiku, 'Did René Descartes Have Exploding Head Syndrome?' *Journal of Clinical Sleep Medicine*, 14 (4), 2018.

6 See the account in Theodore Roszak's *The Cult of Information: The Folklore of Computers and the True Art of Thinking* (New York: Pantheon, 1986).

7 In the twentieth century one of Catholicism's most distinguished philosophers, Jacques Maritain, considered whether Descartes was more reformer than rebutter of the Church in *The Dream of Descartes* (New York: Kennitak Press, 1969).

8 Blaise Pascal, *Pensées*, translated by Alban Krailsheimer (London: Penguin, 1995).

9 Full text available on the website of the United Methodist Church – www.umc.org.

10 Available online thanks to Gale ECCO – Eighteenth Century Collections Online.

11 And was in his turn greatly admired by John Wesley, with whom he corresponded at the end of his life.

12 Some admirers of Swedenborg refer to him as 'the Swedish Da Vinci'.

13 *The New Jerusalem* (London: Swedenborg Society, 2003).

14 *Arcana Caelestia* (London: Swedenborg Society, 2009).

15 In Lutheran Sweden such remarks were taken badly and many of the works were published in England or the Netherlands.

16 So celebrated was it that Mark Twain (1835–1910) felt moved to attack it publicly as imagining 'a mean little ten-cent heaven'.

17 For example, the influential American critic Harold Bloom, in *Omens of Millennium: The Gnosis of Angels, Dreams and Resurrection* (New York: Riverhead Books, 1996).

18 The year of Blake's birth – 1757 – was the one Swedenborg had 'revealed' as the time of the Second Coming, a detail Blake fixated on.

19 See Morton D. Paley, 'A New Heaven is Begun: William Blake and Swedenborgionism', in *Blake: An Illustrated Quarterly* (Volume 3, Issue 2, 1979).

20 *The Illuminated Books of William Blake – Volume Five*, edited by Robert Essich and Joseph Viscomi (Princeton: Princeton University Press, 1998).

21 Blake made little money from his work in his lifetime.

22 *The Complete Poetry and Prose of William Blake*, edited by David Erdman (California: University of California Press, 2008).

23 Ibid.

24 Both incidents are told in the first biography of Blake in 1863: Alexander Gilchrist, *Life of William Blake* (London: Flamingo, 2011).

25 *The Complete Poetry and Prose of William Blake*, edited by David Erdman (California: University of California Press, 2008).

26 Harold Bloom, *Omens of Millennium: The Gnosis of Angels, Dreams and Resurrection* (New York: Riverhead Books, 1996).

27 Ibid.

28 *The Complete Poetry and Prose of William Blake*, edited by David Erdman (California: University of California Press, 2008).

29 Alexander Gilchrist, *Life of William Blake* (London: Flamingo, 2011).

30 From John Henry Newman, *Selected Sermons*, edited by Ian Ker (London: Paulist Press, 1993).

31 John Henry Newman, *Apologia Pro Vita Sua*, edited by Ian Ker (London: Penguin, 1993).

32 John Henry Newman, *The Dream of Gerontius* (New York: Cosimo Classics, 2007).

33 An exhibition of her 'angel children' was staged in 2011 with images from the Victoria and Albert Museum's collection at London's Museum of Childhood.

34 Favell Lee Mortimer, *The Peep of Day* (London: Religious Tract Society, 1900).

Chapter 12

1 'The Bowmen', by Arthur Machen, *London Evening News*, 29 September 1914.

2 In his 1915 introduction to the story collection *The Bowmen and Other Legends of the War*.

3 David Clarke, *The Angels of Mons: Phantom Soldiers and Ghostly Guardians* (New Jersey: John Wiley, 2005).

4   Jane Williams, *Angels* (Oxford: Lion, 2006).

5   Depending on who is included and how the final total is arrived at (for example, whether to include those who died, often after the war ended, but as a result of their injuries).

6   Thérèse of Lisieux, *The Story of a Soul* (North Carolina: Tan Publishing, 2010).

7   He has been accused of turning a blind eye to the Holocaust, and never mentioning it publicly even when he knew it was happening.

8   *Humani Generis*, section 26 – available on the Vatican website (http://w2.vatican.va/content/pius-xii/en/encyclicals/documents/hf_p-xii_enc_12081950_humani-generis.html).

9   Weekly general audience, Wednesday 6 August 1986.

10 Benedict XVI, *Jesus of Nazareth: The Infancy Narratives* (London: Burns & Oates, 2012).

11 Karl Barth, *Church Dogmatics – Volume III, Part 3* (Edinburgh: T&T Clark, 2010)

12 20 April 1962.

13 Karl Barth, *Church Dogmatics – Volume III, Part 3* (Edinburgh: T&T Clark, 2010).

14 Ibid.

15 In some earlier ones, he called himself Nephi.

16 From Smith's 'First Vision Accounts', published online by the Church of Latter Day Saints.

17 The three, Oliver Cowdery, Martin Harris and David Whitmer, all subsequently broke with Smith, though the first two eventually re-joined the Mormons, with Whitmer starting his own church.

18 Revelation 14:6.

19 Walter Benjamin, *Illuminations* (London: Bodley Head, 2015).

20 See Michael Baumgartner, *Paul Klee: Angels* (Berlin: Hatje Cantz, 2012).

21 Jackie Wullschlager, *Chagall: A Biography* (New York: Knopf, 2008).

22 From the 'First Elegy', published in 1923: *The Selected Poetry of Rainer Maria Rilke*, translated by Stephen Mitchell (New York: Vintage, 1989).

23 Emma Heathcote-James, *Seeing Angels* (London: John Blake, 2009).

Epilogue

1   'Pictures of angels helped with *Girls & Boys* play panic attacks', *London Evening Standard* (4 June 2018).

2   'Angels Are Us', *Time* magazine cover story (December 1993).

Illustration Credits

Alamy: 25/photo Gilles Barbier, 40/Tretyakov Gallery Moscow, 50/ Art Collection, 65/Lebrecht Music & Arts, 68/Art Collection, 88/ Ian Dagnell, 98/Peter Barritt, 100/The History Collection, 136/ Interfoto, 166/Heritage Image Partnership Ltd, 176/Art Collection, 199/The Picture Art Collection, 203/The Picture Art Collection,208/ Heritage Image Partnership Ltd, 224/René Mattes/hemis.fr, 226/ Granger Historical Picture Archive, 231/Heritage Image Partnership Ltd, 272/Art Collection, 273/Art Collection, 288/Heritage Image Partnership Ltd, 306/Holmes Garden Photos. © The Estate of Sir Jacob Epstein, photo © Tate London 2018: p32.

Index

Page numbers in **bold** refer to figures.

Index

Index